CLARENDON LAW

Edited by

A. M. HONORÉ AN

GW00360762

CLARENDON LAW SERIES

THE LAW OF PROPERTY

BY

F. H. LAWSON
*Formerly Professor of Comparative Law in the
University of Oxford*

AND

BERNARD RUDDEN
*Professor of Comparative Law in the
University of Oxford*

SECOND EDITION

CLARENDON PRESS · OXFORD

Oxford University Press, Walton Street, Oxford OX2 6DP

Oxford New York Toronto
Delhi Bombay Calcutta Madras Karachi
Petaling Jaya Singapore Hong Kong Tokyo
Nairobi Dar es Salaam Cape Town
Melbourne Auckland
and associated companies in
Beirut Berlin Ibadan Nicosia

Published in the United States by
Oxford University Press, New York

First published 1958 under the title
Introduction to the Law of Property by F. H. Lawson
2nd Edition first published 1982
Reprinted 1984, 1987

British Library Cataloguing in Publication Data
Lawson, F. H.
The law of property.—2nd ed.—(Clarendon law series)
1. Real estate—Law and legislation—England
I. Title   II. Rudden, Bernard   III. Lawson, F. H.
Introduction to the law of property
344.2064'3   KD829
ISBN 0–19–876128–7
ISBN 0–19–876129–5 Pbk

Printed in Great Britain
at the University Printing House, Oxford
by David Stanford
Printer to the University

PREFACE

THIS is an explanatory, not a learned book, designed for two classes of readers: law students approaching the law of property for the first time, and non-lawyers who wish to obtain a rapid and summary view of what is usually regarded as a highly technical and obscure part of English law. In the Preface to the First Edition the author wrote:

The Law of Property has the reputation of being one of the most difficult branches of English law, and its reputation is not undeserved. But its difficulty will be found on closer inspection to be of a different order from that of most other branches. For whereas the law of contract or torts, which in detail seems straightforward enough, only gradually unfolds its real difficulties to the student, the law of property presents its most difficult features to the beginner, but becomes relatively easier as he gradually comes to see what is its general philosophy and purpose. However, the experience of teachers seems to show that it takes the student quite an appreciable time to reach that stage.

Yet it should be possible, by a concerted and deliberate attack, to carry the beginner through this initial difficulty more quickly than has hitherto been the case. That is the main purpose of this book. It proceeds from the belief that there are clear patterns in the English law of property, which are not evident to the student until he has his attention forcibly directed to them. On the other hand, those patterns are to some extent disturbed by exceptions and minor inconsistencies, which are apt to assume undue prominence in elementary books. Some of them are historical survivals whose importance tends to be exaggerated because the bias of teaching in this subject, perhaps more than in any other part of English law, has been historical. Doubtless even now a study of legal history is essential to the complete culture of a property lawyer, but it should come rather later in his education, when he has acquired some notion of the general patterns of the law. He will then be able to recognize and understand the exceptions to them; for the time being it is best to neglect most of the exceptions altogether, apart from a warning that they exist and often trouble the practising lawyer.

Although the Law of Property Act 1922 described itself as 'an Act to assimilate . . . the law of real and personal estate', the last sixty years have seen few text-books take the hint. In this work we try to portray the law of property as a whole, eschewing the familiar divisions into land on the one hand and everything else on the other. There are, of course, irreducible differences between movable and immovable property, which are noted as they occur, but there is a great deal of doctrine common to both; and the things themselves are often interchangeable as component parts of the same fund when, for instance, its managers dispose of the one and invest in the other. It is also our firm belief that, even when land and movables are treated not as parts of a fund but as individual objects, there is much more in common between them than is usually acknowledged.

Perhaps the greatest difficulty in exposition is caused by the course the common law has taken. In large measure its vocabulary is still that of feudalism, giving the impression that the law of property is mainly concerned with field and farmhouse, crops and cattle. In fact this feudal terminology has long been filled with commercial content and applied to stocks, shares, intellectual property, goodwill, futures—in a word to capital which is not merely movable but *mobile*. In an exasperated but illuminating aside, Friedrich Engels once observed that, for our law of property, the relation between the words used and their actual function is as remote as that between the spelling and the pronunciation of the English language. An additional difficulty is that, in this century, the mercantile approach has been applied, perhaps unthinkingly, to things—like the family home—which are not investments but necessities.

Parts of this book are, inevitably, concerned with the modern law of England and Wales. Our main aim, however, has been to explain those basic principles of the law of property which are common to the common-law world. In striving to be elementary we ignore exceptions and name no cases, a course not without its dangers. In this area of law, above all others, simplicity is difficult.

F. H. L.

B. R.

Oxford, January 1982

CONTENTS

I

INTRODUCTION

THE law of property deals with the legal relations between
people with regard to things. Problems about these relations
are bound to arise in any community where human beings live
together and compete for the control and use of relatively
scarce resources. Only in conditions of unimaginable abun-
dance can the principle 'first come first served' be generally
applied—elsewhere it leads straight to 'might makes right'—
and it may be doubted whether any society has ever existed
in which people have not had possessions which are in some
sense their own. In the graves of the oldest skeletons yet
discovered were found beautiful things.

Let us look first at the every-day business of getting things
and then keeping and utilizing them. A person may acquire
a thing by making it, but is more likely to get it from someone else and to have to pay for it. He wants to be sure that he
gets what he is paying for, but is normally far more concerned
with its quality and suitability than with worrying whether it
is the seller's to sell. He is able to take this for granted in most
cases because the law is working, virtually unnoticed, to protect him and, if the deal goes wrong, to provide him with a
remedy. He may, however, prefer to pay for his goods or his
house by instalments; and in such cases no one would provide
credit unless he had some security. The law enables the creditor
to obtain this security by means of devices such as hire-
purchase and mortgage.

Having got the thing, a person wants to be sure that no one
else can take it from him. He may keep and use it in safety,
but there may come a time when he wishes to sell it or give it
away. Furthermore—especially if the thing is of a permanent

nature like a house or a theatre—he may want to share its use
among others either commercially by charging a rent or by
way of gift to his family.

The law of property, as it were, provides him with a bag of
tools with which to achieve all these various aims. The rest of
this chapter will outline the different sorts of tools; their more
precise specifications take up most of the remaining chapters.

1. LEGAL RELATIONS

We encounter the law on many different occasions and in
many different ways, but it is probably working best when
we notice it least. Whether we like it or not we are caught up
in a complex of legal relations, some of which are relatively
static while others exist only in order to be changed. The
former are most simply expressed as relations between a person and a thing, the latter as relations between person and
person. If I say that I own a particular motor car my statement is complete; no other *ascertained* person need be mentioned. But if I say I am owed £100, the obvious question is:
by whom? The relation between a person and a thing is called
by lawyers a *real* relation, or relation *in rem* (from the Latin
word *res* meaning thing) and is distinguished from a personal
relation or relation *in personam.*

In one important sense, of course, real relations are relations
between persons. The statement that I own a particular motor
car is complete only because it is a short-hand way of expres-
sing my legal relation with everyone else in respect of that car:
without my permission no one else may drive it, take it, or
sell it, and if anyone does so I may bring an action against
him. Since English lawyers tend to see law in terms of lawsuits,
they think of legal relations as directly or indirectly giving
a specific plaintiff an action against a specific defendant.

From that point of view, real relations are distinguished
from personal by the number of people affected by them.
The statement that I own a car implies something about the
legal position of everyone else and something which, if all goes
well, will never alter. The statement that I am owed £100 implies something about the legal position of only one other
person, my debtor; furthermore my present relation with him

exists only to be changed—he must pay me the money and end that particular relation. So in the case of the car the identity of the other parties to the legal relation is irrelevant until one of them acts inconsistently with it; whereas in the case of the debt the identity of the debtor is crucial right from the start since only he, and no one else, owes me the £100.

The car and the debt are examples of the two extremes: my relation with one affects all the world, with the other only one person. But it may be that my relation to a thing affects not everyone but only those who know of it or, to use the technical legal term, have notice. Those relations which are protected only against persons who have notice of them play a very important part in the law of property: this is one reason why we have registers of so many things—land, shares, patents, plant varieties, aircraft, ships and racehorses. Sometimes, therefore, the persons affected are not merely those who actually know about the relation but also those who could have found out and so are said to have constructive notice. As will be explained later[1] there are good reasons for treating as varieties of real relations not just those which affect everyone but also those which affect only persons with notice. If they are so treated it may be said categorically that the law of property deals with real relations.

2. PROPERTY AND CONTRACT

The commonest way to acquire things is to buy them. Why then should not the law of property include, besides real relations, such personal relations as arise from contracts about things? The simple reason is that the general part of the law of contract is applicable to many other transactions—contracts of employment, transport, and so on—and the principles governing the formation, performance, and breach of contract and the consequences of breach deal with matters which are remote from the law of property. Some of the effects of a contract, however, are regularly treated in books on property. If the rights created by a contract can be transferred from one person to another, the law regards them as a species of

---

[1] See pp. 58–64 below.

property.[2] Indeed English law calls them 'things', though it uses the old French jargon *choses in action*.

3. PERSONS AND THINGS

To describe a real relation one must deal not only with the relation itself, the link between the person and the thing, but also the person and the thing. Now for various reasons, partly traditional and partly practical, the classification of persons is taken out of the law of property and made the subject of a special branch of the law, that of persons. It would be possible to separate the classification of things from the classification of relations themselves and this was indeed done in the German Civil Code, the most consciously systematic of all codes; but in our law other reasons, again both traditional and practical, have produced a different result. Both the classification of things and the classification of relations between persons and things are part of the English law of property.

Persons real and artificial

Although the detailed study of the capacity and status of different kinds of persons does not belong to the law of property it is convenient to allude to them here in a general way. Persons are classified primarily as, on the one hand, natural persons and, on the other, legal or artificial persons. The former are living human beings, the latter corporations. Among human beings few distinctions are made, the only important ones being that between adults and minors and that between the sane and mental patients. For property purposes aliens hardly differ from British subjects.

Artificial persons, or corporations, are, in our law, always groups of human beings such as municipal corporations or trading companies, or else they are successive, human, holders of an office such as the Crown or a living in the Church of England. In either case it is important to distinguish the corporation, as an artificial person created by the law, from the human beings who are its members or who, for the time being, fill the office. Thus the corporation constituted by a limited company preserves its single legal personality although all its

[2] See pp. 26–32 below.

members change through death or sale of their shares and the corporation sole constituted by the parson of a parish is always the same though human incumbents come and go. Corporations are brought into existence by the law, or by human beings in accordance with the law, in order to simplify the solution of problems connected with holding property and doing business.

Thus if 5,000 people wished to invest their money in an industrial concern, it would be extremely inconvenient to make them own the factory as individuals, to appoint managers, engage workers, and so on. The inconvenience would be greatly enhanced if, as would almost inevitably be the case, the 5,000 investors were constantly changing, whenever, for instance any one of them sold out or died and was succeeded by someone else. Such difficulties are removed if the concern is made the property of a corporation called a limited company and the investors are given shares in the company and not directly in the concern itself. To a very great extent the law treats corporations as persons in the same way as it treats human beings although, of course, the former are not subject to death or the other perils of life.

Things concrete and abstract

This distinction between natural and artificial persons has a counterpart in the classification of things[3] for alongside physical objects such as cattle, ships, houses, and motor cars the law ranges abstract things which cannot be perceived by the senses but only conceived by the mind. Some of these which are most readily apprehended are debts, shares in companies, and intellectual property such as patents and copyright. For the time being all that need be said of them is that, like physical objects, they can be passed from one person to another and are often bought and sold. Just as corporations can ultimately be reduced to human beings at the cost of enormous complications in the practical solving of problems, so these, and other abstract things, can, with a similar sacrifice, be reduced to physical objects. Some such abstract things— though not necessarily those admitted by English law— have, it would seem, to be employed if the relations between

[3] See Chapter II.

human beings with regard to physical objects are not to become intolerably complex.

Still more abstract, perhaps, are *funds*: that is to say, collections of things which are for certain purposes treated as having a separate identity independent of their component parts and in which the latter can be changed from time to time without changing the identity of the fund. Just as a corporation has a separate legal personality apart from its members, so a fund has a separate identity distinct from its parts. The pension fund of a Trade Union, for instance, has an identity distinct from the objects in which it is invested; and these latter may be tangible things like shops and paintings or abstract things like stocks and shares. Just as the changing of shareholders does not affect the legal personality of a corporation, so the switching of investments does not alter the identity of a fund. Other examples are a family trust fund and the capital of a company, which may include not only its buildings and plant but also its constantly changing stock-in-trade, the patents it exploits, the debts it is owed, and the goodwill it has built up.[4] English property law has, indeed, become a law of wealth in the widest sense of that term.

4. REAL RELATIONS

Having sketched in outline the sort of persons that can have legal relations with things and the kind of things subject to those relations, it is time to consider the relations themselves. The obvious ones are *possession* and *ownership* and they are easy to illustrate. If there is a library book on my desk then I have possession of it but not ownership. If I ask a friend to lend me a jug of milk and he does so then I acquire possession of the jug and he remains owner; but I acquire ownership of the milk and *owe him* its value, and he owns the abstract thing which is my debt to him.

Ownership would seem to the layman to be a simple

[4] If a trust fund needs management, and most do, the necessary powers to deal with its component parts will be vested in the trustee, and the power to enjoy and deal with the income produced by it will belong to the beneficiaries. See Chapter VI.

notion. It is merely a question of *meum* and *tuum*. If the thing is mine, I own it; if it is not, I do not. Often the law conforms to this simple way of looking at ownership. Thus, for example, a person may live alone in a house which he has bought and paid for, no one else has any rights over it, and his title is registered in the Land Registry; and he may have in his garage a car which he has bought direct from the manufacturer. In both cases he can correctly say, without qualification, that the thing is his. Or he may reasonably say that he is an absolute owner.

But even in such simple cases it is evident that the words absolute owner are being used to express two quite different ideas: that his ownership is both *indisputable* and that it is *unshared*. The owner is asserting at the same moment that he and no one else is entitled to the house and car, and that his interest in them is exclusive and complete; or, in negative terms, that no other person can regard the things as his and that no other person can do anything which cuts down their use or reduces their value. The one assertion relates to what lawyers call 'title', the other to the content of ownership. In English law, as we shall see, it is perfectly possible to have one without the other.

Title

Some ways of acquiring title are original in the sense that a person is the first ever owner of a thing: if I write a song I own the copyright. Usually, however, things are acquired from someone else. A person buying a thing wants to be sure that it is the seller's to sell. With movable objects there are few problems—the seller's *possession* of the thing is normally good enough evidence of his *ownership*.

In the case of land, however, the matter is rather more complex. The word 'title' belongs to the vocabulary of a purchaser's solicitor who is trying to ensure that his client will be safe in buying the house and cannot be turned out by any-one else. He is concerned to see that his client gets what is called a good title. In the event of dispute the question of who is *entitled* to it—the issue of title—may have to be tested by a lawsuit in which, although the plaintiff's object would be to obtain possession of the thing, he must try to prove that element of ownership which is the right to immediate possession. The actions by which, in our system, a person protects his right to possess are usually studied as part of the law of tort, for the encroachments which give rise to them, the 'trespasses', are torts. But an awareness of these actions, and of the periods of limitation after which they are no longer available, is necessary to a proper view of title.[5]

The actions just referred to were developed by the old Courts of Common Law and are still said to be actions 'at law'. However, side by side with the common-law courts, the Chancellor exercised an 'equitable' jurisdiction and developed interests and remedies which have remained distinct even though common law and equity have been administered by the same courts for over a century. They play an important and even predominant part in the law of property.

The content of ownership

If we have a good title to a thing then it is safely ours and our relation with it is protected against others. We now turn to what the law allows us to do with it—the content of ownership. The law of property does not impose duties on us with respect to the things we own; they are part of the law of obligations (especially tort) and of public law. Instead the law of property is concerned with conferring on us legal powers in relation to a thing. The value of a thing is inferred from what can be done with it and it is the sum of all that can be done with it that constitutes the content of ownership.

The main elements are (*a*) the right to make physical use of a thing; (*b*) the right to the income from it, in money, in kind, or in services; and (*c*) the power of management, including that of alienation.[6] Thus the owner of a car may drive it, hire it out, or sell it. And of course within these areas he may do the same things more generously: take the children for a drive, lend it to a friend, give it away. The owner of a house may live there, lease it, or sell it; and so on.

---

[5] See Chapter III.

[6] The distinction was formulated by the medieval teachers of Roman law as one between the *ius utendi*, the *ius fruendi*, and the *ius abutendi*. The last, which would seem at first to mean the right to use up or destroy the thing, was extended to cover alienation as well. Their economic rationale is explained in R. A. Posner, *Economic Analysis of Law* (2nd ed., 1977) 3.1.

There are certain advantages to be obtained by keeping in the same hands the right or power to do all these things. A buyer normally wants them all and it is inconvenient if the seller cannot give him them. On the other hand, there has always been a need to detach some elements of ownership from others and to vest them in different persons, a need felt most strongly in regard to land. One of the main tasks of the law of property is to reconcile this need with the advantages of simplicity.

The first point to make about the English way of looking at ownership is that there is no objection in principle to breaking it up into fragments. This process takes place in several different ways which will be described in turn, through the use of difficult abstractions such as tenure and estates, to be merely mentioned for the moment and explained later.[7] It is enough to say, by way of example, that whereas the 'ownership' of a house itself may be divided between a landlord and a tenant or a building society and a borrower, the fragmentation directed to provide incomes successively for members of a family has shifted its ground from physical objects to interests in funds managed by trustees.[8]

(a) Physical use of things

Referring back to the distinction between the right to use a thing and the right to derive income from it, we must consider these in turn. We shall find that the discussion will run more easily if we start by assuming that a person using a thing has the full interest in it by being the only owner of the land or the movable.

The law makes a general assumption—which, as regards land, has now worn rather thin[9]—that a person may use a thing belonging to him in any way he likes. He may, of course, bind himself to another person to limit the use of his own property or to allow the other access to the thing, and there is little restriction placed on the relations thus created. But they will usually operate only between the particular parties, and so be a matter for the law of contract. They become part of the law

[7] See pp. 80–4 below.
[8] See pp. 102–3 below.
[9] See Chapter VIII.

of property only when they affect others who acquire the thing—when, in the language of property law, they run with the thing itself. Such burdens attach almost exclusively to one piece of land for the benefit of another piece nearby and are best described by the Roman term *servitudes*. It is rarely possible to attach burdens, such as price maintenance conditions, to goods.[10]

(b) Income derived from things

The last two paragraphs dealt with the case where a person wants to take for himself directly the whole benefit from a thing. But he may, in fact, prefer to divide the benefit in some way between himself and another or even between two or more different persons. Much of the technique employed here is that of the fragmentation of ownership and the law on this subject has been developed most elaborately for land. It does, however, extend to movable property particularly fairly durable things such as patents and electrical equipment. The problems are best understood if the physical use of a thing is distinguished from the enjoyment of the income produced by it; the use of a thing by one person, for example the hirer of a television set or tenant of a house, may provide an income for someone else.

If agricultural land is leased to a farmer or a house to a tenant the landlord reserves to himself an income in the form of rent, but gives up the physical use to the farmer or tenant. The law of landlord and tenant constitutes a great part of the English law of property. But a close analogy may be found in the law of movable property, for a person may hire the use of a car, television set, or other appliance. The technical name for this transaction is *bailment* though nowadays the word leasing is widely used, especially in relation to computers and aircraft.[11] Something more remotely analogous may be found in the licence given by a patent-holder to a manufacturer to make a patented article, or by a copyright owner to a publisher to publish his song.

On the other hand a person may wish to dispose of the income of a thing, not as a business proposition, but as an act of generosity towards others, usually his family. He may

[10] See Chapter IX.   [11] See Chapter XI.

wish two or more persons—say, his children—to have simultaneous rights to the income, or concurrent interests in the thing. Or he may want them to take the income in succession to one another so that, for instance, the income produced by his buildings, patents, shares, etc. is enjoyed say by his widow for her life and then by his children. For reasons which will be explained, however, there must come some moment when his power to say what will happen to his property comes to an end. This will happen at the latest after one generation from his own death.[12]

(c) Power to alienate

The person who is living in his own house and driving his own car can sell either quite easily. Where, however, the income of the thing is being enjoyed by one or more other people it may not be so easy to arrange a sale. In this type of situation the law usually splits the powers of management and sale of the thing from the rights to its beneficial enjoyment, whether in kind or as income, and confers the former on trustees.[13]

An owner may, instead of selling, wish to borrow money on the security of his property—to take his watch to the pawnbroker or mortgage his house to a Building Society. In terms of income value this process is the converse of lease or hire. In the latter the landlord reserves to himself a fixed income in the shape of a rent while the tenant or hirer has the physical use and the undefined residue of the income value. But where a person lends money on the security of a house he gets only a fixed income in the shape of interest on his loan together, of course, with the right to ultimate repayment. Here again it is the person who has the physical use—in this case the borrower—who keeps the undefined residue, if any, of income value; but he has given away a portion of his rights over the thing as security for the debt which he owes and the lender owns.[14]

Finally, instead of alienating or mortgaging a thing, the owner may keep it until he dies. In this case ownership will be transferred to others under his will if he made one, otherwise under the law of intestate succession.[15]

[12] See Chapter XIII.
[13] See Chapter XII.
[14] See Chapter XIV.
[15] See Chapter XV.

5. PUBLIC LAW

Our discussion so far has treated the relations between people with regard to things as if they were purely a matter of private concern. It will be obvious, however, that property involves serious issues of public policy. So far as movables are concerned, consumer protection statutes affect usually the law of obligations, that is contract and tort. It is the law of property in land which, increasingly this century, has felt the impact of legislation enacted in the public interest. On the one hand this reflects the need for control in the interests of public health, public amenities, and the environment generally, so that no longer can a person do what he likes with the land he owns.[16] On the other hand, much legislative intervention has been prompted by the fact that, while land may be an investment for some, it is a necessity for all—we all have to have somewhere to live.[17]

6. CONCLUSION

The preceding pages are strong meat for the beginner, and many students find the law of property both difficult and dull, difficult because there is so much of it, dull because it seems remote from everyday life. It is easy to see what criminal law and tort are all about: something has gone wrong and someone must be punished or made to pay compensation. Parts of property law are rather like these topics in that they deal with problems arising over the physical use of property—disputes among neighbours, for instance, or between landlord and tenant—and, although they may present difficulties, the general familiarity of the subject-matter renders them easy of approach by the student.

But most of us do not commit crimes, injure others, or have rows with the people next door; and (though one might not guess it from the textbooks) few contracts go wrong. Even with this good fortune, however, we need the law, not to settle disputes over events which have occurred already, but to enable us to plan ahead. The main function of the law of property is not to deal with the past but to look forward to the future. People want to acquire things—a car, a house and furniture, a shop, a factory with the necessary plant—and may need to raise money to do so. They need to make arrangements for their property, perhaps because they are getting married, raising children, going into business, or because they will certainly die. To do this as efficiently and securely as possible the law has a selection of tools which may be as abstract as money itself but are of known specification and capability: estate, trust, fund, mortgage, hire-purchase, commercial paper, registers, wills. While some are simple and others very complex, their creation, use, and combination are the heart of the law of property.

II

THE CLASSIFICATION
OF THINGS

THE best way to see what property means for practical purposes is to see what a man of some substance might leave at his death. He would almost certainly own his house; but probably his wife would own it along with him and they might well have been buying it with the aid of a mortgage. He, or they, would own the household belongings and a car, although the latter and some of the household appliances might be being bought on hire purchase.

He might have a life insurance policy, current and deposit accounts at a bank, some money invested in a Building Society, and shares in one or more limited liability companies and some government stock. If he was in business on his own account he might own one office and lease another in a large building, he would have office equipment and perhaps a van and might be leasing a computer. He might have a stock of goods intended for resale and bills of lading for goods consigned to him but not yet delivered and would have petty cash in notes and coin and a balance in his office account at a bank. He might be owed money by his customers and hold patents, trade marks, and the copyright of a book on office management, and the goodwill of his business would also be an asset which could be valued. If his father had been reasonably wealthy and had died leaving a widow but no will he would, along with his brothers and sisters, have an interest in his father's property expectant on his mother's death. And he might well be the executor of the estate of a deceased relative or trustee of a local club or charity.

Abstract things and legal concepts

Now the first thing to notice about the various items which
he owns is that only a few of them are things in the sense of
being physical objects. The home, of course, is one such; but
if there is a mortgage then all that the couple can really call
their own is the difference between what it is worth and what
they owe the lender. The same could be said to be true of the
car or washing-machine being bought on hire purchase. The
other personal belongings and the goods in his business are
physical objects but, of his petty cash, the notes are no more
than pieces of paper bearing a promise and the coins mere
symbols of purchasing power. In his leased office and computer
he has only a limited interest and, although he has an unlimited
interest in the other office, the law would not use the term
'ownership' to describe his relation to the bricks and mortar:
he has only an 'estate' in them, the nature of which must be
explained later.[1] His other belongings are clearly abstract in
the sense that, although they have value, the value attaches
directly not to any physical object but to creations of the
human mind. He may say of his bank account or investment
in a building society 'It's my money' but a moment's reflection
will show that this cannot be true in any physical sense. If his
wife owns the house with him neither could point to any
particular room as their own; nor could he have gone to the
offices of a company brandishing his share certificate and
pointed to some object saying 'That's my share'. Moreover all
the most valuable parts of his property will be of this abstract
unsubstantial kind; and indeed the law is often tempted to
treat even physical objects as though they were abstract
entities.

One of the main difficulties the student of property law
encounters at the very threshold is this presence of abstractions
where he expects to find physical objects. He very soon dis-
covers that the property lawyer takes surprisingly little interest
in land or ships or motor-cars or machinery or animals or food
or drink as such, and not much even in the ownership of such
things, but a great deal in abstract things such as the fee simple
of land, trust funds, stocks and shares, and documents of title

[1] See pp. 84-95 below.

such as bills of lading. Conversely he will discover that what
he takes to be mere rights, such as the right to be paid a sum
of money or the right to use a thing and receive the income
from its exploitation for his lifetime, are treated as things.

The reason why the property lawyer turns all these rights
and interests into things, however abstract they may be, is
that since they have value, people are willing to buy them; and
any valuable asset which is the object of commerce is properly
treated as a thing, just as much if it is an abstraction such as
a share in a company as if it is a physical object such as a ship
or a motor-car. The main reason why far more attention is
devoted to abstractions than to physical objects is that, since
they are creations of the human mind, they can be made to
conform to patterns consciously chosen for their practical
utility and capacity for combination with each other. These
patterns and combinations can be made the objects of a
calculus which is a fit subject of study by lawyers. In comparison with them natural objects such as land or animals are too
individual to serve as mathematical units of this kind.

Perhaps a word should be added to allay any doubts that
may be felt in using the word 'thing' to describe abstract relations. In everyday speech, of course, the word usually denotes
physical objects. This common usage has even been canonized
by the German Civil Code as being the only correct legal use
or the German equivalent. And the English legal philosopher
John Austin states that '*things* are such *permanent* objects,
not being persons, as are sensible or perceptible through the
senses'.[2] This book, however, uses the word to include the
abstract creations of property law—estates, patents, copyright, goodwill, and so on. In doing so it is far from innovation.
The English word, and its counterparts in Latin, and in the
Romance, Teutonic, Scandinavian, and Slavonic languages,
began life to designate relationships, bodies such as assemblies
and courts, then lawsuits, and were only later assumed to
apply just to physical objects.

The work of the conveyancer

A large part of the work of property lawyers with wealthy
clients consists of creating complicated arrangements known

[2] Austin, *Lectures on Jurisprudence* (5th ed., 1911) Vol. I, p. 358.

as settlements.[3] For this purpose they have to work with
elements the nature and potentialities of which are exactly
known. Their position is therefore very like that of a mechani-
cal engineer designing a complicated machine; and just as the
engineer cannot use as component parts natural objects which
he can pick up but must have them made to a preconceived
pattern, so the lawyer making a settlement must work with
abstract concepts which have been made to serve typical
purposes. The property lawyer differs from the engineer in
that he is not free to make and use whatever component parts
he likes, but has at his disposal a limited number of them
which the law provides ready-made. Yet it is surprising what
he can do with them in the way of new combinations.

A great deal of the law of property is concerned with
describing these simple component parts, what can be done
with them, and what has been done with them in the way of
creating standard complex constructions. Here the student
moves in a rarefied atmosphere remote from the physical
world, though by no means remote from social, political,
and economic policy. For these constructions are all made
in order to achieve some purpose, even if only, as has long
been the case, to avoid the payment of taxes. This part of
the law of property, which was worked out first for land and
afterwards extended to cover such permanent sources of income as stocks and shares, is the most intellectually rewarding
for the student, partly because, in its abstractness, it has
strong affinities with mathematics, but partly also because it
shows how an abstract calculus can be made to serve social,
political, or economic policy.

No doubt in all of this the conveyancers, as the most
expert property lawyers are called, have acted and still act as
servants of the propertied classes, and originally very much
under their instructions. Later the law became so technical
that only the conveyancers knew it well enough to know
where it was defective and how to reform it. Even now, when
it has been greatly simplified, it is still something of a mystery
and largely under their control.

[3] See pp. 159–75 below.

Commercial instruments

Some of the same abstractness that characterizes the convey-ancer's side of property law is found also in the property side of commercial law, the essential core of which is concerned with the sale of goods. Here, however, all the more interesting abstractions have been invented by the bankers and merchants themselves, leaving the lawyers to take over, refine, and systematize their creations, without ever completely catching up with the process of invention; while the theoretical elabora-tion of value in the abstract form of money has been the work of the economists, and the lawyers have had little to do with it.

They have, however, taken into property law several instru-ments, such as bills of exchange and cheques, which were invented in order to make money payments without the use of coin, and have to some extent come to treat them not as mere collections of promises but as things which can be bought and sold. They have likewise recognized and accepted the habit which merchants have acquired of treating certain documents which are really receipts for goods to be held on deposit or carried to another place as symbolizing the goods themselves, to such an extent that a sale and transfer of a document operates as a sale and transfer of the goods it sym-bolizes. Here there is first an abstraction by which promises to hold or deliver are treated as equivalent to the goods, and then a materialization of the abstraction, which makes the paper on which the receipt is written or printed equivalent to the receipt. It is in this way that the delivery of a ware-house receipt or a bill of lading is made equivalent to a delivery of the goods.

Public policy

The student enters yet another atmosphere when he enters the part of the law, mainly of land, where the State or other public authorities have intervened directly, to protect agricul-tural, business, or house tenants.[4] Even here he will find the property lawyer at his old habit of detecting or creating ab-stract entities, such as the statutory tenancy under the Rent Acts,[5] but on the whole policy is evident in its naked form.

[4] See pp. 154–8 below.   [5] See p. 158 below.

Here, therefore, the student hardly needs to adjust his style of thinking. His main difficulties are to recognize the precise reasons of policy behind the changes in the detail of the law, and, above all, to assimilate a mass of intricate and often repulsive detail. The land agent can often enlighten him much more effectively than the lawyer, for the land agent is better acquainted with the reasons underlying the law and the lawyer has not yet done much to translate the policy into the abstractions with which he works more securely than with raw fact or policy.

Real and personal property

English law makes a primary distinction between *real* and *personal* property, the former being interests in land other than leasehold interests and the latter movable property together with leasehold interests in land. Real property is often called *realty*, personal property *personalty* or *chattels*, leasehold being, somewhat surprisingly, called *chattels real*, while all other chattels are called *chattels personal*. The distinction is based on historical factors which have no longer any appreciable force; and indeed leaseholds are now always included in books on real property. It is mentioned here only because the student is sure to encounter it later.

Books are still published which profess to deal with real and personal property respectively; and if the one type of book is reserved for land and the other for all other kinds of property, there is something to be said for a division of labour between specialist authors on that principle. For many purposes it is still useful to keep land apart from other kinds of property. It is permanent, almost indestructible, has an income value, and is capable of almost infinite division and subdivision. Accordingly from the earliest periods in the history of English law it has been common to make the same piece of land serve the needs of several persons with conflicting interests. Only in fairly recent times has anything like the same elaborate apparatus been applied to personalty, and even now some kinds of chattels have to be dealt with in a very simple way. Nevertheless, the time has come to emphasize the parts of the law which apply with more or less uniformity to land and chattels, and to relegate as far as possible to the background those which are peculiar to each.

Chattels

Chattels personal are classified as *choses* ('things') *in possession* and *choses in action*, according as they can be enjoyed by taking possession of them or only by bringing an action. The term *chose in action* was first applied to debts, to which alone it is completely appropriate. It expresses the fact that if A owes B £100, the only way in which B can get the money against A's will is by bringing an action against him, whereas if B actually has a book in his possession he can use it at once. However, the term has been extended to all other intangible forms of property, such as patents and copyright. It would in fact be better if the distinction were expressed as one between tangible and intangible things. But, however the distinction may be expressed, it is not always easy to draw. Thus documents which give a right to call for the delivery of tangible things which are known by the name of goods are themselves tangible, but their value depends not on the intrinsic value of the pieces of paper themselves but on the value of the intangible right they symbolize to call for the delivery of the goods; whereas, although bank-notes are merely promises to pay issued by a bank and they are worth much more than the intrinsic value of the paper they are printed on, their tangible character has almost entirely banished from human consciousness the intangible promises they represent. However, as money, they must, along with coins, receive special treatment. Finally, there are collective entities, such as the capital of a company or groups of investments managed by trustees, which are best called *funds*.

Thus we have to consider (1) land; (2) goods, i.e. tangible movables other than money; (3) *choses in action*, i.e. intangible movables such as debts, patents, and copyright; (4) money; and (5) funds. The purpose of this chapter is to explain the main characteristics of these various classes of property, leaving for later discussion the uses to which they can be put and the ways in which they can be protected and transferred.

1. LAND

(a) Definition

We are accustomed to think of land in terms of area, so that a landowner's park is said to be so many acres in extent. That is a good starting-point, but does not include all that the law means by land. Two extensions have to be made, one natural and the other artificial, by the hand of man.

In the first place, if land were only two-dimensional, it would be useless. Agriculture requires a depth of soil, and even human movement requires an air-space above the surface. Thus for practical purposes land must be thought of as having volume, and the only question the law has to answer is how far it should extend in the third dimension, that of height and depth. The solution adopted by English law is expressed in the maxim *cuius est solum eius est usque ad coelum et usque ad inferos*, that is to say, possession of the land extends upwards to infinity and downwards to the centre of the earth. That implies that, except where restrained by other rules of law, a person may build as high as he likes and dig as deep as he likes in search of minerals, which will then belong to him. However, such restraining rules may be very important. For instance, one person may be entitled to prevent another person from building so as to obstruct the light from coming in through his windows; and, most significant of all, a landowner may no longer search for or get any of the coal or oil under his land: they are vested in public bodies. Yet in principle the maxim applies. It is perhaps worthy of mention that land includes lakes and rivers within its boundaries. They are called in the technical language of the law land covered by water.

Further, in principle, whatever is attached to the soil becomes part of it. That means in the first place that things such as seeds or seedlings, which have hitherto existed as individual movable objects, lose their identity when sown or planted in the ground and become part of the land. Similarly, objects such as crops or fruit or trees, which are ordinarily thought of as things in themselves, and which will become individual movable things once they are detached from the soil, are at present part of it. Again, houses and other buildings are inevitably part of the land on which they stand, for they had no identity of their own until they were built on it, and their materials have become merged in them. However, although a building is part of the land on which it is built, it is possible to divide it, not only vertically, as for instance into two semi-detached houses, but also horizontally into flats each of which is a separate piece of landed property, capable of being held not merely by a tenant under a lease but in fee simple, that is to say, in a way which is equivalent to full ownership.

Movables which are merely placed on land remain movable, and doubts sometimes arise as to the status of movables buried in the soil, for instance in order to hide them.

The most difficult questions arise in connexion with what are called fixtures. The primary question is, what is a fixture? It is important where one person buys land and takes a conveyance of it from another, or where one person lends money on a mortgage of land belonging to another. The answer to the question is, generally speaking, that anything is a fixture that is not merely placed on the land, but attached to it with the purpose of making it part of the land. Anything that satisfies this definition will pass with the land on a conveyance or will be subject to a mortgage.

The second question is, granted that a thing is a fixture, may it be removed, for instance by a tenant who has affixed it to the land? Thus if a farmer builds a barn on the land let to him or if a tenant nails tapestry to the wall of a room or if a manufacturer fixes machinery to the floors of a factory which he has leased, disputes have arisen in the past out of demands by the tenant of the land, house, or factory, that he be allowed to remove the fixture. Most of such questions have now been decided in favour of the tenant; but in any case they do not concern the character of the fixtures whilst they are still fixed. The fixtures are certainly part of the land, though they may cease to be so at the wish of the tenant.

(b) Features

By 'land', then, the law understands all immovable property—fields, farms, houses, shops, factories, and so on. It is worth reflecting on some of the obvious characteristics of this species of property because, as will be seen, they have determined the uses to which land can be put and the concepts which English lawyers long ago devised to give effect to those uses.

(i) Permanence The most obvious feature of land, as distinct from movable property, is that it endures. Of course there may be natural calamities, earthquakes, landslides, and so on, but it would be absurd, for fear of these exceptional events, to deny ourselves the possibility of dealing with the normal situation.

(ii) Safety Land is not the only thing of permanence—diamonds, for instance, are forever. But, unlike them, land cannot readily be stolen; in fact it has never been necessary to extend the law of theft to protect land.

(iii) Limited supply While fields may be built on and tower blocks soar there is, none the less, a finite amount of territory available.

(iv) Income value Perhaps the most important feature of land from the point of view of our legal system is that it has an income value. If it is a farm then the crops or cattle which it sustains can be sold and, provided that some of the profits are ploughed back, it will continue to produce an income. If it is an office block or a factory the rents fulfil the same function. What is perhaps a little more difficult to see at first is that a house has an income value for its owner-occupier. Admittedly it produces no cash for him, but he is not paying money in hotel bills to live elsewhere. He is benefitting from what economists call the 'quasi-rent'.

(v) Capital value Not only does the land produce an income, or save outlay, for its owner but, with reasonable management, it does so without depreciation. Its capital value—the amount it would fetch on sale—remains intact. Indeed, given the limited supply mentioned above and the growth of the population its capital value may not only keep pace with inflation but may grow in real terms.

(vi) Necessity Land is necessary to us all. We all must have somewhere to live and work, something to eat and something to wear. The house we live in is land, and our food and clothes are produced, made, stored, and sold to us on land.

(vii) Investment The combination of the features just described has meant for centuries that land is an attractive investment. A successful business man will find in it something that is permanent, safe, limited in supply, income-producing, and appreciating in capital value. When to this is added the feature of necessity its attraction becomes paramount: where better to put one's money than in something that everyone needs. This feature can, of course, give rise to conflicts between the wealthy few and the rest of us and some countries have sought to resolve these conflicts by simply forbidding private investment in land. Our system has not done so but has intervened in particular areas. The impact of public law will be described later.

(viii) Endowment As an investment, land may form part of the balanced portfolio of any wealthy person, company, or pension fund. But it has certain features which take it outside the purely commercial calculus and recommend it as a family endowment. It seems to be a psychological trait of English fathers that, while they love their families, they do not often trust their sons. Not, that is, that they suppose the young man to be necessarily a criminal. They are quite happy to ensure that he has an *income*; but they are reluctant to trust him with *capital* convinced that at worst he will squander it on playthings and at best invest it in some madcap business venture. What they seek, therefore is some means of providing for him while at the same time ensuring that the family fortune is preserved for his children and, if possible, for theirs. The permanence and safety of land of course recommend it for this purpose; but the outstanding feature of English law's response to this quest is the way in which it can detach ownership of the *income*—so that the son may be given that—from ownership of the *capital* which will, in time, vest in a future generation. It is in fulfilling this function that the concept of the 'estate' in land has proved so useful.

(ix) Public power Finally, and as a historical note, it should be recalled that the private ownership of this attractive investment (or 'means of production') conferred public power. Many of the constitutional struggles of our past were about

the allocation of property interests in land. Along with the private ownership of a county, say Norfolk, went the public honour of a peerage and the political power of a seat in the legislature.

2. GOODS

Goods are defined by the Sale of Goods Act as chattels personal other than money or *choses in action*. For the purposes of the law of sale they also include what are called *emblements*, that is to say, the growing crops annually produced by the labour of the cultivator. That only means that emblements may be sold in advance as though they were already goods and that a sale of them does not fall under the rules governing the sale of land. They are actually part of the land, and therefore not goods, until they are severed from it.

A distinction is often made between goods which are fungible and those which are not. Fungible goods are mutually interchangeable; they can be replaced by equal quantities and qualities, and are estimated by weight, number, or measure. Typical fungibles are coins and raw materials. In the ordinary way it does not matter what coins are given to a person as change provided they add up to the right amount. It does not matter which particular bottles of milk the milkman delivers provided they are of the right quantity and quality. But a little reflection will show that there is no class of goods which are always fungible. Not all goods are capable of being fungible; some are always individualized. But even goods which are normally fungible can be treated as individuals. Thus coins, if valued for their rareness or their aesthetic or archaeological interest, are not fungible, because they cannot be replaced by others. In other words, goods are fungible if they are treated as such.

Similarly if the subject-matter of a sale is expressed as so many articles of a class or kind or so many units of weight of a raw material, the goods sold are at that moment unascertained. When so many articles or so much weight of raw material are set aside for delivery to the buyer, the goods become ascertained. Here, too, there are evidently not two classes of goods; the same goods were at one moment unascertained by a process of human selection. Of course for a person to be willing to buy unascertained goods, that is to say, goods to be ascertained later, he must regard them as fungible, that is to say, as not depending for their value on their qualities as individuals.

Yet another distinction is made between existing and future goods. A thing which does not yet exist cannot of course be an individual object, but it can be individualized in the mind of the person ordering it, as where a person gives an order for his portrait to be painted by a named painter. Nevertheless, in general future goods are the anticipated produce of agriculture or manufacture, such as wheat, cotton, or steel rails. As such they are unascertained and also fungible.

In strict analysis unascertained and future goods are not yet goods, but a promise to deliver them implied in a sale vests a specific *chose in action* in the buyer. Such a *chose in action* may in its turn by symbolized by a document, as will be explained later.[6]

Some articles have a value so great and so dependent on their individual characteristics that some sure and permanent means are required of identifying them and the persons entitled to them. This often leads to the formation of registers, sometimes private, such as the stud-book of racehorses, sometimes public, such as the registers of ships and aircraft. Ships are indeed governed by special rules of law and are for some purposes treated almost as though they were floating plots of land.

3. INTANGIBLE MOVABLES

(a) Debts and other choses in action

If one person makes a contract with another person by virtue of which the other person makes him a promise, that promise obviously has some value. But whether it can be regarded as creating a thing will depend on whether the value can be transferred from the promisee to some third person. If it cannot be so transferred all that exists is a relation of a strictly personal kind between the promisor and the promisee, which never escapes beyond the limits of contract. To be transfer-

[6] pp. 31-2 below.

able, or, to use technical language, assignable, a right created by a promise must be of such a kind that it will not change its nature or content upon transfer to another person. Thus if performance is to be to the satisfaction of the promisee, the promisor cannot be forced to execute it to the satisfaction of any other person, and accordingly the benefit of the promise cannot be transferred. Similarly, if the amount that has to be paid or delivered under the promise is apt to change if the benefit of the promise is transferred, as for instance if a company bargains for the delivery of all the goods it will require of a certain kind and is then merged in a larger concern, no such transfer can be allowed to take place. Thus in practice choses in action are almost confined to promises to pay fixed sums of money or to deliver fixed quantities of goods. Even services of a fixed kind can rarely be transferred from one person to another because the transfer carries with it some taint of slavery.

A debt is an abstract thing, quite distinct from the money which will be the creditor's if it is paid. For if X promises to pay Y £5, what belongs to Y is not the note which may possibly be at that moment in X's pocket, but a totally distinct thing, namely the contractual right to be paid the £5. Each of the two things, the note and the right to be paid £5, can be the object of distinct transfers, for X can effectually and quite properly make A the owner of the note and Y can just as effectually and properly make B the owner of the right to be paid the £5.

Choses in action in the nature of debts do not necessarily arise out of contracts, for a legatee may have a claim to be paid his legacy by the personal representatives of the deceased. But mere personal rights of action, such as the right to bring an action for damages for libel or for personal injury, cannot be assigned by one person to another, and so are not considered choses in action. The reason once given for this is that an assignment would be champertous, that is to say, it would amount to trading in litigation and the fruits of litigation; and since the later Middle Ages interfering in the disputes of others, especially for purposes of gain, has been considered dangerous to social peace and therefore against public policy. But perhaps another reason that lay in the way of recognizing such claims as choses in action has been their indefiniteness, for the exact amount of the damages to be obtained cannot be predicted.

(b) Commercial paper

Certain types of written promises to pay money or deliver goods have become standardized and so fully acknowledged by the commercial world as to represent almost, and sometimes quite completely, the money or the goods.

Once a contract for the sale of goods has been made between merchants, then each has the benefit of the other's promise. The benefit is a thing which each owns and can transfer but is, in itself, intangible. If, however, it is expressed in a certain written form the documents themselves are bought and sold as if they were the money or the goods. In the hands of the seller the benefit of the buyer's promise to pay the price is reified in a negotiable instrument, while the buyer receives a document of title to the goods which the seller has promised to deliver.

(i) Negotiable instruments   The best-known negotiable instruments are the bill of exchange, the promissory note, and the cheque. For the law of property the essential feature of a bill of exchange is that it represents, in physical form, the debt which the buyer owes and the seller owns, and the latter may deal with it just as he may his own books or motorcar. Indeed a negotiable instrument is even more suitable to commerce than either of those things. The quality of *negotiability* means that anyone taking the instrument in good faith and for value obtains a good title despite any defect in the title of the transferor. Thus if, in good faith, you buy my books or car from someone who has stolen them from me you must return them to me and are left—for what it may be worth—to an action against the thief. But a thief can pass to an innocent purchaser a good title to a negotiable instrument.

A simple form of bill of exchange, used nowadays in overseas trade, occurs when goods are sold but are still on their way to the buyer. He will get the documents of title described below. But if the seller does not get the cash at once he will take a bill from the buyer which he can then use as if it were cash.

> **Bill for £1,000**
>
> London, 1st January 1982
>
> Three months after date pay me or my order the sum of one thousand pounds for value received.
>
> To: Brian Buyer Esq.   Steven Seller
>
> *Accepted* 1/1/82 — Brian Buyer

The buyer signs the bill for acceptance, gives it to the seller, and has three months in which to find the money. In the hands of the seller, however, the bill of exchange is an immediately realizable asset. He can endorse it, by writing his name on the back, and transfer it by delivery to anyone he chooses. It can then be passed from hand to hand, the holder being entitled to be paid by Brian Buyer when the three months expires and the bill matures. Assuming that the buyer is solvent, and that there are no particular risks in the transaction, Steven Seller will usually endorse and transfer the bill to a bank. The process is known as 'discounting' because the bank will give him for it an amount based on that sum of money which, invested then, would produce £1,000 on the date the bill matures. Thus, during the three months, the claim represented by the bill is an asset which is growing in value; and we shall see later that, in relation to land, the concept of the 'estate' is used to express in legal terms the vital factor of *time* which determines present values.

The bill can then, on endorsement, pass from hand to hand—from that bank to another, or to a customer. Any holder in due course, that is to say anyone who has physical control of the bill at maturity and has bought in good faith, is entitled to be paid the £1,000 by Brian Buyer, even if it had been stolen on its way to him or even if the buyer had a good defence against the seller, because, for instance, the goods never arrived. In other words any transfer of the bill to a purchaser in good faith is a transfer of the right to receive £1,000 from Brian Buyer.

The example just given is of the very simplest type of bill of exchange. Historically, however, the bill evolved to deal with a rather more sophisticated situation. Suppose that when Brian Buyer contracted to buy goods from Steven Seller he was already owed £1,000 by David Debtor. One way to resolve matters would be for DD to send bullion, notes, or coin to BB, and for him then to send them on to SS—a process both expensive and risky. A much cheaper and safer method, especially if DD and SS live in the same place, is for BB to order DD to pay the money to SS. But for DD to be liable directly to SS he must *accept* this order, and so the bill would look like this:

Bill for £1,000   3/1/82   Debtor   London, 1st January 1982

Three months after date pay **Steven Seller** or order the sum of one thousand pounds for value received.

To: **David Debtor Esq.**   Accepted   David   **Brian Buyer**

SS can now deal with the bill exactly as described above, and any holder in due course will have a remedy against DD.

Another form of negotiable instrument is the promissory note, which differs from bills in that it is unilateral, that is only one person signs.

£1,000   London, 1st January 1982

I promise to pay **Steven Seller** or order at the Old Bank, Oxford, three months after date the sum of one thousand pounds for value received.

Brian Buyer

Most people have in their pockets at some time or another examples in the shape of Bank of England notes. The result is rather interesting: a private-law obligation under which, to use the above example, BB owes SS £1,000 is performed by payment—that is, by handing over banknotes which themselves bear a promise to pay. This obligation, however, is strictly one of public law and the nature of money will be briefly discussed later.

The same rules as to negotiability apply to the cheque, which is defined by statute as 'a bill of exchange, drawn on a banker, payable on demand'. This definition is likely to confuse the beginner. Admittedly a cheque looks like a bill of exchange:

1st January 1982

Old Bank Ltd.,
High Street, Oxford

Pay Steven Seller   or order

one thousand pounds/00   £1000.00

Brian Buyer

As however, the bank never accepts the order by signing the cheque it is never directly liable to the payee. When the cheque is presented it should, of course, meet it—for the cheque is a bill of exchange *payable on demand.* This obligation, however, is only to the drawer, BB, and arises out of the bank's contract with him; so that if he has neither credit balance nor overdraft facilities the bank need not pay. In fact a cheque is more like a promissory note, that is a promise by the drawer that his bank will pay.

(ii) Documents of title. The commonest documents of title are bills of lading, delivery warrants, and warehouse receipts. A bill of lading is a receipt given by the master of a ship or its owner's loading broker to the consignor of goods placed on his ship for carriage to the consignee—or, as is generally the case, to the consignee or his order. It is executed in triplicate, and the master gives two copies to the consignor, keeping one for himself. The consignor then sends one of his copies to the consignee. Thereafter the consignee may, if he chooses, endorse and sell the bill of lading to another person and it may pass, like a negotiable instrument, from hand to hand. Here again the ultimate holder may call for delivery of the goods on surrendering the bill of lading, and to that extent the bill of lading represents the goods; but the representation is not so complete as with a bill of exchange—and accordingly the bill of lading is not strictly speaking a negotiable instrument—for

although the master must deliver the goods to the person who presents the bill, if the bill has been stolen from, or lost by, anyone properly entitled to it, that person can recover the goods from the person who has obtained delivery, or indeed anyone who has acquired them from him. The same rules apply to other documents of title unless in some way by custom or otherwise, they have been made fully negotiable. In the United States most of such documents of title are fully negotiable.

(c) Contracts as assets

The previous section described how, in the normal contract of sale of goods, each party's promise becomes a piece of property in the hands of the other, is embodied in some form of commercial paper, and may then easily be transferred. But a contract, even for personal service, may be an asset in another way. Each expects performance from, and has claims against, the other. But there may be situations in which one party needs protection against interference by outsiders in the asset which the contract represents for him. A theatre manager engages a popular musician to appear for a season but a rival manager tries to 'bribe' the artist to break his contract (and be liable for damages) and appear elsewhere. The original manager may well secure an injunction against his rival to prevent this form of poaching. He cannot compel *performance* of the contract; but he can ensure its protection from unjustified interference. Furthermore, as far as he is concerned, he is protected against all the world; that is to say against all his world—that of show-business rivals. It is revealing to note that entrepreneurs in the film industry and the popular music business use the language, not of contract, but of property. They do not say 'I have signed a contract with such-and-such a star' but 'I have a piece of that boy'.

(d) Goodwill

Goodwill is property of a highly peculiar kind. It is the right to enjoy all the advantages of an established trade connexion. Customers who have been in the habit of dealing with a business will probably continue to do so, even if the business changes hands, and this probability is regarded as so valuable that large sums of money are commonly paid for it. So well established a head of property is it that its value must be taken into account for purposes of taxation. Yet it is an odd kind of property since only the person who has transferred the goodwill can be placed under a duty to respect it. He indeed can be restrained from soliciting his former customers and he may also agree not to carry on a competing business. But no third party can be restrained from trading in such a way as to reduce the value of the goodwill. Yet as a marketable object goodwill must be considered property.

(e) Industrial and intellectual property

Also intangible, and therefore often included in choses in action, are certain rights which have recently acquired the name *industrial* or *intellectual property*. Such are patents, registered designs, trade marks and trade names, and copyright. They are really monopolies protected permanently, or for a limited period, by law. The law governing all of them is highly specialized and is handled by experts. All that will be attempted here is a very summary account of their nature and purpose.

These monopolies fall naturally into two classes, the one perpetual, the other temporary. The former really amount to nothing more than the right to identify one's business or its products and prevent others from usurping the advantages which go with them, or, as the phrase goes, 'passing off' their goods as one's own. There is therefore no reason of public policy why they should not last for ever, for they do nothing to prevent or even discourage competitors from producing or trading without using improper means. These perpetual monopolies are trade names and trade marks.

The exclusive right to one's trade name is protected at common law and equity by 'passing-off' actions, in which the plaintiff must prove that confusion has been or is likely to be caused between his name and that assumed by the defendant or between the name attached to his goods and that placed by the defendant on his goods, and that such confusion has has caused or is likely to cause injury to his goodwill. The protection of trade names is in fact only an indirect way of protecting goodwill.

A trade mark is a mark used to indicate a connexion in the

course of trade between goods and the person entitled to use the mark. If registered it gives a protection free from the difficulties which sometimes encounter the plaintiff in a passing-off action. Registration is in the first instance for seven years, but it may be renewed indefinitely for successive periods of fourteen years. A trade mark could formerly be alienated only with the goodwill of a business, but it can now be alienated separately. Thus trade marks have attained an independent status and no longer exist merely to protect goodwill.

The temporary monopolies are the exclusive rights to exploit patents, industrial designs, and copyright. These are all genuine monopolies which operate to exclude competition in manufacture, trade, or the dissemination of literary or artistic work. Now it is the general policy of the law to stimulate competition, in the hope that thereby things will be produced and disseminated in the best and cheapest way. Accordingly, to grant perpetual monopolies to inventors, artists, authors, and composers would be unthinkable. On the other hand, such persons must be given some inducement to produce. Processes of manufacture can indeed be kept secret, but, while present or future employees may be restrained from divulging such secrets, once they are divulged they become public property. Thus, so long as a process remains secret, the public suffers from the existence of a monopoly but the manufacturer also suffers from the ever-present fear that it may at any time cease to be one.

The solution which has been adopted, with variations among the various classes of monopolies, goes back to the famous Statute of Monopolies of James I. It is that in return for immediate disclosure to the public, the inventor shall have a temporary monopoly, which he can dispose of for money if he wishes. After the monopoly comes to an end everybody is free to act as though it had never existed.

A patent is the exclusive right granted by the Crown for twenty years of using, exercising, and vending an invention. On applying for a patent the applicant must lodge with the Patent Office a specification showing the nature of his invention and the method of carrying it into effect. In exceptional cases the specification is kept secret, but in principle the invention must be disclosed to the public, for such disclosure is the consideration for the temporary monopoly granted the patentee. The patent may yet be held to be invalid if the invention be found to contain nothing new, and it may well be imagined that some of the world's most costly and protracted litigation arises out of disputes about patents. Industrial designs can be registered and then receive protection analogous to that of patents. 'Know-how' is the name given to those industrial techniques which, while falling short of patentable inventions, are none the less so valuable that they can be marketed as a kind of incorporeal property.

Copyright is of two kinds. There is first the common law right to restrain the publication of unpublished writings. It is perpetual and survives in the hands of the representatives of the original writer. But its money value is limited since once the writing is published anybody may copy it, so that the person who has paid for the privilege of publishing it may find others making use of what he has paid for. The more valuable copyright is statutory and gives the sole and exclusive right to print or otherwise multiply copies, and, in the case of dramatic or musical works, to perform them. In most cases the right vests in the author automatically without registration, and lasts normally for the life of the author and a period of fifty years after his death, after which anyone may publish or perform.

Patents and copyright would have a very limited efficacy if they operated only within the United Kingdom. Hence every attempt is made to extend them to foreign countries. The only way to do this with patents is to take out a new patent in every country where manufacture might be undertaken by a competitor; and of course the requirements of the patent law of each country must be observed. But for many years a movement has been on foot to make copyright genuinely international, so that if an author acquires it in one country, he automatically has it in other countries also. Most countries now belong to either the Universal Copyright Convention or the Berne Convention or both.

(f) Stocks and shares

The stock issued by governments and other public authorities is really only the acknowledgement of loans made to them and a promise to pay interest at a fixed rate. Some such loans are redeemable, others irredeemable.

A detailed description of stocks and shares in limited companies belongs to Company Law. But an analysis of the nature of a share in a limited company is very much in place.

It is easy to say quite shortly that a shareholder has a share in the capital of a company proportionate to the value he has contributed to it, but such a statement means nothing until it is explained. For a person may have shares, for the time being undivided, in many other things, such as land, or a collection of pictures, or a heap of coal, and in all such cases he may insist on having the property divided and so convert his share of the whole into sole ownership of a specific part; and it might therefore be thought that a shareholder of a company could force a division of the capital and take away, for instance, one particular machine, the value of which was equivalent to his share. But that is not the case. One shareholder cannot force a partition of the assets of a company; the most he can do in that direction is to get other shareholders with a majority holding to join with him in winding up the company. Nor can he sue the company for the value of his share. And yet, as is well known, the various stock exchanges provide an extraordinarily active market in shares. What advantages then does a buyer hope to gain when he buys shares?

It might be said that he hopes to be able to resell them at a profit. That is true—the real value of a share to its holder is now perhaps usually its present or future sales value—but it rather begs the question, for we should still have to ask why he in his turn can find a buyer.

It is not enough to say that he will be entitled to a share in the capital of the company if it is wound up, for as a rule he will hope that it will never be wound up. Is he then entitled to an income in the shape of dividends? Again the answer is no. Neither he nor any combination of his fellow shareholders can force the directors to declare a dividend, though if they have a majority holding of shares they may be able to dislodge directors who do not declare a dividend. However, if a sum of money is set aside for distribution to the shareholders, it must be fairly distributed so that the same dividend is paid on every share belonging to a class. Thus if there are only three shareholders, and each has a single share, any profits that are distributed must be distributed equally among them, and if their shares are unequal the profits must be distributed among them in accordance with the size of their shares. Shareholders have also voting rights at the annual general meeting of a company and may use them in order to elect the directors who are to control the management of the company, but these voting rights are perhaps not strictly speaking property.

Accordingly, from the point of view of property law, a share may best be defined as a hope, often rising to an expectation, of receiving dividends from a company, though not of any definite amount, together with a right not to be differentiated against in respect of any dividend which may be declared by the directors and an ultimate right to a share in the capital of the company if it is wound up. And, as so defined, shares have an undoubted value for which persons will pay good money, though the value may be more or less speculative.

4. MONEY

It has already been explained that money consists now of both coins and promissory notes issued by the Bank of England, and therefore in theory sometimes consists of *choses in possession* and sometimes of *choses in action*. But coins, if used as money, are only symbols of purchasing power and bank-notes are no less. Thus the distinction between coins and bank-notes is quite unreal. Both are alike treated as tangible symbols.

Money must be distinguished from other movables, for it is that with which other things are bought and it is not in itself an object of sale. It has been defined for legal purposes as comprising 'all chattels which, issued by the authority of the law and denominated with reference to a unit of account, are meant to serve as universal means of exchange'.[7] Thus money, to be current in England, must be issued as such by the Mint or the Bank of England, and must be expressed in pounds and pence. Since it is meant to serve as a universal means of exchange the law must allow it to pass from hand

[7] Mann, *The Legal Aspect of Money*, 4th ed., p. 8.

to hand freely and with the utmost security without persons taking it in payment in good faith being concerned to
investigate the title of the person paying it. Thus the rule
has always been that the title to current coin passes by delivery
to anyone who takes it for value in good faith; and the same
rule applies, as we have already seen,[8] to banknotes. It is
often said that money has no earmark, that is to say, that one
coin cannot be sufficiently distinguished from another to be
easily identified, and that that is the reason why a person
who acquires current coin for value in good faith becomes
owner. But it is just not true. Coins can be stolen and they are
frequently marked so as to make detection easier; but the
thief makes the shopkeeper owner of such marked coins if he
uses them to buy goods. The true reason is that any other rule
would make coins less useful as a universal means of exchange.
For over fifty years banknotes have not been convertible,
so that the promise made on an English note is performed
merely by exchanging that note for others; but of course
they retain their character of negotiability.

5. FUNDS

The essential nature of a fund is that it preserves its identity
although its contents change. Thus persons beneficially entitled
to a fund are entitled to be paid the income derived from it,
and can enforce that right and alienate their interests in it,
but the investments contained in it may be varied from time
to time. One example of a fund has already been discussed,
namely the capital of a company. The form taken by that
capital is constantly changing, as debts due to the company
are paid and others contracted, as out-of-date machinery is
replaced and as stock-in-trade is sold and new goods manufac-
tured; yet the capital is regarded as a continuing entity, over
which debenture holders may have a floating charge[9] and in
which shareholders may have shares producing dividends.

   The capital of a company is a fund of a specialized character, for it is the property of an abstract person, the company,
of which the shareholders are members and debenture holders
merely secured creditors; while the power of managing the

[8] pp. 30–1 above.   [9] See p. 201 below.

business, and therefore of varying the investments, is vested in a board of directors, who are mere agents of the company but have very wide powers. It is as members of the company that the shareholders share in the capital and the dividends produced by managing it; they are not brought into immediate contact with either the investments contained in the fund or the fund itself conceived as an abstract entity.

However, it is by no means necessary to interpose an abstract person between human beings and a fund; it can be vested in human beings for the benefit of other human beings, or indeed for themselves. In English law this is done by means of a trust.

Property may be given to trustees for the benefit of persons or for purposes, usually charitable. In either case the trustees have the management of the property, including the power of alienation, subject perhaps to certain restrictions. They may not take any benefit themselves in their character of trustees, unless they are empowered by the instrument creating the trust to charge for their services, and the trust property is not available for payment of their private debts. They must obey the terms of the trust and are under a personal duty to the beneficiaries similar to that which could have been imposed on them by contract. Thus the beneficiaries, if there are any, have personal rights against the trustees. They are also regarded as having a sort of property in the trust fund.[10]

[10] See further p. 59 below.

III

THE PROTECTION OF PROPERTY INTERESTS

1. ACTIONS AT COMMON LAW

THE rules governing the recovery of property vary with the nature of the property. Some kinds of property can be possessed, others cannot. Of the former the possession can be lost and pass into the hands of a person not the owner, and recovery means a recovery of possession. Of the others some, such as patents, copyright, or goodwill, can be infringed, and the only meaning that recovery can have is a suit to restrain infringement and perhaps to obtain damages or a return of the profits made by the infringer. Where a trust fund is concerned, the only remedy can be a suit for enforcement of the trust or, in the last resort, for removal and replacement of the trustees.

Here all that can be discussed is the recovery of possession. There is a difference between land and goods. A person who loses the former can insist on having it returned to him. He can bring an action of 'ejectment', and if he succeeds will obtain a judgment for return of the land. If the defendant refuses to comply with the judgment, the sheriff will be ordered to put the plaintiff in possession of the land. On the other hand, it is a matter for the discretion of the judge whether he will order the return of goods or give judgment for either the return of the goods or payment of their value at the option of the defendant. Thus a person who loses goods can never be certain that he will recover them *in specie*. However, generally he is likely to feel satisfied with payment of the value, whereas, if the article in question is unique, for example, a valuable picture, the judge will usually order it to be returned to him without giving the defendant any choice in the matter.

To recover possession the plaintiff must establish his title to the thing, or, in the technical language of the law, prove that he has the right to the immediate possession of it. Although this is not the same as possession itself, it is so often the case that the plaintiff can prove it only by proving that he or some other person possessed the thing previously that possession is said to be a good root, sometimes the only possible root, of title. It must therefore be described at the outset.

2. POSSESSION

Possession is one of the most difficult concepts in English, or for that matter any other, law. Part of the difficulty of understanding it comes from the fact that the legal meaning of the term does not fully correspond with its ordinary non-legal meaning. The ordinary popular meaning is intentional physical control; if I have such control over a thing that I can, if necessary, prevent anyone else from using it, I possess it. Even if possession is so regarded as a mere fact, its outline may not always be easy to recognize, still less to define; for bystanders may often legitimately disagree if asked to give their opinion whether a person has enough power to prevent others from using a thing to be regarded as possessing it. Such is especially the case if a person is temporarily absent from land. In practice indeed possession is often said to be a social rather than a physical fact, in the sense that a person will be held to possess a thing if he has the sort and extent of control that society, considered as being represented by the ordinary reasonable man, would regard as appropriate to the kind of thing and the circumstances of the case.

But this is only the beginning of the difficulty; for the judges in developing the law have made use of possession for various purposes and in the course of doing so have given it a meaning which sometimes departs from its ordinary non-legal meaning. On the other hand, they have attributed to possessors certain advantages which may be called possessory rights or, more compendiously, the right of possession, to be carefully distinguished from the right to possess, which may, however, sometimes be inferred from it. Thus a possessor has, as such, the right to recover damages for trespass from anyone who intrudes on his possession, but he may in certain circumstances have to prove that he has a right to the immediate possession of a thing. Similarly, the legislator uses the word in quite different contexts ranging from the adverse possession required to benefit under the statutes of limitation[1] to the possession which attracts penalties under the criminal laws against misuse of drugs.

Now in certain circumstances, although a person's possession passes the ordinary tests applied by the average layman, a judge may think it improper to accord such rights to a person whom an average layman would not regard as a possessor; or again he may wish to vary the concept depending on the function it is to fulfil. Thus if money and heroin are slipped into someone's handbag unawares, the owner certainly has possession of the money as against a thief, but not of the drug so as to incur criminal liability.

The proper way to express this divergence between the use of the term 'possession' by laymen and by lawyers is to say that when lawyers use the term they have in mind the legal consequences of certain states of fact which, though they tend to conform to the ordinary layman's notion of possession, often depart from it; and where possession is relevant to the law of property it really means the collection of possessory rights which are collectively known as the 'right of possession'.

In what ensues we shall have to deal with this legal concept of possession and not with possession as it is regarded by the ordinary layman.

Certain persons who have physical control of a thing are held not to possess but merely to have custody of it on behalf of someone else. Thus, although a servant possesses what he has taken on his master's behalf, whether from a third party ·or from nobody at all, the answer to the question whether he possesses something he has received from his master or, on the contrary, his master continues to possess it through him, depends on the circumstances; he does not possess, for instance, his master's silver when he has cleaned it, but he may possess his master's luggage if he is travelling overland to meet him when he steps down from an aircraft. Other difficulties arise with regard to lodgers and tenants; the law

[1] See pp. 51–3 below.

governing the attribution to them of possession of furnished or unfurnished rooms is both complicated and doubtful. Further, the merely temporary control that a guest has, for instance, over the cutlery he is using at a dinner party is not treated as possession. His host possesses it through him. But, generally speaking, physical control does imply possession, and so tenants of land or houses, and borrowers, pledgees, or other bailees of goods possess what they have under their control; though for certain purposes the landlord and, in certain cases, the lender or other bailor are also held to possess at the same time.[2]

Although these principles do not amount to a very neat doctrine, they afford answers to all the obvious problems which are likely to arise except one. Difficulties have arisen particularly where one person has found something in or on land possessed by another person, and the presence of the thing was hitherto unknown to the latter. Does his possession of the land or house carry with it possession of all its contents? Or if the possessor must intend to acquire possession of the contents in addition to acquiring possession of the land or house, will a general intention to acquire the contents suffice, or must he have directed his mind to each specific object, or at least to such specific objects as would not ordinarily be expected to be there? Again, does it matter whether the object in question is on or embedded in the land or again whether it was in or on the land when he took possession of the latter or, on the other hand, came on to it later without his knowledge? The few decisions on this topic are not easy to reconcile with each other and do not tell a very clear story. Some at least seem to turn on the special facts of the case. Perhaps some of them are unsound.

Thus a Viking ship was held to be possessed by the possessor of the land in which it had been buried centuries before, and rings found imbedded in a reservoir were held to be possessed by the owner of the reservoir. But a shopkeeper was not held to possess a five-pound note dropped by someone on the part of the floor of the shop open to the public; and the possessor of a house which had subsequently been

[2] The Theft Act 1968 s. 5(1) treats property as belonging to 'any person having possession or control of it . . .'.

requisitioned by the military authorities was held not to possess a brooch which was afterwards found on a ledge at the
top of a window (though the true reason for the decision
may be that, whatever might have been the correct view as
between the finder and the military authorities, the person
who, as former possessor, brought the action against the
finder, had never actually taken possession of the house before
it was requisitioned).

For the general purposes of property law, however, the
concept of *possession* is useful as a contrast with *ownership*.
Thus if A borrows B's book it is sufficient for most purposes
to say that A has possession and B ownership. Whether all the
problems of chattel bailment can be resolved thus, or whether
the notion of 'estates' might be useful, will be considered in
relation to hire-purchase.[3]

3. TITLE

Title is a shorthand term used to denote the facts which, if
proved, will enable a plaintiff to recover possession or a defendant to retain possession of a thing. Even when a purchaser's solicitor insists that a vendor shall give a good title
to the land, he has at the back of his mind the possibility of
his client's having to recover or defend the possession of it.

A plaintiff seeking to recover possession must prove that
he has a right to the immediate possession of the thing. Before
examining in greater detail the meaning of this statement it
is well to dispose of a number of special considerations.

Exceptional cases

First, a person who, in the ordinary acceptation of the term,
is an owner, may not have a right to the immediate possession
of a thing because if it is land he has leased it, or if it is a
movable chattel he has bailed it, for instance hired it out, to
another person for a fixed term. During the continuance of
the term he cannot recover possession from the lessee or
bailee, whereas, if it comes into the possession of a third party,
the lessee or bailee will recover possession on the strength of
his right to immediate possession, though in order to do so

[3] See pp. 201-3 below.

he may have to prove that, but for the lease or bailment, the owner would have had a right to immediate possession. On the other hand, if the lessee or bailee retains possession after the expiry of the term, the owner can recover possession by merely proving the fact of the lease or bailment and the expiry of the term; for it is said that the lessee or bailee cannot deny his title, since his own title depended on it. Nor, thirdly, can a dispossessor put the person he has dispossessed to proof of his title. All that the latter need prove is that he was in possession of the thing and the defendant took it against his will. But another way of stating this result might be that the former possession of the plaintiff is in such a case conclusive evidence of his right to immediate possession.

Self-help

On the other hand, if the dispossessor can prove his title, he is entitled to remain in possession. Thus a person who has a title but is out of possession can assert his rights by merely evicting the present possessor. But to do so may be dangerous, not merely because a forcible entry on land may be a criminal offence but also because disputes may arise, *inter alia*, as to whether excessive force has been used.

Proof of title

If now we assume that the plaintiff must prove his right to immediate possession against a person who has not directly dispossessed him but has acquired possession through a third party, and also that no such obstacle as a subsisting lease or bailment stands in the way, how is he to do it? The layman's obvious answer would be: Let him prove that he is the owner and all difficulties will be at an end. And indeed that is sometimes possible. There are such things as absolute titles.

The term 'absolute' is here used as meaning that the title cannot be defeated and also that it is not relative. Thus it is not merely better than other titles; it is good and they are non-existent, or at the best bad. This sense of the word has nothing to do with the content of a person's interest in a thing. He may have an absolute title to a merely partial interest or, on the other hand, he may have only a relative title to the

full interest. It will be seen later that the term 'absolute ownership' sometimes alludes to absolute title and sometimes to
the unlimited interest in a thing.

Absolute titles

(i) *Creation* The easiest way to acquire absolute title to
a thing is to create it out of nothing. The writer of a book or
composer of a piece of music acquires, by that act, ownership
of the copyright: protection, that is, against all prohibited
infringements for his lifetime and fifty years. He need do
nothing more, although to obtain international protection
under the Universal Copyright Convention his work should
bear the sign ©.

(ii) *Manufacture* Similarly it is easy in practice—though
not, perhaps, in strict theory—to prove a title to a movable
which is a product of recent manufacture, and it will almost
always be accepted, in the absence of clear evidence to the
contrary, that the manufacturer is the first owner. If that is
so he has an absolute title which he can transmit to others.
Recently, however, sellers of materials which are to be worked
up into finished products by the buyer have sought to retain
title to the materials until their bills are paid. This development is considered later in the chapter on security.[4]

(iii) *Registered title* Absolute titles also occur when the
title to a thing is registered and the law guarantees it. Where
that is the case the holder need not consider whether there
are any outstanding titles in other persons. If the title has been
wrongly registered, the person injured thereby has no claim
against him, but, if at all, only against the person or authority
registering it. Such registered titles exist for a growing part of
the land in England and Wales. The Crown guarantees title to
this so-called registered land and assumes liability to pay an
indemnity to anyone who, without carelessness on his part,
has been injured by the state of the register.[5] In the same way,
a person who has been registered as a holder of shares in a
company is a shareholder for all purposes. But sometimes
registration is only prima facie evidence of title, though it is
usually hard to disprove.

⁴ See p. 203 below.   ⁵ See p. 215 below.

Acquisition in good faith

So far as movables are concerned it would be possible to hold, as do many legal systems, that anyone who, in good faith, buys and takes possession normally obtains a good title even though the possessor from whom he obtained it was not the owner. In that case all that a person alleging title would have to prove would be that he bought and took delivery of the thing, and he could not be met by any defence, save bad faith.

This is *not* the basic principle of the English law of movable property. In this jurisdiction in such a case the general rule is that the true owner can recover his property or obtain compensation for its conversion. Thus if A lends a book to B who sells it to an innocent purchaser C, then C must return the book to A or pay damages; his act of buying the book, however innocent, amounts to the tort of conversion. It is then up to C to claim compensation against B although—since it was A who trusted B with a loan of the book—it might be thought that English law is being somewhat indulgent towards the owner.

The principle just described thus protects ownership as against commerce and is usually expressed in the Latin tag *nemo dat quod non habet*. It is subject to several exceptions which cover typical commercial situations. The main ones reflect the particular needs of business in the age when they were devised and are as follows:

(a) *The medieval exception: market overt*

In earlier times a customer would normally buy goods from the person who made them, or food from the person who grew it. The one great exception was the open market where the sellers might be neither manufacturers nor farmers but dealers. To protect their customers (and incidentally to increase the popularity and profits of the market itself) the rule emerged that a person buying goods in market overt acquired an absolute title to them. The only markets which count as overt for this purpose are those which enjoy the privilege by express grant or prescription; however anything bought in the open part of a shop dealing in such articles in the City of London is held to be bought in market overt.

Further, even if a purchaser obtains an absolute title, he may lose it if the goods have been stolen and the thief prosecuted and convicted, for he may be ordered to restore them to the true owner.

(b) *The nineteenth-century exception: mercantile agents*

With the growth of trade many sellers employed agents to sell for them—they are often called 'factors' in the older law books. Of course such a person can pass a good title in anything he is employed to sell. The difficulty may arise, however, that a customer from him would not know which of the goods the agent was to sell and which not; in the case of particular goods, for instance, his principal might have instructed him not to sell but to display and report offers which the principal could then decide whether or not to accept. Nineteenth-century statutes protect the customer in good faith from such an agent by making the transaction take effect as if the agent were authorized to sell.

A similar problem arose where a person had sold goods (so that they were no longer his) but remained in possession of them. A visitor to his premises could not possibly know which of the goods were still for sale and which had been sold and so statute—now the Sale of Goods Act—gives him a good title. The converse position is also covered so that where a person has agreed to buy goods (but has not yet become owner) and gets possession with the seller's consent, he too can pass a good title to the innocent purchaser.

(c) *The twentieth-century exception: vehicles on hire-purchase*

A person who is acquiring a car on hire-purchase is not the owner and, strictly speaking, has not agreed to buy but has merely an option to do so. Since 1964, however, statute has provided that a private citizen (i.e., not a dealer) who buys in good faith from him will take a good title.

(d) *The general exception: negotiable instruments*

It was explained earlier that, following the custom of merchants, the bona fide purchaser for value—or, as he is called, the holder in due course—of a negotiable instrument gets a good title and the right to demand payment whatever may have happened between the creation of the document and its coming into his hands.[6]

Relative titles

While these may, in theory, be exceptional they are, in practice, far from uncommon. Titles are often not absolute but relative in senses which are best explained by showing what a person alleging ownership must prove and what defences may be set up against him. If a person cannot prove an absolute title by pointing to his act of creation, manufacture, or to a register, then he must rely on a past possession in himself or in some other person or persons.

Now the law says that actual possession implies a right to possession. If, as in the normal case, it is the defendant who has possession and the plaintiff who is seeking to recover the property, then the latter must at least prove that his right to possession is better than that of the defendant. This is usually done by showing that the plaintiff or his predecessor in title, for instance a testator under whose will he claims, possessed the thing before the defendant—which implies that it had since been wrongfully taken by someone. Normally that concludes the case, for an earlier possession which is not barred by the statutes of limitation prevails over a later possession.[7]

But what if the defendant admits that his title is weaker than that of the plaintiff but claims that, behind the plaintiff's earlier possession, there is a still earlier one conferring a better right to the thing on some third party. Can he defeat the plaintiff's claim by pointing to this right of a third party, this *jus tertii* as it is called? Clearly if the plaintiff were allowed to recover from the defendant he could not retain the thing as against the third party, who still has a better title; but can the defendant say that, as he could not retain it against the third party, so he cannot recover it from *him*? The matter is by no means free from doubt and different answers may have to be given for land and movables. In the latter case the Torts (Interference with Goods) Act 1977 allows the defendant to show that a third party has a better right than the plaintiff as respects all or any part of the interest claimed. The purpose

---

[6] See pp. 28–32 above.   [7] See pp. 51–3 below.

of this is to allow competing claims all to be adjudicated in the one action. But when we come to conveyancing the matter assumes a totally different aspect.

Proof of title in conveyancing

The intending buyer of a thing rarely buys from a seller out of possession and so is not often concerned with any title that may be vested in a separate possessor. In buying from a seller in possession, however, there are two risks. Firstly, there may also be someone else in possession. This arises only in the case of land and has caused great difficulty where a buyer takes a conveyance of a house from the husband only to discover that the wife, or some other member of the family, who is also in occupation then sets up a property claim against him.

Secondly there is a risk that, although only the seller is in possession, there may be in existence some earlier title adverse to that of the seller; and the buyer does not want to pay for something which he may lose to the holder of that title. The question is not of great importance in the sale of movables. The title to most unique chattels is usually well known or easily ascertainable. There is a register of shipping which, if not conclusive as to title is almost so; the stud book performs the same function for racehorses; the whereabouts and owner-ship of valuable pictures and jewels are usually well known to dealers. Possession of the registration book is not, unfortunately, a perfect test for ownership of a motor car, but in practice few owners let it go out of their possession. The one exception is, of course, the seller on hire-purchase but, as has been explained, the private citizen who buys such a vehicle is still protected. The various finance houses in the motor trade keep their own private register of such transactions. Most other chattels are hard to trace, and in any case it would slow trade down too much if buyers tried to make sellers prove their title to ordinary objects of commerce. Thus most buyers deal with reputable sellers whose place of business is well known and trust them not to sell what is not theirs; and the law relating to the contract of sale gives buyers a remedy against sellers if the former have been forced to satisfy third persons with a better title. Although there is always the possi-bility that the seller may be insolvent and so unable to make good the buyer's loss, that is a risk which buyers take in the ordinary course of business.

However, people do not buy land, or lend money on it, without investigating title, though they have the same remedies as they would have against a seller of goods; and it leaps to the eye that the title they require will be one which is not likely to have any flaw in it. How can the seller prove that he has such a title? If it is not registered, he can prove only that he got it lawfully from someone else, and that someone else from someone else, and so on. Does that mean what the philosophers call an infinite regress, on the principle that however far he goes back there is always the possibility that someone else will pop up with a better title? The difficulty is avoided by the operation of so-called Limitation Acts. They demand separate consideration.

4. LIMITATION OF ACTIONS AND RIGHTS

A person who starts with a weak title to property or property rights may find his position strengthened by lapse of time, and other persons who are able to contest his title may find their power to do so disappear. This may happen in three different ways. In the first case a person who in fact exercises the right for the period required by law will acquire an absolute title to it, and it follows that any other person who hitherto could contest it on the ground that he had a right adverse to it will no longer be able to do so. In the second case a person who allows another person to exercise for the period required by law a right adverse to his own will lose any right of action against him. His action will be said to be statute-barred. In the third case, not only will his right of action disappear, but his right to the thing will disappear too.

In English law the first of these solutions applies only to servitudes, that is to say, to certain rights which can be exercised over another person's land, such as a right of way. It is so closely connected with servitudes that it will be explained later in dealing with them. The second solution finds its main field of application in personal actions arising out of contract or tort. The solution applicable to property rights as a class is the third.

The difference between the second and third solutions, which might at first sight seem unimportant, is as follows. Suppose A, when visiting B, finds his book, which he lost seven years ago, on B's table. If he tries to bring an action against B to recover it, he will certainly find his action statute-barred and he will fail, for the period for physical movables is six years and the lapse of such a period will at the very least bar the action. If, however, instead of bringing an action, he picks up the book and puts it in his pocket, thus retaking possession of it, he will be able to defend his possession against B if it is only his action that is statute-barred. If, on the other hand, his right is barred also, he will not be able to resist an action by B. Lapse of time has barred the right to land since 1833, but to movables only since 1939.

The difference is of little importance so far as movables are concerned, for, as has already been said, persons acquiring movables seldom trouble themselves with questions of title. But with land the barring of title by twelve years' adverse possession is important.

It operates as follows. Let us suppose that A has the best title to a piece of land which we shall call Blackacre—that is to say, a title which has no known title superior to it—and whilst he is away B takes possession of it. B now, by the very fact that he possesses Blackacre, has a title to it, but one that can be defeated by A. If, however, A does not take steps to recover possession for twelve years, by ousting B or bringing an action against him, he loses his title, and B's title, which was formerly the best but one, becomes the best. But his title does not then become a new one; it is still the same one that he obtained by dispossessing A; and this may have important consequences which are too technical to detain us here.

It might be thought that a purchaser of land would feel safe in limiting his researches into his vendor's title to a period of twelve years in the past. This is unfortunately not the case. For there may be persons who have rights in the land which will entitle them to possession at some future date. Until that time they will have no right to recover possession from an intruder, and the Limitation Act gives them some years from that time and not from the original intrusion in which to recover possession. No limit can be set to the period during which the purchaser should push back his investigations in order to be absolutely safe. However, as a practical matter some period must be fixed and the law has chosen to say that, unless a special agreement has been made to the contrary, a purchaser is entitled to trace back the vendor's title only to some good root of title at least fifteen years old. A good root of title is some document, such as a conveyance on sale, which transferred the interest which the purchaser seeks to acquire, which dealt completely with the title to it in law and equity, and contained nothing to cast doubts upon the title of the vendor.

If, however, the vendor knows of some flaw in the title farther back than that root of title, it will be best for him to disclose it before the contract is signed and to insert a term in the contract binding the purchaser not to object to the flaw. If the flaw is unimportant and not such as to make it probable that the purchaser will ever be evicted because of it, he will probably be willing to accept the title, though perhaps at a slightly lower price, whereas if it is important, he may insist on a serious reduction in price or not sign the contract. But if the flaw is not disclosed and the purchaser is evicted, he can sue the vendor for damages on the covenants for title formerly inserted but now implied in the conveyance of the land.

5. EQUITABLE RIGHTS AND REMEDIES

The rights and remedies which have been discussed hitherto are said to exist or operate at law. Certain other rights and remedies must now be discussed which exist or operate only in equity. This is a distinction which is hard to grasp and which has nothing to do with the ordinary popular meanings of law and equity. Historically it is a distinction between rights recognized and remedies afforded by courts exercising different jurisdictions, on the one hand the old Courts of Common Law and on the other the Chancellor. The Chancellor exercised what was in effect a supplementary jurisdiction, assuming at every point the existence of the common law administered by the Common Law Courts, but making good, as far as possible, its deficiencies. Thus equity never became a coherent system, though it may fairly be said that not only is the common law taken by itself a coherent system, but common law and equity taken together make a coherent system. This is more evident now that both are administered in the same courts and both common law and equitable remedies can be obtained in the same proceedings.

Equity is in no way synonymous with natural law or natural justice, though, like all good law, it aims at justice. It is now a body of technical rules and principles based, like common law, on precedent and in places modified and even codified by statute. Most of it deals in one way or another with property, but only a few of its leading principles and characteristics need be discussed in an elementary account of property law.

Conscience

Equity will act on the person of a defendant only if his conscience is affected in some way. Whereas common law remedies are granted to plaintiffs on the ground that they are entitled to them, equitable remedies are granted because it would be unconscionable of the defendant to do or not to do something to the disadvantage or advantage of the plaintiff. In one sense this may make equitable remedies more restricted than legal remedies, for whereas a person who is entitled to the immediate possession of a thing at common law is entitled to recover it even against a person who has bought it in good faith, if his interest in the thing is merely equitable he cannot enforce it against a person who has bought the thing in good faith without notice of the existence of the equitable interest. On the other hand, equitable remedies may have a wider range than legal remedies because there are many situations where, although a person has a perfect right to possess a thing at common law and is under no duty at common law, contractual or otherwise, to hand it over to another person or to hold it for his benefit, he is bound in conscience to do the one or the other. But it is well to warn the reader that equity has on occasion stretched the claims of conscience rather far, and that in modern times lawyers direct their attention not so much to the conscience which is the ultimate foundation on which equitable remedies are based, as to the specific rules which now govern them.

For the moment it must suffice to examine by way of example one great institution, the trust, and one great remedy, the specific performance of contracts. By so doing we shall incidentally learn much about the ways in which equity works in contrast to common law.

Trusts

A settlor A may wish to give property to his children. The simplest way is to hand it over to them, but there may be objections to this. In the first place the children may be too young to manage the property, especially if it is substantial in value or complex in nature. In the second place a simple transfer is a present of *capital*—but A may want to provide even an adult child only with *income*. In both cases he will be thinking not of an instantaneous present but of a gift which will last over a period. The private trust is basically a gift projected on the plane of time and, meanwhile, in need of management.

So A will probably transfer the property to a trustee B, in trust for his infant son C thus providing for the administration of the property during C's minority; or he may give property to B in trust for his child D for life and after D's death for E. C, D, and E are called beneficiaries—each was once technically known as a *cestui que trust*.[8] In such cases the trustee is bound to hold the property for the benefit of the beneficiary. He must allow him to use it and take the income from it, and he must take all the necessary steps to protect it—if it is a fund, by varying the investments from time to time so as to preserve the capital. The trust property is safe from the trustee's creditors, though available to those of the beneficiary. If the beneficiary is an infant, the trustee may have to apply part of the trust property for his maintenance and education. So stated, the beneficiary has only a personal right, a right *in personam*, against the trustee. He has no right at all at common law, but if the trustee fails in his duties to him, the beneficiary can bring proceedings in equity to have the trust enforced. This may end with an order that the trustee hand over possession to the beneficiary, that he replace trust property or its equivalent if he has got rid of it improperly, or even that he be

[8] Pronounced *settee kee trust*.

replaced as trustee by some more suitable person. These remedies are quite different from common-law remedies, which are only two in number, an order for possession of a thing, and a judgment for a liquidated sum of money or unliquidated damages. Moreover, whereas a common-law judgment is executed against an unwilling defendant by an order to a sheriff to put the plaintiff in possession of land or sometimes of goods, or to seize and sell a sufficient quantity of the defendant's goods to pay the judgment debt, the ordinary sanction of an order issued by a court of equity is imprisonment of the recalcitrant defendant. Equity it said to act *in personam*.

Once courts of equity had elaborated the institution of the trust and a set of remedies to enforce the duties implied by it, the way was open to say that persons who had never accepted the position of trustee, but had property which they ought in conscience to hold for the benefit of other persons, should be treated as if they were trustees. They were said to be saddled with a constructive trust, and to be constructive trustees. That meant in effect that the same remedies could be used against them as if they had been trustees.

Constructive trusts

Hence came some rather surprising developments. If a trustee transferred trust property in breach of trust, the question arose, what was to be the position of the alienee? It might be said that since the beneficiary had a remedy against the trustee, the alienee did not come into the picture; but the trustee might be, and probably would be in such circumstances, insolvent. Could it be said that the alienation in breach of trust was invalid and therefore inoperative? That would have been to deny the full ownership recognised by the Common Law Courts to be vested in the trustee. Accordingly the Chancellor asked whether, in all the circumstances of the case, the conscience of the alienee could be held to be affected in the same way as that of the original trustee, and to this question different answers were given according to the circumstances. If the alienee had known when he took the property that it was being alienated in breach of trust, then he had no merits and he must be treated as a constructive trustee and would hold the property on the same terms as the original trustee. If, although he had no notice of the breach of trust, he had acquired the property by way of gift without paying for it, then, as between a person who was getting something for nothing and another person who would actually lose by his getting it, the choice was easy: the former must suffer. Thus the gratuitous alienee of trust property became a constructive trustee. More difficult perhaps was the question whether, if the trustee's property was insufficient to satisfy both his creditors and the beneficiary, the creditors who took the trust property should hold it in trust for the beneficiary. In the end they too became constructive trustees. The only person who succeeded to the legal rights of the trustee without becoming a constructive trustee for the beneficiary came to be a person who took the property for value in good faith and with notice of the breach of trust. Moreover, even if he had no actual notice he would still become a constructive trustee if he would have had notice had he taken the steps to investigate the trustee's title which a reasonable man would have taken. He would then be said to have, not actual, but constructive notice. Constructive notice has played a great part in legal history, though its importance has been diminished by recent changes in the law. For, as will be explained in greater detail later,[9] almost all interests to which a beneficiary is entitled now fall into two groups. One of them, which has seldom any relation to trusts, has been made registrable, with the effect that registration is held to be equivalent to actual notice, and failure to register is fatal to the claims of the beneficiary. On the other hand, trustees are now almost invariably empowered to sell the trust property without breach of trust and reinvest the proceeds, and it is to the trust fund in its new form that the beneficiary is then entitled; his interest is said to be 'overreached'. Of course, when the sale is not in breach of trust any notice that a purchaser may have is irrelevant; he will acquire the trust property free from the trust. However, though it can happen only rarely today, a sale in breach of trust to a bona fide purchaser of the legal estate without notice of the trust gives the purchaser a clear title like that of the holder in due course of a negotiable instrument

[9] See pp. 61, 106–13, 215

or a buyer of goods in market overt. The reason for this is that the Chancellor could not act against someone who had bought the legal title and whose conscience was clear. The purchaser's defence was the most powerful of all: a plea to the jurisdiction of the court. The defrauded beneficiaries would still have a claim on the money received by the trustee.

Nature of the beneficiary's interest

So unlikely was it that trust property alienated in breach of trust should come into the hands of a bona fide purchaser who had no notice, actual or constructive, of the breach of trust, that the beneficiary's interest became almost as secure as if it had been protected by the Common Law Courts. Accordingly, in recent times an academic controversy arose whether it was still only a right *in personam* and not really a right *in rem*. The great historian Maitland, while admitting that it was almost equivalent to a right *in rem*, thought that the possible existence of a bona fide purchaser for value, who could cut off the right of the beneficiary, prevented it from quite attaining that status. The better opinion seems to be that of Professor Austin Scott, that it is in no worse position than almost all rights *in rem*, which can be cut off under the Limitation Act by a person who succeeds in retaining possession of an object for a long enough time against the will of the person entitled to it, and so is a true right *in rem*, though slightly more likely to be defeated than the interest of the trustee himself. In other words, most rights *in rem* are defeasible in some way or other, and the beneficiary's interest is not so defeasible as to forfeit the title of right *in rem*.

The question whether a right is *in rem* or *in personam* must be distinguished from the question whether a remedy is *in rem* or *in personam*. For example, a possessor of Blackacre has a right *in rem* not to have his possession intruded on, but his remedy against a trespasser will be *in personam*, that is to say, an action for damages. On the other hand, although a purchaser of Whiteacre has only a right *in personam* against the vendor, his remedy, if the latter does not convey, is specific performance of the contract, which operates directly on Whiteacre, by giving him a title to it, and so is *in rem*.[10]

[10] See further p. 68 below.

Tracing

The beneficiary can therefore follow, or trace, trust property alienated in breach of trust into the hands of any person other than a bona fide purchaser for value without notice of the breach of trust or anyone who subsequently acquires it from or through him even with notice of a previous breach of trust. The full implications of this ability to trace trust property will be considered later in relation to the fragmentation of ownership.[11]

So far *tracing*, as thus described, is used only to substitute one trustee for another in respect of the specific objects originally subject to the trust, and to ensure the continuance of the equitable interest in them. But *tracing* can be used not merely to follow the same identifiable objects into the hands of one person after another, but also to follow the same fund into all the various specific objects which it may from time to time comprise through successive changes of investment, whether it remains in the hands of the original trustee or comes into the hands of other persons, as constructive trustees or otherwise.

Thus X may be the trustee of a fund which is entirely composed of a block of government stock. He may sell out in accordance with the terms of the trust and reinvest in industrial shares. He may then sell these in breach of trust at an undervalue to Y and disappear with the money, Y being aware of the breach of trust. The beneficiary can trace the trust property in its new form of industrial shares, so that the fund remains the same though its contents have changed, and also into the hands of Y, who will become a constructive trustee.

But it would have been just the same if X had sold the government stock in breach of trust and reinvested the money. The beneficiary would have been able to trace the trust property into the new investments and either treat them as part of the trust fund or take their value in money.

Having gone so far equity will go farther. Trustees must keep trust money in a banking account separate from their own private account. If now X paid the purchase price of the government stock into his private banking account and mixed

[11] See p. 101 below.

it with his own money, it might be thought that what had taken the place of the government stock was no longer identifiable. However, equity is prepared to say that the trust fund still comprises so much money in the trustee's private account as corresponds to the purchase price.

This is perhaps not very easy to understand. The normal relation of banker to customer is that of a debtor if the customer has money in his account, and of a creditor if the customer has an overdraft. If therefore X pays the purchase price into his own account, which is at the time in credit, the banker owes him just so much more money. It might therefore be thought that the beneficiary could at best say to the banker, Pay me instead of X any money that you still owe to X, and that all other creditors of X could say the same, with the result that the beneficiary would have to compete with them on equal terms if X became insolvent. That is not, however, the case, for the beneficiary is allowed to trace the proceeds of the sale into the banker's hands. He is given what is called a charge[12] on the money still in X's account to the extent of the purchase price. This really means that if X becomes insolvent, and there is not enough money left in the account to satisfy all his creditors in full, the banker must pay the beneficiary out of what is still in X's account in preference to the other creditors. It is therefore simpler to say that where tracing is allowed, the beneficiary is a creditor with a preferential claim to be paid before the other creditors.[13]

Tracing is not limited to trust funds. Thus persons other than beneficiaries may sometimes treat a mass of money or investments as a separate account on which they can draw whatever may be the claims of other creditors against the

---

[12] See further p. 199 below.

[13] This process by which one specific object can be replaced by another object as part of a fund is known to continental lawyers as *real subrogation*. If one person guarantees the repayment of a loan and is forced to pay, he is said to be subrogated to the rights which the creditor has against the debtor; in other words, he has any remedies against the debtor which the creditor would have had. The substitution of one thing for another in a fund is obviously analogous to the substitution of one person for another in a contractual claim. Hence the term real subrogation, the word *real* being added to show that it is a thing which is substituted and not a person. It would be convenient if the term was naturalized and regularly used to express a process which is indeed much more generally applied in England than on the Continent.

person or persons who own it. Moreover, equity often gives one person a charge for a certain amount over property belonging to another. Although the latter is not called a trustee, this is really an extension of the trust concept, and its effect is to give the person entitled to the charge a preferential right to be paid out of the value of the property charged before any other creditors. This technique will be discussed later in relation to security.[14]

Specific performance

The imputation of a trust or charge is thus a very powerful equitable remedy, though trusts and charges are themselves equitable interests and not remedies. Specific performance, on the other hand, is an equitable remedy which has the indirect effect of creating equitable rights.

The only remedy common law affords for a breach of contract is a money judgment, either for a liquidated debt or for unliquidated damages. Thus if one person promises to transfer property to another, he cannot at common law be compelled to perform his promise. However, a court of equity will usually decree specific performance, ordering the promisor to convey the property, and, if he is recalcitrant, itself executing his promise through its officers.

Moreover, once a promise to convey property has come into existence which a court of equity will enforce specifically, the promisee is regarded as already having an equitable interest in the property; speaking popularly, he is regarded by equity as already the owner, although, for purposes of common law, he may not become owner until actual conveyance.

One principle of equity must be emphasized. It is said that equity will not assist a volunteer. A volunteer, for this purpose, is a person who has not given consideration, that is to say, has not given value—usually money—in return for a promise. Thus a mere promise of a gift will not be specifically enforced, even though, if it is contained in a document under seal called a deed, an action for damages would lie at common law in favour of the promisee if it is not fulfilled. Equity will not intervene to perfect an incomplete gift. So far does this refusal go that equity will not construe an incomplete gift as a trust.

[14] See pp. 199-201 below.

Nor will it in general enforce an imperfectly constituted trust, that is to say, where the settlor has neither declared himself to be a trustee nor completely divested himself of the trust property in favour of the trustee.

On the other hand, not only will equity enforce a promise for consideration to transfer some kinds of property, for instance, a promise to sell land, but it will even, in favour of a person who has given consideration, treat an imperfectly constituted trust as a promise to create a trust and enforce it as a trust, as though the trust were already in existence.

Finally, specific performance will be decreed only if a common law judgment for money would be an inadequate remedy, and never for the performance of personal services. Thus only contracts for the transfer of unique objects will be specifically enforced, since if the subject-matter of the contract is not unique, the successful plaintiff can take the money awarded him as damages and go into the market and buy its equivalent. By far the commonest object of a decree of specific performance is land, for every piece of land is unique. But a sale of a specific block of shares will be specifically enforced, and if so, the shares are regarded by equity as the property of the buyer as soon as the contract is made. We shall see later that at common law too physical chattels such as specific goods, ships, and racehorses are usually the property of the buyer from that same moment. These points will be taken up again in treating of the transfer of property.[15]

Effects of equitable remedies

These equitable remedies have had enormous effects on English law. For as they have been extended to protect beneficiaries against increasing classes of persons, they have conferred on them rights which, though starting as rights *in personam*, have become almost as good as rights *in rem*. Indeed, from a general point of view, their most interesting effect has been this weakening of the distinction between rights *in rem* and rights *in personam*, which is absolutely essential to Roman law and the laws strongly influenced by it. Equity is usually prepared to treat a contractual right relating to property not only as a right *in personam* entitling one person to a performance from

[15] See pp. 67–70 below.

another person in respect of that property, but as a right *in rem* analogous to ownership of the property.

This transformation of contractual into real rights operates, first, only in favour of a person who has given consideration,[16] that is to say, money or money's worth, for them and, secondly, never against a person who has given consideration without notice of an infringement of the personal right.[17] Thirdly, the property affected must be identifiable and unique; but a trust fund and a banking account are identifiable and unique enough.[18]

Of all the various equitable interests protected by these equitable remedies the most permanent is that enjoyed by the beneficiary of a trust fund. The others, such as the equitable interest in a thing arising from a claim to specific performance of a contract, are usually very short-lived because in the ordinary course of events the contract is soon performed or specifically enforced. But a person may have an interest in a trust fund which will last all his life or which will be so permanent that he can transmit it to successors by will or on an intestacy.

One word of warning is needed. A court of equity may be willing to enforce an equitable right against one person, for instance, the other party to a contract, without being willing to enforce it against any other person, even if he has acquired property from him with notice of the right. In other words, by no means all equitable rights attach to or, in the recognized slang of the lawyer, *run with* property. Some are personal and therefore are not equivalent to interests in property. The distinction is an important one and has recently come into prominence in connexion with what are called licences, under which one person is permitted by another person, without a lease or tenancy, to occupy property belonging to him. The protection which equity is prepared to give a licensee against his licensor has recently been enunciated in very wide terms, the licensee being entitled, if he has given value for the licence, not only to bring an action for damages if the licensor wrongfully revokes the licence, but also to be maintained in enjoyment of the property. On the other hand, recent attempts to

---

[16] See pp. 61-2 above.   [17] See pp. 57-8 above.
[18] See pp. 59-60 above.

treat such licences as creating equitable interests in land have been much criticized, and the law remains uncertain. A separate chapter is devoted to licences.[19]

Beneficiary's use of legal remedies

Although the normal remedies for the infringement of equitable interests are equitable remedies, a beneficiary may be deeply interested in the title to a legal right and the legal remedies that protect it. In the first place, if the legal right is not secure, the equitable interest may topple down with it, for the ultimate basis of the latter is the ability of some person having the legal right to deal with it as a court of equity directs. But, secondly, the beneficiary may, and often does, have possession of the subject matter of the trust property. If that is the case, he may use the same legal remedies as are available to any other possessor.

[19]   See Chapter XVII.

IV

ACQUISITION OF
PROPERTY INTERESTS

1. TRANSFER OF PROPERTY

THE modes of transferring property vary with the different kinds of property transferred. Moreover, sometimes the actual transfer is and sometimes it is not preceded by preliminaries which are almost as important as the transfer itself. Thus the actual transfer of land on a sale is almost always preceded not only by a contract but also by an investigation of title; indeed at the present day the actual signing of a contract is preceded by inquiries which would not themselves be made unless they were preceded not only by negotiations but also by something in the nature of a pre-contract. On the other hand, when goods are bought for cash in a shop, contract and conveyance are rolled into one, there are usually no negotiations, and there is certainly no investigation of title. Buying a patent or copyright lies somewhere between the two. More time and care are taken than in buying ordinary goods, but there is not the same elaborate succession of stages as in the purchase of land.

Acquisition by consent

The details of these various types of conveyance can be found in the textbooks, but it may be worth while to try to generalize as far as possible. In the first place all the transfers of property discussed here are consensual, that is to say, they require agreement between the parties. This is obvious enough where there is a sale, for the seller must agree to transfer the property and the buyer to acquire it. Where there is a gift, the agreement may seem rather more shadowy, for English law does not require any actual acceptance by the donee; however, since he is at liberty to refuse the gift, from his failure to do so it may be presumed that he is willing to acquire the property in question. There are transfers of property which take place not only without the consent but against the will of the person losing it, as for example when the property of a bankrupt vests in his trustee in bankruptcy, but such transfers are best kept apart from those which are now being discussed.

Factors at work

The next question to be asked is, agreement being admitted to be necessary, what is its effect?

The law is complicated by the interaction of three different principles, which are, moreover, subject to exceptions.

First, a distinction is made between transfers which operate merely between the parties and transfers which are good for all purposes. In principle, for the former nothing more is needed than the intention of the parties that the property shall pass; for the latter something more is needed such as delivery, a sealed document, or notice to some third party.

Secondly, any transfer which is good as between the parties also binds the transferor's creditors; though sometimes they may be able to have the transfer set aside, for instance if it is in fraud of them.

Thirdly, since the law does not readily enforce promises to make gifts, gratuitous transfers do not ordinarily operate even as between the parties unless they are also done in a way which is good for all purposes; but this is subject to an exception which is hard to explain and even harder to name.

A further complication is introduced by variations in the requirement of written evidence. It would serve no useful purpose to discuss them here. It is enough to say that, in the interests of safety and clarity, it is always advisable for a transferee who does not immediately gain possession of a physical object or a document of title to get a written statement from the tranferor.

Operation between parties and operation against all the world

The distinction between transfers which operate merely between the parties (though binding the transferor's creditors) and those good for all purposes is best explained by means of examples. Thus the property in ascertained goods passes from the seller to the buyer when the parties intend it to pass, and very commonly the goods will become the property of the buyer even though they are left by him in the possession of the seller. If, as is common, they express no intention, the ownership of specific goods in a deliverable state passes at the moment of contract, even though the buyer is not to collect and pay for them until later. If now the seller, in fraud of the buyer, sells and delivers the goods to a second buyer, who is in good faith, that is to say, has no knowledge of the previous sale, the second buyer becomes owner of the goods. The Sale of Goods Act explains this result by saying that the seller must be taken to have had the authority of the first buyer to sell the goods to the second buyer. It is perhaps easier to see what happens if one adopts the language of an 1821 Massachusetts decision that the property in the goods passes when the parties intend it, 'only as between seller and buyer'; and sections 16 to 20 of our Sale of Goods Act have the subheading 'Transfer of Property as between Seller and Buyer'. On the other hand, if, while goods sold to the buyer are still in the seller's possession, the seller goes bankrupt, the trustee in bankruptcy, who acts in the interests of the seller's creditors, cannot resist the buyer's demand for delivery of the goods, for he is entitled only to the property of the seller, and the goods are no longer the seller's but the buyer's.

On the other hand, once the goods have been delivered by the seller to the buyer, they are the buyer's for all purposes. Even without delivery the same result would be produced if notice of the sale could be given to all persons who could possibly buy the goods subsequently from the seller in possession; but that is in practice inconceivable.

Sales of land are ordered somewhat differently. In principle, and as a matter of the modern common law, the title to land can be transferred only by a deed, that is to say, a sealed writing executed by the transferor. A deed is necessary to pass the legal title to legal estates and interests in land and also to transfer interest in ships. It is an alternative method of perfecting a gift of physical movables. To be effectual, a deed requires to be signed, sealed, and delivered by the person making it. The seal need not be his personal seal; indeed most usually nowadays it is no more than a small circular piece of red paper gummed to the document. But a deed executed by a corporation must bear the corporate seal. Delivery would normally be physical delivery to the person in whose favour the deed is made, but need not be so. It is enough for the deed to be put in circulation, for instance by the maker saying to some bystander that he delivers it as his act and deed. Even if he then locks it up in his desk it is properly delivered.

However, as soon as a vendor agrees to sell land to a purchaser a court will in the exercise of its equitable jurisdiction normally grant specific performance of the agreement and hence the purchaser is regarded as having already an equitable interest in the land.[1] Now, that equitable interest is perfectly good against the vendor and also against any person who acquires the legal estate in the land otherwise than as a purchaser for value without notice of the previous sale. Thus, a person who has agreed to purchase land is in at least as good a position as a buyer of goods, though technically the latter already has a legal title whereas the purchaser of land only has an equitable title. But if the purchaser registers the sale in the appropriate register, his equitable interest is good as against any subsequent purchaser, for registration is equivalent to notice; whereas if he does not, it will be good against no subsequent purchaser. This power of registering the sale makes the position of a purchaser of land better than that of a buyer of goods. It can be made better without inconvenience to third parties because the transfer of land is a more leisurely process than the transfer of goods, and so purchasers have ample time to search a register.

An example may help. A agrees to sell to B his car for £1,000 and his house for £30,000; and the latter contract satisfies the requirement relevant to land of being evidenced in a signed document. As regards the legal position between the parties, ownership of the car has passed to B as has equitable ownership of the house; and if A goes bankrupt then, B is still entitled to both, though he must, of course, pay for them. Formal ('legal') ownership of the house will not pass to B until A executes a deed (and, if the house is registered land, B should enter his name as proprietor).

If, however, the car is still in A's garage then a sale and delivery by him to an innocent purchaser, X, will take

---

[1] See p. 61 above.

ownership of the car from B and vest it in X. A will be liable in a personal action by B, for he has broken his contract and converted B's property, but if he is insolvent B will merely be an ordinary creditor along with the others. If A—again in breach of contract—sells and conveys the house to X for £40,000 then, if B has not registered his contract, he has no remedy against X. If he has, however, he can compel X to effect a formal transfer of the house to him, paying X £30,000. He can thus obtain specific performance of a contract against someone with whom he never made a contract and with whom there is no 'privity of estate'.[2] X would have to look to A to recover the £10,000 he has lost.

Choses in action are subject to yet another régime. For the assignee of a legal chose in action, such as a debt, to be able to sue the debtor in his own name, without joining the assignor either as plaintiff or as defendant, the requirements of the Law of Property Act must be fulfilled, among which appear the rules that the assignment must be in writing and that notice in writing must be given to the debtor. But if either, or even both, of these requirements are not fulfilled, the assignment may take effect as an equitable assignment, so long as the assignor has done all he can to divest himself of all his interest in the debt to the assignee. If, however, the debtor pays the assignor before he has notice of the assignment, the assignee cannot enforce a second payment to him; and if the assignor, in fraud of the first assignee, makes a second assignment to a second assignee who succeeds in giving notice to the debtor before the first assignee, the second assignee will take priority over the first. Yet in spite of all this an assignee who has not yet given notice to the debtor will be preferred to the trustee in bankruptcy of the assignor. In other words, the assignment may be complete as between the assignor (or his creditors) and the assignee before it is complete as against bona fide third parties.

Beneficial interest in a fund held by trustees are subject to similar rules as are *choses in action*. Assignments may be valid as between the parties (and their creditors) but to bind others the assignee must give notice of the assignment to the trustees of the fund. Thus the Trust Instrument, on which notice of

[2] See pp. 152-4 below.

the assignment may be entered, acts as a kind of private register of dealings in the beneficial interests in the fund, just as the public Registers do for dealing in formal, legal ownership.

Gratuitous transfers

So far we have been considering transfers in a general way, without reference to the question whether they are gratuitous or not, though for the most part they have been by way of sale. It is vital to grasp the distinction between *making* a present to someone, and *promising* to do so. Thus if A wishes to give B money or a bicycle for his birthday, he should hand it over. That legal transaction is quite different from a promise made by A to B to give him the things. We must now consider the complications introduced by the refusal of the law to enforce informal promises of gifts.

It does not affect transfers which are good for all purposes. Such transfers are always more than mere promises, that is to say, they are out-and-out grants by way of delivery of goods or documents or by deed or by written declaration coupled with notice to a third party. But it does usually affect transfers which are good only between the parties. Thus if one person promises gratuitously to give money or goods to another person, no transfer takes place even between the parties; and a promise of a gift of land raises no equitable interest in the donee. On the other hand, a promise of a gift made in a deed is binding on the donor, for promises by deed are an exception to the rule that gratuitous promises are not binding. However, a deed is also a means of transferring property not only between the parties but for all purposes, and so the only difference between a valid promise of a gift and an out-and-out gift is in the intention of the donor.

So far there is no real difficulty. But there is sometimes a difficulty when a chose in action is assigned but no notice has been given to the debtor or other person under a duty to the assignor. To give a neat result the law should say that an assignment perfected by notice and so good for all purposes should operate even if it is gratuitous, but that an assignment not perfected by notice and therefore at best good only as between the assignor and assignee (and also as against the assignor's creditors) should be treated only as a promise to assign and should therefore not even operate to that limited extent if it is gratuitous. But that is not the case. Between the gratuitous promise and the out-and-out gift, good for all purposes and against all comers, equity interposes a *tertium quid* which has no name of its own.

Equity takes the same view of gratuitous promises as common law. It will not perfect an incomplete gift. If, therefore, something remains to be done in order to make the donee owner of a thing, the donor remains owner in equity as well as at common law. Generally speaking this means that something must be done, even to satisfy equity, which will make the transfer of the property good for all purposes. However, equity does not really consider the giving of notice to a debtor a part of the transfer of a chose in action, but merely as something determining priorities among claims to be paid the debt. If, therefore, the assignment is complete but for the giving of notice, it is a good equitable assignment, even though the lack of notice makes it impossible for the assignee to sue the debtor under the Law of Property Act in his own name without joining the assignor.

Even so, equity would normally require, in order to perfect the gift of a chose in action, the delivery of a document of title or a declaration of trust by the assignor. But there are occasions where all that the assignor could possibly do would be to make a declaration, if necessary in writing, that he is assigning the chose in action to the assignee; and in that case there is a good equitable assignment which, even if gratuitous, operates to transfer the chose in action as between the parties, though for lack of notice it is not good for all purposes. This in effect covers simple money debts not enshrined in a document of title and interests in trust funds—and probably nothing else.

Rationale of the main distinction

It is not unreasonable that the parties should be able to regulate according to their own wishes the transfer of property as between themselves, and, provided he furnishes sufficient evidence of his intention, that the transferor should bind those who have already given him credit; for the creditors will be fairly well protected by the power with which a trustee in bankruptcy is invested, to resume anything which third parties have acquired from the transferor whether by way of recent gift or in fraud of his creditors.

However, it is not thought reasonable that the bare agreement of the parties, even if evidenced in an informal writing, should be conclusive against a third person who acquires the thing afterwards from the transferor for a consideration, or gives him credit on the security of it, in ignorance of the informal transfer. Almost invariably some further step must be taken to bind bona fide subsequent acquirers. Usually the books state quite shortly that these further steps are necessary for the property to pass. In fact, as we have seen, they are usually necessary not as between the parties, but only if third parties are to be bound to respect the transfer.

Notice and registration

As has already been said, notice is not so much a part of certain transfers as a supplement to a transfer designed to make it good against third parties. Registration plays the same role, and indeed the two are more alike than would appear at first sight.

The purpose of giving notice of assignment of a debt or an interest in a trust fund to the debtor or the trustees is to prevent them paying the assignor instead of the assignee, and also to secure priority to the assignee over any subsequent assignees. But the matter may be looked at from another point of view. A person who is buying, or lending money on the security of, a debt or an interest in a trust fund is well advised to apply first to the debtor or the trustees to see if it has already been assigned, and, if so, to what extent, at the same time warning them of the forthcoming assignment to him. Thus the debtor or trustees keep, as it were, a private register of assignments.

Where land or physical chattels are concerned, such private registers would be both unsatisfactory and hard to establish. Hence public registers have been set up for various classes of things. For the présent it is enough to say that registration serves two purposes, to protect third parties and to render easier and cheaper the investigation of title. Moreover, the property in registered land is transferred by entering the purchaser's name in the register.[3]

___
[3] See further pp. 213–16 below.

2. ORIGINAL MODES OF ACQUISITION

By far the commonest mode of acquiring existing property is by transfer from one who has the title to it. But there are other modes, some of which are fairly important.

Occupation

Some things can be acquired by merely taking possession of them. Even if only possession is acquired, it carries with it advantages which have already been explained. The possessor can maintain his possession against a mere intruder and can if necessary recover it from him. But possession may in some cases give the sort of title that is usually designated as ownership. This is so where the thing of which possession is taken has been up to that time without an owner.

This can hardly occur where land is concerned, for there will always be some person with a title to a piece of land. When a squatter takes possession of land it is almost always because the true owner is away or has mistaken the boundaries of his holding or even, as occasionally happens in some parts of the country, because he cannot be bothered to look after it. The true owner then loses his title only after the period of limitation has run against him.

The three cases where title is gained immediately by taking possession are where a person takes abandoned goods; where he finds goods without a present possessor and the owner of which cannot be traced; and where a person reduces a wild animal into possession.

The first case is rare, although a collector of used toffee-papers could acquire ownership of any thrown away by catching them. In the second case the only difficult question of law that occurs in practice is whether the thing found was at the time without a present possessor. There seems to be a general tendency at the present day to hold that a thing lost on premises is in the possession of the possessor of the premises; but, as has already been explained,[4] the various decisions are not easily reconciled. There may also in any particular case be a doubt whether anyone else will claim the lost property and a further doubt whether a claimant can prove his title.

[4] p. 43 above.

These doubts make it necessary for the finder, if he is to feel safe, to advertise his finding, or, better, to report it to the police. But there is no doubt whatever that if no possessor or owner can be found the finder becomes owner.

Animals

The law relating to the ownership of wild animals is rather complicated. A distinction must first be drawn between the killing of animals and the possession of living animals. The law as to the latter is relatively simple. Any person who takes or confines a wild animal so as to possess it is owner so long as he retains possession. He is said to acquire a qualified ownership *per industriam*. As soon as it escapes and resumes its wild character he ceases to own it, though he is allowed to retake it so long as he keeps it in sight and has the power and right to pursue it. This latter requirement has been held to deprive of ownership a person whose bees swarmed into the garden of a neighbour who refused him entry to retake them. Mere temporary absences will not deprive a person of title to animals which are in the habit of leaving his land and returning, but if they lose the habit, and therefore what is whimsically called the *animus revertendi*, they cease to be his. A qualified ownership is also acquired *propter impotentiam* over animals on his land which are too young to escape, and is of course lost when they can escape.

As regards the killing of wild animals the vital question is, who has the right to kill? If such a person kills he obtains permanent ownership of the dead animal, which does not cease to be his merely if he loses possession of it. The right to kill ground game, that is to say hares and rabbits, is vested in the occupier of the land on which they are found; and he cannot be deprived of it by contract or any other means. The right to kill other game is sometimes vested in a person *propter privilegium*, by royal grant or prescription, but it is usually vested in the freeholder, by whom it can be detached and let to tenants of sporting rights. A trespasser who kills does not acquire ownership.

Accession and alteration

Other modes of acquisition, which play a less prominent part in English than in Roman law, are accession and alteration. When an accessory is added to a principal object, its identity is merged in that of the latter; and so, if they belonged to different persons, the owner of the accessory loses his title. The most important cases, where buildings or other fixtures accede to land, have already been discussed in defining land.[5] Where movables accede to movables, in most cases the owner of the principal object has already acquired ownership of the accessory before incorporating it.

Alteration of objects gives rise to problems of ownership where one person manufactures a finished object from material belonging to another. Probably the Roman solution would be accepted, namely, that if the object can be reduced to the original materials it would be the property of the owner of the materials, but if not, the manufacturer would become owner. Until recently, there was very little authority for the following reason. The owner of the materials could in any case obtain their value from the manufacturer in an action for converting them; while, if he went farther and claimed possession of the finished object, the judge would have a discretion whether to accede to his request or not, and, if he did, could probably make him pay for the value added to it by the manufacturer. Thus the question of title would hardly arise. Of late, however, sellers of raw materials have tried to retain ownership, not for its own sake but in case the buyer does not pay and becomes insolvent. This is best dealt with in the chapter on security.[6]

---

[5] pp 21–2 above.
[6] pp. 203–4 below.

V

THE FRAGMENTATION
OF OWNERSHIP

ONE of the greatest difficulties encountered by students of
property law comes from the English habit of splitting what
may in a general way be called ownership into its component
parts and making of each of them an abstract entity which,
if not quite the same as a thing, is not very different. A full
explanation of this fragmentation of ownership must come
later and indeed will not be accomplished within the two
covers of this book. Here it is intended to give the student a
first look at some of the more important ways in which fragmentation occurs, with as full an explanation as will be intelligible for the time being.

The law governing this topic was worked out in the first
instance for land and later applied to funds comprising both
land and more permanent chattel interests such as stocks and
shares. It has never been applied in its entirety to physical
chattels, not usually because of any objection in point of
principle but from lack of opportunity.

Land and chattels

For the fragmentation of ownership to be worth while the
thing in question ought to be capable of yielding an income
for a considerable time and its whereabouts should always be
readily ascertainable. Now land possesses both these qualities
in the highest degree. It is immovable and virtually indestructible. When the law was being worked out, trust funds either
did not exist in sufficient numbers or were not considered
important enough to be prime objects of doctrinal development, but later they were found to possess the same characteristics as land to a sufficient degree to make it appropriate

to extend to them the same technique of fragmentation; for although they were and are less immune from destruction than land, they exist solely in order to furnish an income for beneficiaries, and although they are not immovable, they can be traced with sufficient ease and security into the hands of successive trustees. But physical chattels, with comparatively few exceptions, are too destructible and can be got rid of too easily for it to be worth while to split up the ownership in them among several persons according to many different principles. Ships indeed escape this generalization to some extent, and so do valuable heirlooms such as pictures and jewels. But what are rather vaguely known as 'consumer goods' have too temporary an existence and can be spirited away too easily for the law to apply to them the full apparatus of fragmentation. They will appear only occasionally in the following pages.

However, lawyers, more especially when, in the course of writing books on law, they stand a little away from their subject, feel a strong desire to generalize. In this they do not differ from other scientific thinkers. But they have also a practical end in view. The law cannot provide in advance a detailed solution for every conceivable specific problem. It must develop principles and techniques which can be applied uniformly over fields of varying extent. Hence the need to generalize.

Now the full extent to which a general principle or technique can properly be made to apply is hardly ever apparent. from the start. Accordingly, generalization tends to be progressive; partial generalizations are seen to yield to wider generalizations. The process is often easy enough, though awkward exceptions may have to be admitted. Sometimes it is difficult because, whereas the common elements in two bodies of doctrine or technique may now seem to outweigh in importance the differences between them, at an earlier period the differences seemed so serious that generalization was expressly rejected.

This has been the case with realty and chattels. Above all, extremely fruitful generalizations such as the notion of tenure and the doctrine of estates have been excluded on principle from the law of chattels, for the very good reason that what at the time would have been the most important inferences to be drawn from those generalizations were clearly not applicable to chattels. But those inferences, as will be seen later, can no longer be drawn for realty either, and so the question must now be raised whether the elements common to the law of realty and the law of chattels are not important enough to justify new attempts to generalize more thoroughly the whole law of property, and in particular to apply to the somewhat rudimentary law of chattels the highly developed doctrines and techniques hitherto commonly recognized to apply only to realty. A conviction that such attempts are justified must explain what may at first sight appear to be an excessive preoccupation with obscure problems raised by bailments, and especially with the questions whether the notion of tenure and the doctrine of estates can be applied to them.[1]

Abstraction

At this point the student enters a new world, much less familiar than the one he has just left. So far he has been concerned in the first instance with remedies, and rights have appeared only as implied in those remedies. He has lost something and wants to get it back, or he wants to stop someone else from interfering with it. The atmosphere became rather more rarefied when he had to understand equitable rights and remedies, but he was still in the sort of world that the ordinary man usually regards as peculiarly legal, the forensic world of the courts, of 'going to law'. The transfer of property made him acquainted with another form of legal activity, that of conveyancing, but there also there was nothing very surprising, for all he was really interested in was making certain that he got something that would stand up to a lawsuit. He was still dealing with corporeal things or with such familiar incorporeal things as debts, stocks and shares, or copyright.

Now he will find himself brought face to face with a new activity of the conveyancer and with a type of conveyancer whom he probably never knew to exist, the expert barrister who sits in his chambers in Lincoln's Inn and hardly every goes into court, who spends his time like a spider, weaving webs of legal gossamer in which to tie up corporeal things and the incorporeal things which are the immediate objects of commerce. The purpose of all his activity is to ensure, as

[1] See pp. 81, 96-7, and 202 below.

far as the law can ensure it, that the property interests he is dealing with shall move from one person to another for an appreciable time in the future in a perfectly predictable way and that they shall be managed in the cheapest and most efficient way, attracting the lightest possible burden of taxation. As has already been remarked—but the point is worth making repeatedly—he works with abstract entities which it takes a prolonged effort to understand completely, for only such abstractions can be, as the Americans say, 'tailored' to fit a particular purpose. What is more important for the moment is that they are precision instruments of known form and potentialities; and it may be consoling to know that there are basically only three of them: estate, trust, and fund.

In other words, the student has now left the forensic world, peopled by vague and hardly definable notions like possession and title, whose only purpose is to help judges deal as best they may with things which have gone wrong, a world where purchasers either trust to luck and neglect to investigate title or are willing to accept a good holding title which will probably not be attacked. He is entering the precise, sharp, logical world of the expert conveyancer, who is constantly using the most refined abstract tools in order to create complex arrangements for the future which cannot, so far as the law is concerned, go wrong and to provide with equal certainty for the happening of untoward events. The student has had a slight foretaste of this in the law of negotiable instruments and documents of title. Indeed that highly abstract thing called money lends itself, and is intended to lend itself, to something of the same precision, and the banker, who handles money most expertly, tries to make the results of his operations as predictable as does the expert conveyancer. But the more profound study of money and banking falls within the confines of commercial law.

The topics which will be discussed at this point are (1) tenure, (2) co-ownership, (3) time, (4) words of limitation, (5) rent and rent-charges, (6) powers, and (7) the distinction between management and enjoyment.

1. TENURE

The earliest fragmentation, which made all others possible, was an essential part of feudalism. That was a system of land-holding which had for its main purpose the quartering of an army on the soil. In a society short of the precious metals, and therefore unable to pay for services in money, the most convenient way of providing for an expensive force of armed horsemen was for the king to give parcels of land to men of substance (so-called tenants-in-chief) upon the terms that they should provide a certain number of knights to serve for forty days a year, and then for the tenants-in-chief, as mesne lords, to give those knights, as demesne tenants, lands to hold in subordination to them. This is only the core of what was a most complicated system of landholding, under which some cultivated the land for the benefit of others besides themselves, in return for protection and justice. But it gives sufficient information to explain what is meant by tenure.

Tenure is a relation which looks both ways, towards a parcel of land and towards a lord. The tenant-in-chief held his land of the king, and the demesne tenant held his land of his mesne lord, the tenant-in-chief. In this sense tenure was a relation between lord and man, but with regard to the land itself it expressed a fragmentation of ownership among a number of persons, each of whom was regarded not as owner but only as tenant of the land. In the older books on Real Property law one often comes across the generic term *terre-tenant*, as the exact technical equivalent of what in ordinary language is called a landowner.

Tenure is a notion which the student is bound to encounter when beginning the study of property law. He must be warned not to devote much attention to it. It still exists at two points, in the quite meaningless and indeed inaccurate statement that no subject can in the technical sense 'own' land, even though he has the exclusive benefit of it, since only the sovereign can own land and all others hold it of him, and in the law of leases, which is familiarly called the law of landlord and tenant. Of the relation between a tenant-farmer or the tenant of a house and his landlord three things must be said: first, it is the only form of tenure that still has any practical meaning, secondly, it never really fitted into the feudal system, being an alien commercial element which had to be brought into some sort of artificial relation to it, and, thirdly, the relation between landlord and tenant is now in the main contractual, though controlled by modern statutes.[2]

However, tenure, since it denied in principle the unity of ownership, created a mental atmosphere favourable to the division of ownership on other lines also. If ownership could be divided between landlord and tenant, why not between persons related to the land in other ways? In legal systems which have been greatly influenced by Roman law there is a standing inhibition against the fragmentation of ownership, which is allowed only grudgingly when practical considerations exert overwhelming force.

Bailment

Tenure has no place in the law of personalty. Nevertheless, a very close analogy to the relation of landlord and tenant is to be found in that between bailor and bailee. Whenever a physical movable is delivered by one person to another for a purpose upon the understanding that it is to be returned upon the accomplishment of the purpose, there is a bailment. Now between the bailor, who hands over the thing, and the bailee, who receives it, there is a personal relation, for the bailee is under a duty to the bailor to take reasonable care of the thing and to return it in due course. But a bailment for a term also confers possession on the bailee, to the exclusion of the bailor. Thus the bailee, and not the bailor, can bring an action of trespass against an intruder, and can alone recover possession from a dispossessor. If the bailment is at will, the bailee's position is precisely the same, though it is said on rather doubtful authority that the bailor also has possession, with the rights it confers. So far there is nothing to differentiate in principle a bailment for a term from a lease of land. Moreover, such interest as the bailee has in the chattel is derived from that of the bailor, as is shown by the rule that, just as a lessee cannot be heard to deny his lessor's title, so a bailee cannot be heard to deny that of his bailor. Thus a bailment presents the same sort of mingling of real and personal relations

[2] See pp. 147-58 below.

as a lease, and to say that there is tenure between bailor and bailee would be no great offence against terminological propriety.

2. CO-OWNERSHIP

Ownership of the same thing at the same time and in the same way by a number of persons has been general from early times. Indeed, some students of primitive law think that ownership by communities such as families, tribes, and clans everywhere preceded ownership by individuals. Roman law admitted common ownership and it has survived everywhere in one form or another.

Even in the modern world there are many occasions on which this may happen. A man may, for instance, die intestate leaving two unmarried sons who go on living together in his house; they do not choose to divide it into two self-contained flats but use most of the rooms in common. In many countries marriage usually makes some at least of what was hitherto the separate property of each of the spouses their common property; and in England it is common for husband and wife to operate a joint banking account. Or two men may run a business in partnership, which involves using the same factory or office in common.

English law has always known two kinds of co-ownership, in accordance with which several persons enjoy what are called concurrent interests. They are called respectively joint ownership and ownership in common. In speaking of land the terms joint tenancy and tenancy in common are used, but this is used of freehold owners and has nothing to do with the law of leases. The difference between them is that whereas if one owner or tenant in common dies, his share passes to his successors, whether by will or on an intestacy, one joint tenant's share accrues on his death to the other joint tenants, so that when all the joint tenants but one are dead the last survivor becomes sole owner or tenant.

Lawyers have tried to explain this right of survivorship in a thoroughly artifical way by saying that whereas tenants in common are regarded as holding undivided shares in the land, each share being capable of being alienated, joint tenants do not own shares, but each joint tenant owns the whole, subject to the concurrent ownership of the other joint tenants. When one dies the others do not in theory acquire anything that they had not already, but are merely relieved of the presence of a competing tenant.

The phrase 'undivided shares' has a long history and is much used in modern statutes, so it is a burden we must accept. But it would be meaningless to call a share 'undivided' if by that were meant not separate from the other shares. The simplest way to grasp the position of tenants in common is to think of shares in a company. The shareholders each have a separate thing which they can alienate or leave to pass on their death. It is the property in which the share subsists—the company—which is undivided. So two tenants in common of a house each have a separate, though intangible, asset; it is the house which is not divided into distinct 'shares'.

Thus, if property is given to A, B, and C as joint tenants or without any additional words at all they take as joint tenants because there is nothing to show that they are to have shares in the property. But if property is given to A, B, and C with the addition of words which show that they are to have shares in it, for instance the word 'equally', they become tenants in common.

The right of survivorship at first sight gives such unfair results that it is difficult to see how anybody should want to give property in joint tenancy or joint ownership. A moment's reflection will, however, show that joint tenancy or ownership is an extremely convenient form of ownership for trustees. For the ownership of trustees is for the purpose of management and not enjoyment. Now it is only where a number of persons have concurrent rights to enjoy a thing that the right of survivorship produces unfair results; on the other hand, it is very convenient that the interest of one of a number of managers should not devolve on those who succeed him on death, but should vest automatically in the survivors. If one looks upon the trustees as a committee, all that has happened is that a member of the committee has disappeared, and the others carry on as if he were still there, taking steps to add to their number if it becomes too small. Thus, joint tenancy or joint ownership is appropriate to management, tenancy or ownership in common to beneficial enjoyment of property. For this reason and others, as will be seen later, the Legislature in 1925 restricted tenancy in common of land to equitable interests.

Property other than land may also be held by concurrent owners. Partners, for instance, may well be tenants in common of—that is, have separate shares in—the goodwill of their business, debts due to it, patents, copyrights, and the like. Movables may be held in a similar way: racehorses owned by a syndicate are one example and aircraft another, although in the latter case a legal person, a company, is usually interposed.

3. TIME

So far we have considered cases where a person's ownership of property is limited by the competing existence, first, of a landlord or tenant, and, secondly, by that of a co-owner. In both cases their interests coexist simultaneously with his. But there is another case where the interests are really simultaneous, though they seem at first sight to be successive.

Successive enjoyment of property

Most legal systems find it necessary to allow one person to be given property for a limited time and for a second person to be assured during that time that he or his representatives will take the property after him, not as his successor but independently of any relation to him. A simple example is a grant of property to A for his life and then to B absolutely. There are many forms of legal technique by which this can be effected. The English technique is peculiar and at first sight difficult to understand. None the less a firm grasp is absolutely vital to an understanding of the basic principles of our law of property. The student is urged to take the next few pages very slowly.

It may make an explanation of this crucial concept easier if we take a simple example. Suppose that S owns property worth £1m. and that this capital—it may be invested in farmland, shops, offices, shares, patents, and so on—brings him a return of 5 per cent; an income, that is, of £50,000 a year. Suppose also that there is no taxation and no inflation, for if we can construct a model for such a perfect world we could then load in factors to deal with either.

Yesterday, using the correct legal machinery, S gave his property to A for life, and then to B absolutely. Today all three of them ask the question: how much am I worth? Not, how much was I worth yesterday, or will be in the future, but what is the present value of my asset. The answer to S is easy: nothing. He may have split his wealth between two others, giving neither of them the whole, but he has saved none for himself.

To answer A's enquiry as to his present worth we must look more closely at what exactly he has been given. He is certainly rich, but there are two elements to be considered in order to arrive at an assessment of his present wealth. The first is the income, which we know to be £50,000 a year; A is entitled to that for as long as he lives. But these last words bring in the element of time. Suppose—to keep the arithmetic simple—A is a healthy fifty-year-old and an actuary, consulting his life tables, would say that, statistically speaking, A could expect to live to the age of seventy. This means that we are actuarially certain that A will receive £50,000 a year for twenty years. This adds up to £1m.; but A is *not* a millionaire today. He owns something which is dwindling—a 'wasting asset'—rather like a gold mine that will produce a profit of £50,000 every year but, at the end of twenty years, will be worked out and worthless. No one would pay £1m. today for either the life estate or the mine; for if, instead, he kept his money and invested it at 5 per cent not only would he get the same income as if he had bought but, at the end of twenty years, he would still have the million. An actuary would capitalize the present value of A's entitlement over his lifetime by working out what sum would need to be invested today to provide, by payment out of both capital and income, for twenty annual instalments of £50,000. There would then, of course, be a speculative element for A might in fact die sooner or later. An actuary could load this in and the actual figure of the present value is roughly half a million.

Let us now turn to see what B is worth today. At one extreme an apparent answer might be nothing, for after all he can look forward to no cash from S's generosity until A dies.

But if that answer be correct, something strange has happened. Yesterday S had a million; today he has nothing and A has a life estate worth half a million. So if B's interest has no *present* value, things have gone very wrong. What has happened is that S has given the income to A for his life, but the remainder belongs to B at this moment. It currently produces no income for B because all the income is going to A. But it is absolutely certain that A will die—an actuary gives him twenty years—and that B's interest will not. It does not matter that B himself may die before A, for his interest will outlive him and pass on his death.

When A dies B's remainder will, as the lawyers put it, 'vest in possession'. All this means is that, at that moment, B will be entitled to both the capital and the *income* produced by it. The present certainty that this will happen is valuable today. It does not, however, mean that B is worth a million at this moment; for, if he were, he would, at 5 per cent, be worth £1.001m. in a week's time, £1.05m. at the end of a year and, in twenty years, £2m. So to ascertain the present value of his interest we must calculate the amount of money which, invested today at 5 per cent and left to mount up, would in twenty years reach a million. Our actuary will then incorporate the risk that A might live longer, and the resulting figure is about half a million. So if we look at the position today we see that S's million has been divided: A's life estate is worth about a half and B's remainder the same. If we look at the figures on A's death in twenty years time we see that A will have collected a million over that period and B will then have a million of income-producing property. But since, over that period of time, the original million will, at 5 per cent, have generated another, the arithmetic still holds good.

One other point must be made. To say that A and B are each worth a great deal of money today implies that each now owns an asset which he can immediately put on the market. But who, it may be asked, would be prepared to buy their interests? The likeliest purchaser from A would be B who might well be prepared to 'buy him out' both for tax reasons and because B might think that he could make a better job than A of managing the property and its various investments. The likeliest purchaser from B would once have been a monastery, for the certainty of immortality made them ready to plan ahead. Nowadays it would be an insurance company or the trustees of a pension fund. Both are in a business where, in return for annual income payments—premiums—they undertake to provide capital sums in the future. So it may make good investment sense for them to balance their risks by buying from B in a transaction which involves their parting with capital now (which, if kept, would produce an income) against the certainty of acquiring a larger amount of free capital when B's interest falls into possession on A's death. There is, in fact, a thriving market in what the dealers in them call 'reversionary interests'.

Now what is it that B would be getting if he bought out A or that any outside purchaser would be buying from B? In one sense what is being bought is time, the right to have now what one might have to wait a long time for. It might also be said that the outsider buys from B the property, subject to A's life interest. But it would not be so easy to say that an outsider in buying A's life interest was also buying the property. What is clear is that in buying whatever they do buy they have an eye to value and that the value of what they buy depends partly on the value of the property and partly on the probable duration of some person's interest in it. On the other hand, it is probably better to say that they buy, not the value, but something to which the value attaches, but in that case each thing to which a separate value attaches must have a present existence.

It need not therefore cause any surprise to find that English law said that the thing bought and sold was something that in some way represented the property but also contained the notion of duration, and that that duration could be cut up into slices. Now land itself in its physical aspect could be cut into slices amounting to this or that fragment of area, or even of volume, for instance, if one floor of a house is sold apart from the other floors. But although land exists in time as well as space, it is difficult—perhaps impossible—to cut the physical stuff itself into slices each of which amounts to a period of time. For it is of no use, if you are thinking on these lines, to say that one person has the land now and the other will have it in the future; that future holding has a present market value and therefore should be treated as a present thing.

Estates

In relation to land the solution long ago adopted by English law was to create an abstract entity called the estate in the land and to interpose it between the tenant and the land. Since the estate was an abstract entity imagined to serve certain purposes, it could be made to conform to a specification, and the essential parts of the specification were that the estate should represent the temporal aspect of the land—as it were a fourth dimension—that it should be divisible within that dimension in respect of time according to a coherent set of rules, but that the whole of that dimension, the estate, should be regarded as existing at the present moment so that slices of the estate representing rights to successive holdings of the land should be regarded as present estates coexisting at the same time. Thus, although B might have to wait for A's death to enter upon the land, his estate was not later in time than A's life estate but existed simultaneously with it. We have just seen how it can be at once valued and marketed. This difficult idea may perhaps be rendered more intelligible if one takes the analogy of a musical score. We shall not in the ordinary course hear the fourth movement of a Beethoven symphony until we have heard the first, second, and third movements in that order; but they are all present at the same moment in the score.

This technique, giving a legal explanation to the present market value attaching to successive rights to hold property, was first worked out for land. It has since been applied to funds, and indeed some of what has just been described now applies more to funds than to land, as will appear later. It is generally said not to apply to corporeal movables, but the matter is uncertain. In practice it would seldom be worth while trying to apply it to them.

It is a fascinating technique, supple and allowing great liberty together with security in dealing with interests in property; but its main service has probably been, by attaching ownership not to the land itself but to an abstract entity, to familiarize property lawyers with the possibility of inventing abstractions which should conform to specifications chosen with considerable freedom to serve particular purposes. With that development the law of property ceased to be earth-bound.

Since that lesson had been learnt there was no reason why other abstract entities should not be invented to serve other purposes. Henceforth it could be no objection that by adopting a particular technical solution one made it difficult, if not impossible, to discover the owner of a thing. If one could attach ownership to one abstract entity, one could attach it to another. Of course one ought not to multiply such entities unnecessarily, and one should always have practical needs in mind; but inhibitions based on the need for keeping one's eyes fixed on the physical object were quite out of place.

With a little patience it is possible to express all estates in quite precise formulae. The basic concept contains only three elements, although their explanation and combination require some care.

(a) Possession

Every estate involves possession, now or in the future. 'Possession' is here simply the word used to express in legal terms the economic factor of income value. If the asset involved is an office block or a number of shares in a company, then its possession gives entitlement to the rents of the offices or the dividends on the shares. If the asset involved is the owner's home then his occupation of it is saving him the money he would otherwise have to pay to live elsewhere; or, to put it another way, he is foregoing the income he could get by way of rent if he leased the house to a tenant. We represent the element of possession by the letter p.

(b) Time

Every estate also incorporates the notion of possession (now or in the future) *for a time*. If we take the case of the ordinary owner of a thing—the 'tenant in fee simple' if the thing be land—that time is for ever. To the economist, income for ever equals capital value. So if we represent eternity by the infinity sign we can combine the two elements to give

$$(p\infty)$$

(c) Alienation

As we have seen, instead of relating the owner directly to the thing, English law interposes this abstraction—$(p\infty)$—and says that that is what is owned. But what you own you can give away; and so the third element to be added is the legal power of alienation, here represented by a, to give

$$a \ (p\infty)$$

One more precision must be added. The estate owner can give away not only $(p\infty)$ but also the power to give it away; for the purchaser does not have to hang on to possession for ever but can sell to another, who may, in turn, sell. So the estate owner has the power to alienate the power to alienate the power to alienate . . . and so on to infinity. In other words he can alienate a itself, and so this should be raised to infinity to give, for the fee simple absolute in possession

$$a^{\infty} \ (p\infty)$$

(d) A deliberate omission: title

Finally it must be emphasized that one element does not figure in the formula: that representing *title* in the sense of the best right to the thing. If a person occupies another's land adversely then his title is weak, since he may soon be evicted. Meanwhile, however, and as far as the rest of the world (excluding the dispossessed owner) is concerned it makes good sense to say that he has an estate in the land—a fee simple, since it may last for ever. It does not seem right to English law to deny him the attributes of estate owner as far as the rest of the world is concerned just because of the possibility that one particular individual may turn up and claim a better title.

So far the formula given expresses only possession granted now and to last for ever. There are, however, only three other estates in land—entail, life, and lease—and the last two can be readily understood even at this early stage. The main classifications of estates follows.

(i) Estates in possession and estates in expectancy

The first is into estates in possession and estates in expectancy. If a person's estate gave him a right to the immediate possession of the land, it was said to be an estate in possession. If, on the other hand, he would have to wait for his right to possession to take effect, he had only an estate in expectancy. Thus, a grant to A for life and thereafter to B gave an estate in possession to A but only an estate in expectancy to B. However, although B's possession would be in the future (and, if his estate were for life, might never fall into possession owing to his predeceasing A) his estate, though itself often called a future estate, was really a present estate in the land. If B's interest were to last for ever and we use the letter l to denote A's life expectancy, we may formulate the two estates thus:

A's life estate absolute in possession $\quad a^{\infty}(pl)$

B's fee simple absolute in remainder $\quad a^{\infty}(p(\infty-l))$

(ii) Reversions and remainders

The second classification is of estates in expectancy, which are divided into reversions and remainders. If a person, A, who has an estate in Blackacre, for instance a fee simple, gives to another person, B, an estate of smaller duration than his own, for instance, a life estate—it is called a particular estate because it is only a fragment *(particula)* of A's estate—and says nothing about what is to happen after B's death, the land is said to revert on B's death to A or his successors in title, and the residue of A's estate after B's particular estate has been subtracted from it is called a reversion. If, on the other hand, A were to direct that Blackacre should go to C for life and thereafter to D, the land would be said to remain away from A, and D's interest would be a remainder. The technical words used in such a case would normally be 'grant to C for life remainder to D'. In the two examples just given A would be called a reversioner and D a remainderman.

Vested and contingent remainders

It is also advisable to explain at once the difference between a vested and a contingent remainder. If at any moment the remainderman would be able to take possession of Blackacre should the particular estate come to an end, which would normally be by the death of a tenant for life, then his remainder is *vested*. This would be the case if the identity of the remainderman was perfectly ascertained and no contingency still needed to be fulfilled. Both he and the *quantum* of his estate were known. Hence he had a present estate *vested* in him. It was said to be *vested in interest*; it would *vest in possession*, if at all, only when the particular estate came to an end. But Blackacre might have been given, for instance, to A for life remainder to the eldest surviving son of X, who already has children; or to Y when he reaches the age of twenty-one; or to the eldest son of Z, who is still a bachelor. All these remainders depend for their coming into effect on contingencies. Thus, in the first example, the remainder will fail unless X has a surviving son, and, moreover, the identity of his eldest surviving son cannot be ascertained until X dies. Hence there can be no present estate in remainder for want of a known person in whom it can vest. In the second example, the identity of Y is known, but he cannot take until he reaches the age of twenty-one. Hence he has no estate at the present moment. In the third example, there are two contingencies: first, Z must marry, and secondly he must have a son. Again there is no person who can have an estate. In all three cases there is nothing but a possibility that an estate will come into existence on the happening of the contingency. Hence these remainders were called contingent remainders. They were never considered to be estates; but the probability that the contingency would happen might be very great and might be worth paying for. So it is not a matter for surprise that contingent remainders eventually became alienable, like vested remainders; and they are known as future *interests*. Reversions are of course always *vested*, for the identity of the reversioner is always known and he is always ready to take if all particular estates should come to an end.

Contingent interests form a large class, of which contingent remainders are only one example. The law relating to them was at one time extremely complicated.[3] Even after the simplications introduced by the 1925 legislation it is still complicated and presents many traps for the unwary framers of settlements and wills.[4]

[3] See pp. 119–20 below.
[4] See pp. 178–86 below.

(iii) Freehold and leasehold estates

The third classification is into freehold and leasehold estates, the former having an indefinite, the latter a definite duration, or one which can be made definite at the will of one of the parties concerned. The simplest examples of freehold estates are the estate in fee simple and the life estate.[5] A fee simple lasts for ever.[6] It is in the ordinary course of events perpetual and is the nearest thing to full ownership of land found in English law. The indefiniteness of its duration lies in the fact that although it may come to an end, no one can say at any given moment before its termination when that will be. That a life interest will come to an end is certain, but the time of its termination is indefinite. On the other hand, not only is it certain that a lease for five years will come to an end, but it is also certain that, if nothing happens to terminate it prematurely, it will come to an end precisely five years after its creation. In fact lawyers have been so impressed by the definiteness of a lease's duration that when they allude to the lease as an estate rather than as an arrangement giving possession to the lessee, they always designate it as a *term of years*, or, more shortly, a *term*; and they call the lessee a *termor*.

Not all leasehold estates arise from leases in the strict sense of the term. Some are more properly called tenancies, and are of various kinds. The most frequent and most important are so-called periodical tenancies, for example, from week to week, from month to month, or from year to year. Periodical tenancies so created continue until they are brought to an end by a notice to quit on the part of either the landlord or the tenant varying with the period of the tenancy and terminating on one of the anniversaries of the original grant. They have, as it were, a definite duration for the time being and the definiteness of its duration starts up again whenever the

[5] A third freehold estate was the fee tail. In principle it lasted as long as the tenant had issue in the direct line, but was usually turned into a fee simple by being 'barred'. See pp. 164–8 below. All freehold estates other than the fee simple absolute in possession were in 1925 called equitable *interests*. See p. 103 below. However, much of what could be said of freehold *estates* is still true of what may by analogy, but somewhat inaccurately, be called freehold *interests*. The statutory change in terminology is not helpful in an introductory book and has often been ignored in the text.

[6] If the present holder dies intestate and without close kin it will go to the Crown. In the past it would 'escheat' to the feudal lord.

proper day for notice has passed without notice being given. The other possible tenancies are tenancies at will and at sufferance. The former means what it says: the landlord may terminate it at any moment by ejecting the tenant and the tenant likewise may throw it up at any moment. However, the payment of rent by a tenant at will, on a yearly basis, makes him a tenant from year to year, subject to termination by a half-year's notice. But for its capacity for enlargement into a yearly tenancy the title of a tenancy at will to be called a leasehold estate would be doubtful enough. A still weaker title would be that of a tenancy at sufferance, which arises when a tenant holds over, that is to say, wrongfully continues in possession after the expiration of his term or his tenancy, but is not ejected by the landlord. But they were, both of them, like all other leaseholds, accounted smaller in *quantum* than even the shortest freehold estate.

The distinction between freehold and leasehold estates has a practical justification which has remained virtually the same from the thirteenth century to the present day. Leasehold estates have always been thought of on commercial lines. Persons have always been willing to invest in terms of years, whether by purchase, or by taking them as security of loans of money, or merely in order to secure possession of land for a guaranteed period as tenants of farms or shop premises. Long terms of as much as ninety-nine years have commonly been granted at low rents to persons who undertake to build on the land. On the other hand, although freehold interests other than the fee simple have a present actuarial value, they are not marketable to the same extent as leasehold interests; and certainly no one would at the present day give a life interest to a person with the intention that he should turn it into ready money. A life interest is meant to provide an annual income for an indefinite number of years. In other words, freehold interests, other than the fee simple, have always been used mainly in order to provide for different members of a family, whereas leasehold interests have been used as objects of commerce.

Since, like the other estates, a lease confers possession for a time, it is possible to express the legal relations by means of the formula described above. If land be let (say for 21 years) and then sub-let (say for 7 years) there exist simultaneously three separate estates, each with a market value: the freehold, the head-lease and the sub-lease. We use T to indicate the term of the head-lease and t that of the sub-lease (numbers will not do since each term is diminishing daily) and R to indicate the rent reserved by the head-lease and r that of the sub-lease.

Fee simple $a^\infty \left(p(\infty - T) + RT \right)$
Head-lease $a^\infty \left(p(T - t) - RT + rt \right)$
Sub-lease $a^\infty \left(pt - rt \right)$

Estates and chattels

It has always been an article of faith that the doctrine of estates does not apply to chattels. In the Middle Ages, when the doctrine of estates came into existence, hardly any movable property was permanent enough to produce the same sort of periodical income as land, or the stocks and shares of the modern world. Hence there was little temptation to carve estates out of them such as life estates or estates tail. Nor were chattels permanent enough to be made subject to tenure. Thus it was neither against principle nor inconvenient to say that a person could own chattels. To be sure one might want to lend or hire out or pledge a chattel, and so, by what lawyers call a bailment, to deprive oneself temporarily of the physical use of it. But this would be done in the way of business or friendship and not in order to provide successively for members of the family. It was sufficient therefore to distinguish only ownership and possession and attribute the latter to the borrower, hirer, or pledgee as a bailee.

Since there was no marked tendency to use chattels to endow successive generations of a family, neither life estates nor estates tail were in principle allowed; and the doctrine of estates was never applied to chattels. However, all these limited interests, whatever be their subject-matter, works of art or other heirlooms or, much more commonly, stocks and shares, are always created by way of trust and therefore in effect exist in funds rather than specific movable objects. From the mere fact that the doctrine of estates—or something closely analogous to it—can exist in trust funds it does not by any means follow that it can also exist in specific physical chattels such as ships or horses or motor-cars.

It is still certain that the *legal* ownership of such objects
cannot be carved up so as to create in them life interests or
entailed interests; but, as will be explained later, in that they
do not now differ at all from land. The real question is whether
a bailment creates what might be fairly called a limited estate
in a physical chattel comparable to the periodical tenancy or
the term of years created by a lease. We have already seen that
there is good reason to regard the relation between bailor and
bailee as something equivalent to tenure.[7] Can we find something equivalent to an estate?

Bailments and estates

Bailments do indeed raise very interesting theoretical questions
which do not seem to have called for a solution. They have
usually been discussed in terms of ownership and possession,
but as conferring possession they differ in no way from leases
of land. Do they then, like leases, confer real rights to their
objects and are they in fact, though not ostensibly, subject to
a doctrine of estates in the same rather imperfect way? Certainly the word 'lease' is commonly used of chattels such as
computers.

Some bailments, for example by way of pledge, undoubtedly
confer real rights good against purchasers from the owner of
the chattel. Bailments at will, under which the bailor can resume possession at any moment, cause no difficulty. Of course
the purchaser can oust the bailee. There is some authority for
saying that if a person charters a ship for a term, any other
person, such as a purchaser, who has notice of the charter-
party must take the ship subject to it. Apart from ships, which
in many ways strongly resemble land, there seems to be little
authority on the question whether a purchaser could oust a
bailee for a term such as a hirer for a fixed period. In fact a
would-be purchaser would almost always have notice of the
bailment and, unwilling to risk the trouble and doubtful success of an attempt to oust the bailee, would probably either
refuse to buy or pay only for the right to have the thing after
the bailment came to an end.

In that case he would really be buying a reversion. That term
is commonly used in such a connexion. But is it rightly so used?

[7] See p. 81 above.

There are one or two cases which allow the owner of a chattel out of possession, and therefore not entitled to bring an action of trespass, to bring an action for damage to the reversion, that is to say, permanent physical damage to the thing itself. Thus there is warrant for the use of the word reversion. The only doubt—it goes mainly to classification and does not affect the substance of the law—is whether by calling the owner's interest in the chattel the reversion the law subjects it to a doctrine of estates. Perhaps the best answer that can be given to that question is that the doctrine of estates was not invented to deal with terms of years, to which it has always been applied with some difficulty and with more than the usual amount of artificiality, and that bailments of chattels present no greater difficulty. Certainly the interconnected elements of time and *quantum* which went to make the doctrine of estates are present in both. We shall return to this question in the discussion of hire-purchase.[8]

4. WORDS OF LIMITATION

In an exact art such as conveyancing it has always been important to draft documents in the most precise terms and for that purpose to develop a technical vocabulary leaving nothing in doubt. Once fragmentation of ownership according to time was admitted it became necessary to distinguish estates at their creation; and fixed forms of words had to be used to create certain kinds of estates. Although some of the formalities have been relaxed in course of time, others have been retained or even made more rigid.

A distinction has always been made between words of purchase and words of limitation, the former designating the person to whom the estate is given and the latter the nature of the estate. Thus, if land is given to A for life or in fee simple, the words 'to A' are words of purchase and the words 'for life' or 'in fee simple' are words of limitation.

The basic rule of the modern law is that if land is given to a person without words of limitation, for instance, 'to A', he acquires all that the donor has to give. If the donor has a fee simple, A gets a fee simple; if he has only a life interest, A

[8] See p. 201 below.

gets only a life interest, or rather, an interest *pur autre vie*, that is to say, one which will last for the life of the donor. If, therefore, a person who has a fee simple in Blackacre wishes to give only a life interest in it to A, he must make his meaning clear. He will usually do this by giving it 'to A for life', but this is not strictly necessary. Anything in the instrument creating the life interest which indicates his intention will suffice. Thus a grant 'to A remainder to B' shows that A's interest is to come to an end in order that B may take after him, and the most natural inference is that A shall take only a life interest.

Normally it is not now necessary to use any words of limitation if the donee is intended to get a fee simple. A grant to A will suffice. But it is customary, in order to avoid doubts, to use words of limitation, thus, 'to A in fee simple'. Occasionally even now an alternative form is used, namely, 'to A and his heirs'; it was much commoner in instruments executed before 1926, and before 1882 it was the only permissible form. The words 'and his heirs' were necessary at common law in order to show that A had an estate capable of continuing after his death and of descending to his heirs if he died intestate, but since A had acquired the full power of alienating his fee simple, the succession to it was not guaranteed to his heirs and hence the grant gave nothing directly to them. Thus the words 'and his heirs' are not words of purchase but only words of limitation.

In contrast to this relaxation in the words necessary to create a fee simple, the requirements for an entailed interest, which played an essential part in the so-called strict settlement, have been made stricter. Since 1925 the words of limitation must include the words 'and the heirs of his body' or 'in fee tail' or 'in tail', whatever the kind of instrument in which they occur.[9]

5. RENT AND RENTCHARGES

The income derived from the exploitation of a physical object must always be produced ultimately by some physical use made of it. But it is not at all necessary that all the persons who enjoy the income should do the physical work of producing it. Commonly some person or persons work on the

---

[9] Entailed interests are explained at pp. 164-8.

thing but share the income from it with others. A similar situation may arise in relation to monopolies such as patents or copyright. Others besides the manufacturer or publisher may derive an income from them.

In theory the sharing of the profit could take any one of three forms: the user could take a fixed sum paying the whole of the residue to another person, he could pay a fixed sum (which might vary from time to time) to that other person and keep the residue for himself, or they could share the profit according to a fixed or variable proportion.

The first relation would in fact take the form of a contract binding the user to manage the property for a fixed salary or wage; he would have no right *in rem* to the property and the service would be temporary lest it should smack of slavery. The third relation is known in France as *métayage* and in the Southern States of the United States as *share-cropping*. It occurs especially where the landlord has to provide not only the fixed plant of a farm but also some or all of the working capital and prefers to go into a sort of working partnership with the cultivator instead of merely employing him; though the cultivator has a right *in rem* to the farm. This arrangement is not used in England.

In the second solution the actual user of a thing pays what may in the general way be called a *rent*, though for physical movables it is often called a *hire* and for patents and copyright a *royalty*. The relations of the party to the thing may vary greatly. Where corporeal chattels are concerned, there will almost always be a bailment and the limited interest, such as it is, will be in the bailee. A manufacturer or publisher may exploit a patent or copyright either under an out-and-out assignment or under a licence which will leave the ownership of the patent or copyright unchanged. The same variety exists in respect of land.

If a landowner wants to get his land back eventually, he leases the land to a lessee in return for a money rent, and both lessor and lessee have rights *in rem* over the land. On the other hand, he may be quite willing to sell the land and so dispose of his interest in it for good, but may be prepared to meet the needs of a relatively indigent purchaser by accepting, as was often done in Manchester and Bristol, in place of a lump sum down, a perpetual rent, or, as it was often called, a fee farm rent. Where that was the case, he retained no estate in the land and so had not the security for the annual payments that the lessor automatically had. Accordingly he required the purchaser to execute a deed creating a rentcharge on the land, which gave him certain powers of enforcing a payment of the rent. It was in reality a form of security. No such rentcharges may now be created and the old ones are being redeemed.

6. POWERS

Another division of property rights results from the use of powers. Normally the ownership of an interest in property carries with it the power to manage and dispose of it. This power can indeed be restricted without any portion of it being vested in another person. Thus, if one person holds the fee simple of land in trust for another person in fee simple, although he has the legal estate in the land, he can be restrained by a court of equity from alienating it without the consent of the beneficiary.[10] Such restrictions, though of little importance as far as land is concerned, can be quite important for chattels such as valuable pictures or furniture. They produce a restriction rather than a fragmentation of ownership.

However, fragmentation does occur where one person has the enjoyment of an interest but another person has powers of managing or of alienating it or of otherwise determining who shall enjoy it. A clear functional distinction can be drawn between three different kinds of powers.

Some powers exist to enable persons who have no beneficial interest, or at most a limited one, to manage property and, in so far as they include the power of sale, it is for the purpose of preserving the capital by getting rid of one investment and acquiring a better one. A second kind exists for the purpose of enabling a person who has acquired a security, such as a mortgage, over a thing, to sell it for instance in order to enforce his security and so obtain the money to which he is entitled. The third kind of power is used to make the beneficial enjoyment of property move more flexibly among a number of persons.

[10] See further p. 103 below.

The first kind of power forms much of the subject-matter of the next section, which deals with the distinction between management and enjoyment;[11] the second is best studied in relation to security;[12] the third falls to be discussed at once. These powers are called powers of appointment.

Powers of appointment

It is quite possible for a person, A, who is settling property on marriage or by will, to give a life interest to B followed by a gift to such person or persons as B shall appoint. In other words, the donor of the power, A, delegates to the donee of the power, B, the task of selecting the persons to take after B. If the power is expressed in that unrestricted form, it is said to be a general power. B can, if he chooses, appoint even himself and so a general power is equivalent to ownership in the donee. But since there is no obvious advantage to be gained by giving a person a general power to appoint to an interest instead of giving him the interest itself, general powers are not often met with in practice. A much commoner kind of power is the so-called special power of appointment, in such a form as 'to B for life remainder to such of his children as B shall appoint'. The appointment can then be made only within a class, and since the class does not include the donee, the power is not equivalent to ownership. Moreover, if the donee uses a special power to obtain an advantage for himself, by extracting, for instance, a payment to himself from the person appointed, he is guilty of a fraud on the power and the appointment is void.

A power is not itself an estate or interest but merely enables the donee to create an estate or interest in himself or some other person or persons; though for many purposes a general power is regarded as an interest.

7. THE DISTINCTION BETWEEN MANAGEMENT AND ENJOYMENT

The freedom of invention developed in handling estates has proved particularly useful in enabling the distinction between management and enjoyment of property to be expressed in

[11] See p. 79 below.   [12] See pp. 190, 193-5 below.

terms of law. It must, of course, first be decided as a matter of policy whether management shall be allowed to be divorced from enjoyment, or whether on the contrary a person who is to enjoy the benefits of property should not also be forced to undertake, if not the actual management of the property, at least to the full extent the risk of mismanagement by others. It must be said at once that English law has taken the former view; it allows, though it does not of course compel, the management to be detached from the beneficial enjoyment.

Trusts

It is also obvious that there must be some personal relation between the manager and the beneficiary, under which the former may be made liable to the latter if he wrongfully mis-manages the property. That relation is in English law called a trust. The manager is *trustee* for the beneficiary. But the question still remains, what are the relations of trustee and beneficiary to the thing held in trust? It would have been possible to say either that the trustee owns the property but is under a duty to manage it for the benefit of the beneficiary, who has nothing more than a correlative personal right against the trustee, or on the contrary that the beneficiary owns the property but gives full powers of management to the trustee, who stands in no direct relation to the property but acts merely by delegation of property rights vested in the bene-ficiary. English law has taken neither course, but has in effect said that both trustee and beneficiary own the property in different ways, or, more accurately, that neither owns the property in the strict Roman sense of the term ownership, but each owns a different interest in it, called respectively the legal estate and the equitable interest. It says that to ask in such a situation who owns the physical object is an improper question, just as it would be improper to ask whether a tenant for life or a person entitled to the land after his death owned the land itself.

The legal and the equitable estate

We have already seen that not only the trustee but the bene-ficiary has a right *in rem* over the trust property, for the beneficiary can trace it into the hands of any holder of it who has not taken it bona fide for value without notice, actual or constructive, of a breach of trust.[13] There might none the less have been some tendency to treat this right as a mere *chose in action*,[14] that is to say, as the property aspect of the personal rights which the beneficiary may have against the original trustee or later constructive trustees. But it became necessary to treat it as a separate equitable estate comparable to the legal estate; for the same desire to divide up the trust property successively among several beneficiaries arose as had led to the development of the doctrine of estates. That made it inevitable that the beneficial interest in the trust property should itself be treated as an estate, susceptible of division into several estates giving successive rights to possession; and since it was protected by the Chancellor in the exercise of his equitable jurisdiction, it became known as the equitable estate, in contrast to the trustee's interest, which, since it was protected by the Common Law Courts, came to be known as the legal estate. By the 1925 statutes (and for no good reason) the term equitable interest has been substituted for equitable estate. So there is not one object of ownership, a physical thing, but two separate ones, the legal estate owned by the trustee for the purpose of managing the land, and the equitable estate or interest owned by the beneficiary for the purpose of enjoying the land.

At the present day it would be easier to satisfy anyone who wanted to know who owns the land itself, for the trustee can almost always sell the land, and holds the proceeds of the sale in trust for the beneficiaries. Thus the sale will hardly ever be in breach of trust and there can seldom be any question of the purchaser's being a constructive trustee of the land.[15] Since the beneficiary can very rarely insist on the trustee's retaining the land, his equitable interest really exists not over the land but over a trust fund, of which the land is only the present manifestation. This would not be quite so true of corporeal

---

[13] See p. 57 above.

[14] See p. 20 above.

[15] There is one real exception. If I convey land to X in trust for Y and Y is of full age and in his right mind, there is no settlement, and X cannot convey the land to a third party free from Y's equitable interest in it, unless, of course, the third party takes for value without notice either actual or constructive. But Y can force X to convey the legal estate to him.

movables, for the trustee would not be able to sell them as a matter of law, but in practice he is almost always given an express power of sale. Thus it would not now be grossly inaccurate to say that the trustee owns the individual assets comprised in the trust property, though his ownership is limited by the rights enjoyed by the beneficiary, and is not available to the former's creditors.

These various divisions of ownership are cross-divisions; no one is a subdivision of any other. Thus they may or may not coincide at the will of the donor or settlor, as the person who establishes a trust is called. For instance, A, who has a fifty-year lease of Blackacre from B, may give it to C and D (who will be joint tenants of the legal estate in the land, which they will hold as tenants of the landlord, B) in trust for E for life and thereafter to F and G as tenants in common (each of whom will have a present equitable interest analogous to an estate in the land). But almost anything in this settlement could be altered without implying any alteration in what was left. Thus, if the land placed in trust had been not leasehold but freehold (in which case the only tenure would have been the shadowy tenancy under the Crown), nothing else need have been changed. Or again the land might have been vested in only one trustee, for instance, a trust corporation such as a bank; in that case there would have been no joint tenancy, but again nothing else need have been changed. Or again the only change might have been to settle the land in trust for only one beneficiary, or, on the other hand, there might have been only one remainderman. However, some changes would necessarily have implied others. Thus, if F and G had been given an absolute interest immediately without the interposition of a trust, they could not have taken the legal estate as tenants in common, but must have become joint tenants of the legal estate; and we shall see later[16] that E could not now have a legal life estate or F and G legal estates in remainder.

[16] p. 83 below.

VI

THE RECONCILIATION OF FRAGMENTATION WITH THE NEEDS OF THE MARKET

So far our attention has been concentrated on the possible ways in which several abstract things can be made to exist in relation to one physical object; and in so doing we have been thinking of property mainly as income-producing capital. But physical objects demand attention on their own account, for the ultimate source of income must be the use made by someone, however remote, of a physical object or collection of objects. A share in a mining company may be treated as a separate abstract income-producing thing, but there would be no income without the mine which the company exists to work.

Now people do not want to limit their purchases to fragments of income-producing capital. They need also to buy actual physical objects, such as, for instance, machinery and land to build a factory to put machinery in. Moreover, the policy of the law may well be to have as free a market as possible for physical objects, so that they may be bought and sold without difficulty; and one difficulty which will then have to be avoided will be that of having to obtain the consents of several persons with fragmentary interests in them. For this purpose the fact that each abstract thing connected with the physical object is itself freely marketable is irrelevant, for not all the owners of such interests may be willing to sell at the same time and to the same person; moreover, some interests may not be vested in any living persons but may have been limited, as we say, to unborn persons. This difficulty occurs much more rarely with corporeal chattels because they are not permanent enough for an income arising from them to be divided among several persons in succession. But it is important for land and for such incorporeal chattels as stocks and shares or copyright.

Now, if one is impressed with the need for a free market and if at the same time one thinks almost entirely in terms of physical objects, one is forced into accepting the view that the ownership which attaches to physical things must in principle be indivisible; and if one is also forced, as seems inevitable, to allow real rights less than ownership to exist over physical objects, one must limit their number and treat them generally with suspicion. If, on the other hand, one thinks in terms of abstract things and if among those abstract things one admits the possibility of creating trust funds, one can reconcile the need for a free market for physical things with the need for flexibility in the handling of income-bearing lots of capital.

Voluntary methods of reconciliation

This can be done either voluntarily or compulsorily. It can be done voluntarily by a settlor if he deliberately vests in trustees the legal estate in physical things to its widest possible extent, conferring on the trustees full powers of management and alienation. The physical things thus constitute present investments of a trust fund and can be varied from time to time by the trustees, who may, however, be restricted by the trust deed or by the law as to the new investments they may make of the proceeds of any sale. This makes the physical objects freely alienable without the consent of any persons other than the trustees. On the other hand, great freedom can be allowed to create a most luxuriant growth of simultaneously existing abstract things, such as concurrent or future interests, within the ambit of the equitable interest, for all these will amount to limited rights to shares in the income arising from the trust fund, whatever it is invested in for the time being. Of course there is a danger that the trust fund may, by unwise or fraudulent management, be reduced in value or even disappear, but that is a necessary price to pay for freedom to buy and sell physical objects. This is the solution commonly adopted in the United States.

Compulsion by statute

It is perfectly admissible for a settlor in England also to give the full legal interest in property, together with full powers of management and sale, to trustees in trust for a number of beneficiaries in succession. But English law has taken a further step. Since 1882 by statute and whether he likes it or not, a person who settles land on several persons in succession finds that he has automatically separated the control of the land itself from the beneficial interests existing in it and has given to some person or persons, who may indeed include a beneficiary, wide powers of managing and alienating it.

The need for keeping physical objects freely alienable could be most effectually reconciled with the desire to carve up into fragments the right to income from them if it were enacted that the only interest that could be held in a physical object was absolute ownership, while at the same time such objects were allowed to become component parts of a trust fund and the income from the fund to be divided up with the utmost freedom.

In practice this solution cannot be accepted without qualification. Some fragmentation of the legal estate in the physical object must be allowed and some restrictions must be placed on the power to carve up the equitable right to income produced in the trust fund.[1]

Some place must be found for leases, under which the legal interest in the land itself is divided between lessor and lessee, and for mortgages or other charges, under which the mortgagee or chargee can have a legal interest in the land as well as the mortgagor or chargor. If it were not possible to have leases a farmer would always have to buy his land outright and one could not adopt the very convenient arrangement under which a landlord provides the fixed capital and the tenant farmer the working capital necessary for carrying on the farm. For if the only legal interest in the land itself were vested in the farmer, the landlord could not get adequate security for the payment of rent, the more so if at the same time it was made impossible for him to take a mortgage giving him a legal interest in the land. If only the landlord was given

---

[1] A discussion of these restrictions is postponed to pp. 176–87.

an interest in the land, he could sell the land over the farmer's head and force the latter, at best, to accept a money compensation, which would be not at all what the farmer intends or needs.

Similarly, if the mortgagee alone had a legal interest in the physical object, he could force the mortgagor out of it in return for compensation, whereas if only the mortgagor had a right to the physical object the mortgagee could only have a slice of the income arising from a trust fund, and a trust fund is by no means as safe as the physical object itself.

Rationale of the distinction

Thus, a certain amount of fragmentation of the ownership of the physical object itself is necessary, and the most that the law can do is to keep it down to a minimum. This it can do by allowing fragmentation only where it is necessary to give one person the physical use of an object and at the same time to give another person a right to hold or to take the physical object as security for a right to income or even capital. Thus the tenant farmer needs the land, but the landlord cannot be satisfied with a mere right to the share in the income produced by the land which is constituted by the rent. He is not sufficiently secure if he has to accept the farmer not merely as his rent-paying tenant but also as the trustee of a fund out of which the rent is to be paid.[2] The mortgagee needs such protection even more, for without powers exercisable over the land itself he would have nothing more than a preferential right to receive his interest and eventually his capital.

The Law of Property Act

Accordingly, in 1925 Parliament provided, by Section 1 of the Law of Property Act, that the only legal estates that could be held in land were to be the fee simple absolute in possession and the term of years absolute. Those were to be the only interests in land which could guarantee the holder continued possession of the land and ensure that no one else could sell it over his head and force him to accept money compensation.

---

[2] The landlord of an efficient farmer is now very much in that position in consequence of the legislation designed to protect tenants; but this was not so at the time when the 1925 legislation was being prepared.

Mortages were to be made by giving the mortgagee a term of years or a legal charge, either of which in effect gave the mortgagee certain powers to enforce his security, notably by selling the land or acquiring the full interest in it for himself.[3]

The fee simple, as we have seen, approximates to absolute ownership, and this approximation is enhanced by the rules that, to be a legal estate, it must be absolute, that is to say, it must not be liable to come to an end if a condition is fulfilled or be given to last until the occurrence of a future event, and also that it shall give a right to immediate possession, that is to say, that it shall not constitute a future interest. Estates in fee simple which break these rules, for example such as exist in reversion or remainder, though they may subsist as equitable interests, that is to say, as interests in a trust fund, cannot be legal estates. However, if the owner of the fee simple demises the land to a lessee for a term of years, although he is said to give the lessee possession and to be henceforth a reversioner, that is only for one purpose; since he is entitled to the rents and profits of the land, he is for that purpose regarded as still possessing the land and so is held to retain the fee simple in possession. The fee simple in possession and the term of years in possession coexist as legal estates throughout the term.[4]

To be a legal estate, a term of years also must be absolute, but it need not be in possession since a current tenant may want to take now a grant of a legal lease to commence when his present lease expires. However, a term must be limited to take effect not more than twenty-one years after the date of the instrument creating it.

There is nothing in all this to prevent a person *possessing* land by virtue of a grant for life or for an entailed interest or having a right to possession in the future as a reversioner or remainderman; but since all these interests can only exist as equitable interests, they are liable to be overreached, that is to say, converted into money or some other object, and so are in reality only interests in a trust fund of which the present form is land. There will always be some person or persons who can sell the land itself, though, as will be seen

---

[3] See further p. 193 below.
[4] See further pp. 149–50 below.

later,[5] there are ways and means of preventing them from doing so where a sale would be improper.

LPA 1925 s.1 is merely machinery. Section 2 is, if anything, more important. It is the great over-reaching pivot which provides that, in four major areas, a purchaser of the legal estate will take the land free from equitable interests such as life estates or fees in remainder, even if he knows all about them. His only duties are to act in good faith and to pay the purchase money to the right people: to the appropriate trustees if he is to over-reach successive or concurrent interests; to personal representatives to take free of any interests under the deceased's will or intestacy; to the selling mortgagee to over-reach the borrower's interest. These equitable interests then subsist in the money so paid (and any investments thereof).

Tenancy in common and infants

A single subsection of the Law of Property Act, 1925,[6] brings together into what is at first sight a strange juxtaposition tenancies in common and infants, for it declares that 'A legal estate is not capable of subsisting or of being created in an undivided share in land or of being held by an infant'. There is, however, a common element in the extreme difficulties which both tenancy in common and infants may cause to conveyancers.

Any property interest which is vested in an infant is for the time being immobilized. Thus if the land itself which is comprised in a settlement is to be freely alienable, the legal estate must always be vested in some person or persons who have power to convey it. An infant cannot convey, and so steps have to be taken to vest the legal estate in persons of full capacity. On the other hand, there is no reason whatever why the infant's right to receive income from the land comprised in the settlement should be tampered with at all during his infancy, and so he is left with an equitable interest.

It has already been explained[7] that, whereas tenancy in common is appropriate to the beneficial enjoyment of land, joint tenancy is much more appropriate to the management of property by trustees. Moreover, for the conveyancer joint

[5] See p. 144 below.   [6] S. 1 (6).   [7] See pp. 82–4 above.

tenancy has another great advantage over tenancy in common. Since all the joint tenants own the whole, there is only one title, whereas since tenants in common each hold a separate, though undivided share, there is a separate title to each share. Therefore, if a purchaser wants to buy land from a number of tenants in common, he would not only have to get all the tenants in common to concur in conveying the land to him, but he would also have to investigate the title to each undivided share. That could easily become a very burdensome task, for each original share might in course of time have become vested in quite a number of other persons, so that a purchaser might have to consider the validity of one transaction in respect of one share, two transactions in respect of another, three transactions in respect of the third, and so on. It has been known for as many as a hundred separate titles to exist in respect of the same piece of land, and for it to be more expensive to investigate all these titles than the land was worth. Accordingly, it is much more convenient for a purchaser to deal with joint tenants than with tenants in common, and as it is the legal estate in land that a purchaser usually wants to buy, an easy solution was found in the Law of Property Act, 1925, namely, that a legal estate in land cannot be held by tenants in common, but only by joint tenants.

On the other hand, there is not the same objection to the holding of equitable interests in common, and, since they represent rights of enjoyment, there is everything to be said for excluding the unfair operation of survivorship. Thus equitable interests can be held in common and indeed in a few cases equity presumes such a holding. If, therefore, it is now desired to give land to A and B in common, the legal estate must be vested in them as joint tenants on trust for sale, in trust for themselves as tenants in common. The Act also provided that the number of legal joint tenants of a piece of land must generally be limited to four, to ensure that the assent of not too great a number should be needed for an alienation of the land.

Joint tenancy can be turned into tenancy in common by a process known as severance. This can be done deliberately by agreement between the joint tenants, or by one serving notice of severance on the others, or by one alienating to an outsider. Now as we have just seen, the 1925 legislation insisted that legal tenancies in common should not exist, but that they should subsist only as equitable interests behind a trust for sale of the land itself. Consequently, in order to reconcile the wish to permit this fragmentation of ownership with the need for easy marketability of land, two further steps had to be taken. Firstly it was made clear that, on severance, a legal joint tenancy did not become a legal tenancy in common but that the legal title continued undisturbed. Secondly, even where two people hold jointly, not because they are trustees for others, but because they want to be joint beneficial owners, the law was forced to impose a trust for sale from the outset. Having decided that, whenever a tenancy in common arises, the legal estate in the land must be held on trust for sale, it was not possible to make this event occur at whatever particular moment a joint tenancy happened to be severed.

An example may help. Land is given to A, B, C, and D as joint tenants on trust for sale in trust for themselves as joint tenants. A dies. He simply drops out of the picture and the surviving three now hold the legal estate on trust for themselves. B then severs by writing a letter in those terms to C and D. This has no effect at all on the joint tenancy—the legal estate is still held by all three on trust for sale—but the trusts have changed. They now hold in trust as to one-third for B, and for C and D as joint tenants of the other two-thirds. C now dies. The legal estate is held by B and D, still as joint tenants, but on trust for themselves as tenants in common with B having his one-third share and D, who took by survivorship from C, the remaining two-thirds. On B's death the legal estate is held by D as sole survivor of joint tenants and he holds as to two-thirds for himself and one-third for B's estate. If he wishes to sell the land he is free to do so but will appoint another trustee to sell with him; a purchaser who pays both is not in the least concerned with what happened to the beneficial interests.[8]

It must be said that this scheme—so elegant and efficient where the land is treated merely as an investment—is nowadays

[8] When he severs, B will protect himself against the risk of a sale by D alone by, if the title is registered, making the appropriate entry or, if it is not registered, by writing notice that he has severed on the conveyance to the four of them. In any sale by D he would have to produce this.

ill-suited to the most common case of co-ownership. It is not easy to explain to Jack and Jill who have just got married, pooled their savings, and bought a house that they hold the matrimonial home on trust to sell it.

Personalty

In theory precisely the same considerations should apply all along the line to chattels as to land. It would seem that there is the same need to keep the physical object or the specific stocks and shares or other securities marketable, to allow the income derived from them to be divided among several persons, and to allow physical objects to be parted with temporarily for use. However, there has never been much tendency to keep physical chattels, other than pictures or other heirlooms, inalienable; stocks and shares, other than shares in private companies, have always been regarded as marketable commodities, and settlors have therefore usually given trustees full power to sell them and reinvest the proceeds; and whereas the unique character of each single piece of land naturally creates monopoly conditions, which must be counteracted as far as possible by making all land in principle freely alienable, such monopoly conditions rarely exist in physical chattels and, at any rate, have nothing to do with alienability or the reverse.

Whatever may have been the precise force of these considerations, the question of alienability has never been for chattels a matter of public concern as it has for land. Thus when in 1925 it was made a matter of principle that land should be freely alienable and that therefore, with very few exceptions, trustees should have wide powers of sale, no alteration was made in the law governing trusts of personalty. It was apparently thought unnecessary to abolish fixed trusts of personalty in which trustees are given no power of sale, or perhaps they were overlooked. The only provision made for undivided shares in chattels in the LPA 1925 (s.188) allows the owner of a half-share or more to ask the Court to order physical division.

VII
OWNERSHIP

It is now time to see what meaning, if any, can be given to the word *ownership* in English law.

It must be said at the outset that the word is not very often used in the professional literature of English law, that is to say, in authoritative writings such as enactments and reports of decided cases; and that where the word *owner* is sporadically used in statutes it has been given many different meanings, sometimes in the definition sections of the statutes. The 1925 legislation usually speaks of a person 'entitled to an estate in land'. On the other hand, no book on Analytical Jurisprudence would be complete that did not contain a full discussion of the nature of ownership.

The analytical jurists have this concern for ownership because they have for historical reasons had their eyes fixed on Roman law and the so-called civil-law systems which are in large part derived from it. Now, one of the most striking institutions of Roman law was *dominium*, upon which all the civil-law systems have modelled their treatment of ownership. *Dominium* was, in the final form it received in the *Corpus Juris* of Justinian, as near to being absolute as any private-law institution can be. The owner had an absolute title, he had an absolute right to dispose of the thing he owned, and his right to use it was limited by so few restrictions of a public-law character that it, too, could almost be called absolute. The kinds of incumbrances with which it could be burdened were kept down to the lowest possible number, and where they existed they were carefully distinguished from the *dominium* over the thing, which was regarded as retaining its character of a general undifferentiated right over the thing capable of resuming its original plenitude by the mere disappearance of the incumbrance.

Now, the concurrence of these various absolutes in a single institution was really a very remarkable peculiarity of Roman law. Doubtless it was and still is very convenient for a person to be able to say: 'This thing is mine; my title to it is absolute; I can do what I like with it subject to certain very obvious restrictions that have to be put on the use of everything of the kind; and, if I wish, I can vest all these rights in another person by transferring the thing to him.' Many persons can say those things at the present day in England. A tenant in fee simple with the legal estate in registered land is in that position, at any rate if his holding is subject to no incumbrances. If he grants a lease he parts with the use of the land for the time being, but when the lease comes to an end there is no need to revest the right of user in him; he automatically resumes it as part of the fee simple.

However, as we have already seen, absolute titles are rather rare in English law, and so it is not surprising to find that when the term *ownership* is used in relation to title, it is merely contrasted with *possession*, and means little more than *title*, or at most a title with no obviously better title outstanding. The owner is a person who has something better than mere possession. But no technical significance attaches to the term, for what he alleges in an action to recover possession is that he has a right to the immediate possession of the thing which is almost invariably relative.[1]

As regards use of the thing, ownership rarely comes in question. Where the right to use a thing or to enjoy the income from

[1] In actual practice the Roman position cannot have been very different. If a plaintiff was protecting his possession or seeking to recover it from a defendant who had dispossessed him directly, he merely proved his possession; if the defendant had come into possession peaceably and indirectly, for example by acquiring the thing in question from one who had dispossessed the plaintiff, the latter had in principle to prove his ownership. But this meant that he must prove that he had previously acquired the thing by what an English lawyer would call a good root of title and had kept it for a certain length of time. Moreover, if the defendant had not possessed the thing before the plaintiff, the latter need only prove an earlier possession starting with a good root of title. There is little that looks 'absolute' in this, and what there is is further diminished by the rule that no one could become owner of stolen goods however good his root of title or the length of his possession. See for a fuller discussion Buckland and McNair, *Roman Law and Common Law* (2nd edn.), pp. 76–81.

it is divided among several persons nothing is gained by attributing ownership to any one of them. The situation is described much more clearly by talking of bailor and bailee, lessor and lessee, tenant for life and remainderman, and the like. Ownership of a thing does not generally impose duties—they are dealt with, logically enough, by the law of obligations, i.e. contract and tort. Thus it is the occupier, not the owner, who is normally liable to visitors or neighbours (and for rates). It is the driver, not the owner, of a car who is liable in neligence. Nor does the law of property normally limit an owner's power to destroy his thing. By statute nowadays buildings may be 'listed' and trees protected under a preservation order; but the owner of one of the few Vermeers in the world is, under English law, free to put the painting on a bonfire.

When the question is asked whether a person can alienate a thing to a third party, for land the answer is quite clear: he can alienate his estate or interest; and the same is true of interests in a fund. For chattels the matter is not quite so clear; lawyers do often speak of the owner as having the right to alienate, and indeed the policy of that law has always been to concentrate interests in movables as far as possible so as to make them marketable. We have seen that the same policy has been extended to land.

Since it seems a pity to have to jettison excellent words like *ownership*, *owner*, and *own*, the last of which, as a verb, has no real equivalent in many other languages, and since English law is not at all committed to any particular usage, there are two alternatives open to us. We can say that the owner of a thing, whether land or a chattel, is the person who can convey the full interest in it to another person, i.e. the person who is already often called the owner of a chattel or the person who has the fee simple of land, or on the contrary that what a person owns is an estate or an interest in a trust fund or generally his interest in a chattel. In the former case we attach ownership to the physical object at the cost of reducing the number of owners; in the latter we enlarge the number of owners but attach ownership in every case to an abstract entity. At present the usage, for what it is, is ambiguous, for whereas the Sale of Goods Act clearly speaks of the owner of goods, the Law of Property Act speaks of an *estate owner*, who is defined as the owner of a legal estate, which includes, not only the fee simple absolute in possession of land but also a term of years absolute. The Land Registration Act speaks indifferently both of the 'proprietor' of land and of an estate in land.

VIII

THE IMPACT OF
PUBLIC LAW

PROPERTY law has always been considered the heart of private
law. Indeed, three and a half centuries ago every lawyer contrasted government and property. Bacon, for example, said: 'I
consider that it is a true and received division of law into *ius
publicum* and *ius privatum*, the one being the sinews of property, and the other of government.' In so far as a distinction
can be made in England between public and private law, property belongs to the latter.

Nevertheless, it would give a totally false impression of the
present status of property in this country if public law were
left entirely out of the picture; and in fact property lawyers
now devote much more of their attention to public law than
to what would formerly have alone been considered to deserve
the name of property law. A solicitor acting for his client in
purchasing a house may take comparatively little trouble over
the investigation of title—which belongs entirely to private law
—knowing from past experience that the title is almost certainly good; he will, however, be extremely careful to find
out whether public law imposes awkward restrictions on use.
Similarly, whereas the old conveyancers were anxious to draw
their settlements in such a way as to carry out a purely family
policy and within the four corners of it to protect each person
concerned against possible encroachments on the part of the
rest, their successors are willing to quite a great extent to trust
those persons to behave decently towards each other, if only
they can protect all of them against the big bad wolf, the tax-
levying state.[1] Finally, more and more property becomes vested

[1] See further p. 123 below.

in the Crown and other public authorities, whether local authorities such as counties or public corporations such as the National Coal Board and the British Railways Board.

Historical development

From the Reformation to the middle of the nineteenth century the development of property law was almost entirely in the hands of the conveyancers and the merchants, who were constantly inventing and trying out new combinations of the simple elements provided by common law, equity, and the older statutes. The efficacy of their efforts was constantly being tested in the Courts, which produced an immense mass of case law; and this again was brought into systematic form by a number of very remarkable eighteenth- and nineteenth-century writers of whom the most famous were perhaps Fearne[2] and Butler.[3] During the whole of that time, Parliament intervened little to alter the law, mainly because the conveyancers and merchants were able, by manipulating the existing law, to satisfy the needs of the great landowners and men of business who between them governed the country. Moreover, the whole tendency of the time was increasingly in favour of leaving each man to manage his affairs for himself. Towards the end of the period the followers of Jeremy Bentham were able to get rid of unnecessary fictions and to bring the forms of conveyancing more into line with the substance, but without making much change in the latter.

Since that time, however, there has been increasing intervention by the legislature. Almost all of it relates to land. So far as movables are concerned, consumer protection statutes affect usually the law of contract or tort. The law of property in movables has received little attention from the public power, presumably for the reason well expressed by Napoleon in the discussions on the draft Civil Code: 'It matters little how an individual disposes of some diamonds, or of some pictures. But the way in which he disposes of his land is of concern to

[2] Charles Fearne (1742–94), best known for his *Essay on Contingent Remainders and Executory Devises.*
[3] Charles Butler (1750–1832), best known for his edition of *Coke upon Littleton.*

society. It is for society to lay down the rules and the limits to his right of disposition.'[4]

The impact of public law has been felt in two ways which, though the historical background may be similar, can be distinguished. The first reflects the general public interest in the physical state of land and buildings, regardless of who occupies them and will be dealt with in the following pages. The second concerns the effect on certain people—the tenants of farms, business premises, and dwellinghouses—of leaving them entirely dependent on the private law. This topic will be discussed in the chapter on leases and the hire of goods.[5]

Public Health   The Industrial Revolution and the rise of the population led to enormous urban growth which the private law of nuisance could not effectively control. Accordingly since the middle of the nineteenth century Parliament has intervened to empower local authorities, by means of bye-laws to control sewage, cemeteries, gasworks, and the like.

Housing and slum clearance   The common law gave no assurance to one buying or renting a dwellinghouse that it would be fit for human habitation or, if rented, kept in repair. The justification for this was thought to be that a prospective purchaser or lessee would inspect the premises and the state of repair would be reflected in the money he was willing to pay. While the wealthy might be able to look after themselves, however, those not so fortunate had to take what they got, and the result of the common-law rule was the growth of the great urban slums. From the end of the nineteenth century local authorities have been given powers of inspection and repair of individual insanitary houses and power to remove those incapable of improvement. Under slum clearance programmes they may acquire compulsorily housing unfit for habitation and have obligations to rehouse the occupiers. The question arose as to what compensation should be paid to the owners and Parliament eventually decided that the only value to be taken into account was that of the site cleared of buildings. In other words the owner of slum houses could be deprived of them without compensation. It is true that this

[4] Fenet, Travaux Préparatoires du Code Civil, Vol. 14, p. 57 (Paris 1829).
[5] See pp. 154–58 below.

legislation could be treated as merely extending the boundaries of nuisance; an insanitary house was a nuisance and its owner could be forced to abate it by allowing a public authority to acquire it without paying compensation. None the less property rights were less secure than they had been.

Town and country planning

Even though nineteenth-century statutes limited a land-owner's powers in the interests of public health and decent housing, he could generally develop his land in any way he chose, provided he did not infringe the rights of other individuals. By the early years of this century, however, it was becoming obvious to far-sighted people that slum clearance was not enough: the growth of slums should be prevented by town planning. Little was done, however, save under the initative of isolated local authorities except for the attempt in 1936 to solve one particular part of the general problem, namely ribbon development which, although profitable to builders and houseowners who were saved the expense of making up roads and laying sewers, made the suburbs sprawl in a way inconvenient to agriculture and dangerous to traffic.

It would serve no useful purpose to recount the history of the law on this topic. The present position is briefly as follows.

Local planning authorities must prepare general structure plans for their areas and submit them for approval by the Secretary of State for the Environment; in addition they may draw up more detailed local plans for any particular part of their area. The plans themselves, however, do not automatically permit the developments envisaged therein. The most radical feature of planning law is the requirement that, before any development of the land takes place, permission must be obtained from the appropriate authority. 'Development' means not merely building works but any material change in the use of the land. An applicant may appeal against refusal of planning permission to the Secretary of State or his inspector; but development in breach of the local authority's disposition may result in a fine and, in the case of unauthorized building, forcible removal of the offending structure at the cost of the owner.

Allied to the notion of development is the problem of the

increase in value which may accrue to private land by the activities of other individuals or of public authorities. A farmer who sees the nearby town gradually growing in size until his land is on the outskirts and close to hospitals, shops, schools, sewers, and public utilities will find that the worth of his fields as building lands far exceeds their agricultural value. If he obtains planning permission to develop them he will take the benefit of this increased value although none of it is attributable to his own labours. Since almost the beginning of this century attempts have been made to ensure that not all of this extra wealth is a windfall to the private owner. The schemes have been various, ranging from the use of the tax system through the device of imposing a development charge as the price of planning permission to attempting to ensure that all substantial development takes place on land which is in, or has passed through, public ownership. The changes have varied with the political allegiance of the party in power, but none of the schemes has been conspicuously successful.

Property of public authorities

Much property, including large areas of land, now belongs to the Crown, other public authorities and public corporations such as the National Coal Board, the British Railways Board, the BBC, and the Port of London Authority. In other countries such public property is often governed by an entirely different system of law and is excluded entirely from the law of property. In England there is no such distinction of principle. Of course, property such as government buildings in Whitehall or town halls or other municipal buildings seldom come into the market; property acquired compulsorily for specific purposes, such as building a railway, cannot be used for other purposes; the Crown has certain peculiar rights and privileges by virtue of the Royal Prerogative; and such bodies as the National Coal Board and British Rail, by the fact that they have a statutory monopoly, cannot alienate their property in such a way as to constitute competitors. But if none of these peculiar factors comes into play, public authorities and public corporations hold or own property in precisely the same way as private persons. Thus Crown Lands are governed by legislation closely modelled on the Settled Land Act.

An important part of the stock of publicly owned land is that on which are built dwellings owned by a local authority and occupied by 'council tenants'—some 30 per cent of the population is housed in this way. Until 1980 they were subject, in theory, to the ordinary law of landlord and tenant, but in practice enjoyed the security of knowing that, if they paid the rent and behaved reasonably, they would not be evicted. In 1980, however, council tenants were given formal security of tenure and power to buy the freehold.

Compulsory purchase

Public authorities and public corporations can acquire property in the same way as private persons, that is to say, normally by purchase. But sometimes the purchase is compulsory, in the sense that the private owner from whom it is sought to acquire it is forced to sell. In normal times the right of compulsory purchase applies only to land, for there is not usually the same monopoly of chattels that there always is in practice in land. Although compensation must always be paid for land taken under compulsory powers, the amount payable is often restricted to such a degree as to produce partial confiscation.

Powers of compulsory purchase are also available to private citizens in two main areas. Council tenants may buy the freehold—that is may acquire public property. And, under the leasehold enfranchisement statutes, certain tenants may compulsorily acquire private property. This legislation covers residential property held on long leases at a 'ground rent'. Here, the original landlord would have leased merely the ground, imposing on the lessee the obligation to build. Such tenants may now, subject to certain conditions, buy out the landlord's estate. These bare allusions to compulsory purchase must suffice for an elementary book on property law.

Taxation

The idea of levying taxes on the ownership of property has a long history; for technical reasons it is usually easiest to do so when the property changes hands. In the Middle Ages the 'feudal incidents'—sums payable by an heir on succeeding to his ancestor's land—were a form of taxation and were one of the reasons for the invention of the device which we now know as the trust. Death duty—now capital transfer tax—was introduced in 1894; and it is significant that, although not passed by reason of war or even in contemplation of war, it helped pay for an important measure of naval rearmament. Since that period the taxes, whatever their name, levied when property passes on death have imposed a heavy burden on people of wealth. Like their medieval predecessors, they have sought to avoid the burden, typically by giving away their property while alive; and each new avoidance scheme provokes Parliament to legislation. Income tax also bears particularly heavily on that 'unearned income' which is the fruit of property ownership—dividends on shares, rent on lands, interest on loans, and so on.

The burden of taxation has had three marked effects. Firstly, it has forced on to the market a great deal of property—particularly land and works of art—that would not otherwise have been sold. It has therefore intensified the need for cheaper conveyancing, for land has changed hands just as much as movables. Secondly, it has reduced enormously the proportionate amount of land and other property subject to settlements of one kind or another, for the very simple reason that on the whole such regimes were set up only by the richer classes, and there has been a considerable levelling of wealth. Finally, it has changed radically the usual form of settlements. The old strict settlement formerly used by the aristocracy or landed gentry, with the primary intention of keeping land in the family, attracts taxation in the most disastrous way, whereas now the main purpose of settling property is to avoid taxation. This form of legal activity has long been known in America by the euphemistic name of 'estate planning'. We call it, more brutally, 'tax planning'. In truth, everywhere in all Western countries no important decisions are taken by business men or property owners without considering the possible incidence of taxation. It may make all the difference between prosperity and ruin.

IX

THE PHYSICAL USE
OF PROPERTY

1. GENERAL

WE have now to consider the use that can be made of physical
objects and the explanation will be clearer if we start with
persons who enjoy the fullest right over things that the law
recognizes, that is to say, the full ownership of movables and
the fee simple absolute in possession of land.

It is often said proverbially that a man may do what he likes
with his own. Although the many restrictions placed on the
exercise of powers by an owner make that statement false, it
is still the best way of dealing with the content of ownership
to start from the presumption that an owner can make unlimited use of a thing he owns and then to outline the restrictions placed on such use.

Such restrictions may be imposed by the general law, and
if they are infringed, tortious or criminal liability will ensue.
The property lawyer is not concerned with most cases of tortious liability for the use of things, and in all probability never
where the thing used is a movable.

There are rational grounds for regarding liability for the use
of movables in this way. In the first place, movables normally
pass from hand to hand so often and so rapidly that it would
be difficult to restrict their use unless they are of an obviously
dangerous kind. On the other hand, one can say quite simply
that a particular use of one piece of land will reduce the value
of a neighbouring piece of land, so that it is appropriate to
think of the two pieces of land without troubling about the
persons who have them.

That is not to say that a person may do what he likes with,
for instance, a motor-car or a gun; but if he damages another

person, attention will be directed not to the motor-car or the gun but to his conduct in using it. He will be liable if he has used it negligently or intending to hurt the other person, and the peculiar nature of the thing used will come into consideration only in deciding whether more or less care should have been taken in using it. Sometimes, indeed, the nature of the thing is more directly relevant; thus there are statutes and regulations governing the storage of explosives. But such restrictions depending on the nature of the object almost always belong to public law.

Conversely, the value of a person's property may be increased if he is able to do something to the property of someone else. Here again, there is little to say about movables. A person is hardly ever empowered to make use of movables belonging to anyone else unless he has bargained for such use by way of contract; and his right is then strictly personal to him and affects the movables only as long as they are owned by the other contracting party. Moreover, it is impossible to create permanent relationships of this positive kind between one movable object and another.

However, such rights can be created in such a way as to give the owner of one piece of land rights over another piece of land in such a way as to enhance the value of the former.

The law itself (but not the law of property) imposes restrictions on occupiers of land in favour of their neighbours in the absence of any agreements they may have entered into. Thus they must not commit nuisances, that is to say, they must not do anything that interferes to an unreasonable degree with the comfort of their neighbours or the proper use of their land. The law of nuisance is habitually dealt with in books on criminal law and the law of torts, and all that need be said here is that it imposes liability on an occupier to pay damages for any injury caused by excessive noise or the escape of fumes, smells, or electric current or by interfering with his neighbour's natural right to support for his land or the natural flow of water in stream, and that he can be restrained directly by an injunction or indirectly by a prosecution from allowing the injury to continue.

2. SERVITUDES

But a person may feel the need to impose other duties on his neighbours if he is to obtain the full value out of his occupation of land; and, while not imposing those duties itself, the law may enable him to stipulate for them by agreement with his neighbours or to acquire some of them by exercising them peaceably for a long time.

An owner may always lawfully bargain with his neighbour for any advantage whatever, so long as it does not fall within the very narrow class of what is illegal or immoral or against public policy; and such advantages may even include the right that his neighbour shall perform a positive act, such as keeping a wall in repair. But most bargains of this kind will operate only in the law of contract, that is to say, they will bind only the actual person making the promise, or his personal representatives,[1] to the person to whom it is made; though the benefit of the promise will pass to anyone acquiring the land of the promisee, provided it 'touches and concerns the land'. It will not bind anyone who buys or otherwise acquires the land of the promisor. If the advantage is one strictly personal to the promisee, then the benefit of it will not pass either.

Now, this is by no means satisfactory for the promisee, who wants to secure an advantage which will exist permanently and irrespective of the identity of his neighbour. Otherwise he will have to make a new bargain every time the neighbouring land changes hands; and he is likely to be held to ransom every time. It is not sufficient for the benefit to 'run with' his own land; the burden must 'run with' the neighbouring land. In other words, what is needed is not merely a personal right against the original promisor but a real right over his land, a species of property in another person's land.

Now, the law allows such property rights to be created, but subject to definite rules, far more restrictive than those which control the formation of contracts. For a contract creates rights and duties only between the contracting parties, and they are usually temporary; although contractual rights can be transferred to other parties, yet the restriction of contractual

[1] i.e. his executors or administrators; see pp. 205, 210–12 below.

duties to the original promisor in itself restricts the operation of contrast so closely that the law can refrain from imposing any further restrictions. But real rights operate so widely and are so apt to affect all comers that the law is bound to limit the kinds of real rights that can exist. Moreover, there is a serious danger that real rights, especially if they are unrestricted, may make land subject to them of so little value as to be unmarketable.

Thus, with one unimportant exception, which will be discussed later, real rights over another person's land must be 'appurtenant' to one's own land. That means that there must always be two pieces of land—not only a 'servient tenement', which is burdened with the duty, but also a 'dominant tenement', for the benefit of which it exists. This has two separate implications. In the first place, the burden on the servient tenement must be of permanent value to the holder of the dominant tenement, whoever he may be. It must exist to accommodate the dominant tenement and be reasonably necessary for the full enjoyment of it. Thus the diminution in value of the servient tenement caused by the existence of the duty may be expected to be roughly made up by the enhancement in the value of the dominant tenement. If, however, the advantage to be expected is personal to the then holder of the dominant tenement stipulating for the right, there is merely an uncompensated diminution in the value of the servient tenement.

Secondly, although the original person stipulating for the right can in some cases enforce it, if need be by an action for damages, against the original person granting it, no one can enforce it against any subsequent holder of the servient tenement unless he is himself holder of the dominant tenement.

All these rights are best designated by the Roman law term *servitudes*, and are of three kinds, easements, *profits-à-prendre*, and rights created by restrictive convenants.

From the point of view of the holder of the servient tenement servitudes are negative, in the sense that they impose no duty on him to act but only not to act or to suffer the holder of the dominant tenement to do something on the servient tenement.

(a) Easements and profits

No one has yet been able to frame a satisfactory definition of an easement, but easements can be described as comprising two classes of rights, namely, first, rights to do something on the servient tenement other than taking something from it and, in the second place, exceptionally, a strictly limited number of rights to prevent the doing of certain specific acts on the servient tenement. Thus, from the point of view of the owner of the dominant tenement, easements are said to be either positive or negative.

Positive easements, which, it must be remembered, confer a right on the person entitled to them merely to do something positive on the servient tenement and not to exact a positive act from the owner of the servient tenement, are unlimited in variety and number, provided, of course, that they obey the rules which have been set out above as governing all servitudes. They can include, besides the more obvious rights of way, such non-apparent rights as that of laying gas mains or electric cables, with the ancillary rights to enter the land in order to inspect and repair them, and such at first sight surprising rights as those of going upon the land of another to open sluice gates or of storing casks and trade produce on land. Nowadays the right to park a car on neighbouring land, or even to use the aircraft landing-strip next door, may be recognized as easements. If, however, the right granted is basically part of a business deal, its protection will depend on the law of contract, not property. Thus a person with land adjoining a canal may be given a valid easement to put boats on it; but an *exclusive* right to do so is a business monopoly which may bind the grantor in contract but will not enable the grantee to proceed against third parties.

Negative easements, which give a right to restrain activity on the servient tenement, seem to be strictly limited in number, and comprise only (1) the right to light, that is to say, that the light flowing to a window shall not be unreasonably obstructed, (2) a corresponding right to the free flow of air through a defined aperture, such as a ventilator shaft, (3) the right of support to buildings, that is to say, a right to restrain any use of the servient tenement or buildings on it which will

interfere with the support afforded by them to adjoining buildings on the dominant tenement, and (4) a right to restrain any
interference with the continued flow of water through an artificial watercourse. There is a good reason, which will be explained shortly, for limiting such negative easements to a small
number of well-defined instances. It is worth mentioning at
once that although they are all in a sense negative, they all start
at the earliest with some act on the part of the owner of the
dominant tenement, namely, the creation of a window or
ventilator or the erection of a building, or the construction of
an artificial watercourse.

Profits-à-prendre, or, more shortly, profits, are rights to take
part of the soil or of the produce of the soil of a servient tenement, for instance, to take game or fish, to pasture one's
animals, or to cut turf. They may for practical purposes be
divided into two classes. Some, which conform to the usual
rule requiring the presence of a dominant tenement, are survivals of old manorial customary arrangements, whereby the
tenants of a manor had the right, for instance, to pasture their
animals on the waste of the manor. They were, like easements,
necessary for the proper cultivation and use of their holdings.
On the other hand, some profits are said to exist *in gross*, that
is to say, may belong to a person as such and not as holder of
a dominant tenement. Thus he can alienate them freely. If a
landowner grants a lease of shooting or fishing rights for a
defined term, a profit of this kind is created. Probably most
existing profits in gross have this sort of origin.

(b) Restrictive covenants

Restrictive covenants always impose purely negative duties,
such as not to use land for the purpose of building a factory
or a shop or carrying on any trade which would be unsuitable
for a residential neighbourhood. Such covenants often take
the form of binding a landholder to use premises only as a
private dwelling house. This, although apparently not restrictive in form, is certainly restrictive in substance.

Restrictive covenants have an entirely different history from
easements and profits. In the first place, the first case in which
a restrictive covenant was enforced upon the holder of a servient tenement was decided in the mid-nineteenth century,

whereas easements and profits go back to the Middle Ages. In the second place, easements and profits have always been protected at common law, for a person who infringed an easement was liable to an action of nuisance and a person who interfered with a profit could be sued for trespass. Both easements and profits have always conferred rights *in rem*. In the third place, easements developed to cope with only the most basic needs of landowners—rights of way, support, and the like. Restrictive covenants, by contrast, protect *amenity value*.

Restrictive covenants started as mere contracts between vendors and purchasers of land. A person on selling part of his land would exact a promise from the purchaser not to do certain things which would reduce the value of the part of the land retained by the vendor. At first such a promise bound the actual purchaser to the actual vendor; no other person could be bound and no other person could have the benefit of the promise. However, it came to be thought that a subsequent purchaser who had notice of the restrictive covenant and had perhaps paid less for the servient tenement because of the existence of the covenant, would be acting unconscionably if he disregarded it, and in the year 1848 such a covenant was enforced against a person who had purchased land with notice of it. The land in question was subject to a covenant against building and was the area in the middle of a square of houses in central London. The value to them of this tranquil amenity is obvious. It was not till a hundred years later, however, that the logical step was taken of allowing householders around such a square to have easements over it. It would be strange if the central greenery could be preserved by a restrictive covenant, enforceable by the householders, and yet they were not permitted to take their ease in the open space. After a good deal of hesitation restrictive covenants were subjected to the general requirement applied to other servitudes, that they must exist for the benefit of a dominant tenement. But they differ from other servitudes, and especially from easements, in several ways.

In the first place, they started by being enforceable only against persons who had notice of them. For that requirement has now been substituted in most cases a requirement that they shall be registered; and, since registration is held to constitute notice, a registered restrictive covenant is now good against anyone who acquires the servient tenement. Easements and profits operate automatically even though the owner of the servient tenement had no notice of them when he acquired it. It is often said that easements and profits are notorious in the sense that their existence can be detected by anyone who inspects the land. That is true enough of rights of way, and perhaps even of rights connected with watercourses. It is not certainly so of profits, and it is certainly not so of easements connected with underground mains. But doubtless there is a better chance of detecting most easements by inspection than restrictive covenants.

However, the most important difference between restrictive covenants and easements is in the ways in which they can be acquired.

All these various rights over another person's land can be expressly created by an act on the part of the owner of that land. In the case of an easement or profit, it will be what is called a grant by a holder of the servient tenement or a reservation in a conveyance to a holder of a servient tenement by a holder of a dominant tenement; in the case of a restrictive covenant it will be an express promise, but one which has long since acquired most of the characteristics of a grant. Easements are often at the present day acquired by grant or reservation, but, unlike restrictive covenants, they can also be acquired by what is called prescription, that is to say, a person can effectually claim the right to exercise them on the ground that he has actually exercised them for a long time.

Prescription

The detailed rules of the law of prescription, which is fictitiously presumed to rest on a grant made by the holder of the servient tenement in the remote past but the evidence of which has since been lost, need not be considered here. It is enough to say that the exercise of the right on which the person seeking to prove his right relies must have been uninterrupted and as of right; and the exercise is as of right if it is not by force against the will of the owner of the servient tenement, or secretly without his knowledge, or with his permission. Thus it is always open to the latter to prevent prescription from operating by either interrupting the exercise, for instance, by locking a gate across a path, or by insisting on the payment of some sum of money, however small, as an acknowledgement that the exercise is by his leave. Both of these practices are in fact very common.

Now a restrictive covenant cannot be prescribed for; the restriction established by it must always have a definite beginning in an actual covenant by the owner of the servient tenement. But it may be asked, why should not the restriction be imposed by way of negative easement, or rather, why should not one person claim that, having had the benefit of a restriction uninterruptedly for a considerable time, the restriction has become established permanently in his favour; for, as we have seen, the difference between the grant of an easement and the establishment of a restriction by way of covenant is illusory. The answer is surely obvious.

He has not had the benefit of a restriction but merely of a particular kind of inactivity. Now the owner of a piece of land need not use it at all if he does not want to; at least none of his neighbours can claim that he should do so, whatever the public law of agriculture, or town and country planning, may have to say. Thus it is hard to see how the mere inactivity of one person can even look like the exercise of a right by another. Or look at the matter in another way. As a famous nineteenth-century judge once said: 'You cannot acquire any rights against others by a user which they cannot interrupt.' The only way in which a person could interrupt the use of a purely negative right would be by actually doing the thing which it was going to be claimed that he could not do. Therefore he would have to do periodically every single thing that he thought his neighbour might possibly object to in the future. But the number of such things would be infinite.

Negative easements

It may be said that the so-called negative easements break this chain of reasoning. To this objection there are two answers. In the first place, as has been said above, although they are restrictive, the user has a definite beginning which is notorious to the person against whom it may operate. Accordingly, the requirement that he shall interrupt it or demand payment for it in order to prevent prescription, is not at all burdensome. Secondly, since they are definite and few in number, they escape the difficulty that arises when restrictions are sought to be derived from mere general and indefinite inactivity. In fact the need for them became obvious long before restrictive covenants were ever enforced as servitudes against owners of servient tenements. At a time when most work was done by hand in houses and shops in the narrow streets of congested towns, it was very important that occupiers should not be deprived of necessary light by the building operations of their neighbours; and in the circumstances at the time this result could be obtained only by the creation of negative easements.

It is the availability of prescription as a means of acquiring easements which leads the courts to limit them, especially in the case of those negative easements which curtail the servient owner's freedom.[2] Thus it is often said that there cannot be an easement of view or of delight; and yet this is precisely the kind of facility that restrictive covenants provide. The reason is clear; if, for centuries, a house has enjoyed the view over the neighbour's sweeping acres, that of itself is no reason why the neighbour should not build. If the householder wishes to secure the view he should take from his neighbour a covenant against building—*and pay for it*.

Functional difference

Thus there is a valid distinction of a rational and conceptual kind between easements and restrictive covenants. But there is also a difference of function. In the first place easements appear at a much earlier historical period than restrictive covenants. There has never been a time in the history of English law when easements did not exist, whereas the first case on restrictive covenants occurred as recently as 1848. Easements confer those rights over neighbouring land or buildings which are necessary for the proper use of land or buildings but are not conferred by the law itself. The oldest of them arise out of farming needs; one farm is made to accommodate another farm so as to enable it to be used effectively. Thus easements are usually simple and affect only two pieces of property, the

[2] Prescription is also the reason why easements are not registrable.

dominant and the servient tenement. Moreover, although they are valuable, they are valuable because they allow the performance of some physical act. They are as much part of the farmer's plant as his land, his seeds, and his stock. On the other hand, restrictive covenants are best understood as instruments of planning. They date from a time when large landowners wanted to lay out large estates for building according to a permanent plan and arrangements which were intended to protect purchasers of property in it against each other, while at the same time they wanted to divest themselves, by sale of the land, of all further interest in it. As long as a landowner was content to let out all the portions of an estate on lease he could bind his lessees not to use their lands or houses in any way adverse to the interests of the estate as a whole. Thus he could keep the whole estate as a residential estate or could restrict shops or factories to specific sections of it. It was not so obvious that he could maintain these restructions if he sold the land outright. It was still less obvious that any one of his purchasers could enforce them against any other of his purchasers. But if this was impossible, town and country planning would become impossible, for there was no question until the present century of either the State or local authorities starting to plan as a matter of public law. Thus restrictive convenants operating reciprocally between neighbours as part of a comprehensive plan for the development of an estate became necessary if landowners were not to do as they liked and incidentally ruin the market value of neighbouring land.

In fact large residential estates were laid out on these lines in both towns and suburbs until quite recent times, and the law had become satisfactory and complete. Where the proper steps had been taken by the vendor, each owner of a plot was able to hold every other holder within the estate to his covenants. Before 1914 there was no need to plan the countryside on similar lines, largely because it was still to a very great extent in the hands of large landowners but also because motor transport had not yet caused the towns to spread inordinately or ribbon development to make its appearance along the main roads. In this century, as was explained in Chapter VIII, the use of land is subject to a good deal of public control.

3. PRICE MAINTENANCE CONDITIONS

Generally speaking, a person who sells goods has no further interest in them, but within the present century manufacturers have frequently adopted a policy of maintaining retail prices for their goods and have attempted to attach conditions to them binding any person into whose hands they may come not to sell them for less than a fixed price. This is a restriction on the use of the goods for the only purpose for which dealers acquire them, namely resale. This policy has had a chequered career. In the past the courts refused to enforce such conditions directly except where the goods were patented; but they also refused to treat as an actionable conspiracy an agreement among manufacturers to blacklist persons who sold at less than the listed price.

Nowadays, by statute, blacklisting is outlawed and resale price conditions generally void. As regards certain classes of goods, however, the supplier may apply to the court for permission to impose them and, if it is granted, the condition—like the restrictive covenant on land—binds anyone taking with notice. Such notice, for instance, frequently appears at the beginning of books.

X

THE COEXISTENCE
OF PROPERTY INTERESTS
IN SEVERAL PERSONS

1. GENERAL

WE have just been considering the physical use of things by
persons who have the entire and exclusive interest in them. We
have now to consider cases where the interest in property is
divided among several persons. In explaining the concept of
the estate, we dealt with the basic principles.[1] In this and the
following chapters we turn to the machinery for handling them.
One case we have considered sufficiently already, namely that
in which several persons enjoy a thing in common, sharing
simultaneously either the physical use or the income derived
from it or both. The other cases fall under two general heads,
leases and settlements.

The immediate enjoyment of a thing may be divided between
two persons who have interests adverse to each other. On the
other hand, one person or group of persons may enjoy the thing
completely and exclusively for a time, being then succeeded by
one or more other persons or groups of persons in succession.
The former division is effected by leases of land and bailments
of chattels by way of hire, the latter by settlements.

In lease or hire one of the parties, the lessee or bailee, has
the exclusive physical use of the thing and pays a periodical
rent, which, from his point of view, is the price of his enjoyment. From the point of view of the lessor or bailor, the rent
is the return from an investment, and the thing is that which
produces it. Thus the income value is divided between the
parties, for both derive something of pecuniary value from it,
but only the lessee or bailee has the physical use of the thing.
The two parties enjoy the thing in different ways.

[1] See pp. 84–97 above.

On the other hand, if a piece of land or the income from a trust fund is given to A for life with remainder to B, A has the exclusive and complete enjoyment of the land or trust fund during his lifetime, including not only the whole of the income from it but also the physical use of any land or physical chattels which are included in it. When he dies, B will have the same kind of enjoyment of it that A had. From the present point of view it is irrelevant that B has already a present interest in the land or trust fund which he can sell and turn into money.

However, whether the division of interest arises from a lease or bailment or from a settlement, the person who has the physical use of the thing has it only for a period of time and after that time the possession will fall to another person, whether he be a remainderman or a lessor or bailor. Thus the former has only the income, in the broad sense of the term, and the latter the capital. Now certain problems always arise when one person is entitled to the income from property and the other to the capital. These are essentially the same whether one is dealing with leases or bailments or with settlements, though the solutions are not precisely the same.

From this point onwards we shall be dealing with complex entities rather than the simple elements that have hitherto engrossed our attention. To adopt the language of technology, we shall now be dealing not with the equivalents of hand tools but with machines. Moreover, just as machines, though compounded of various elements which could conceivably be put together in an infinite number of ways, tend to become themselves standardized, so the leases, settlements, and mortgages tend to assume a relatively small number of stereotyped forms. This is common enough in all parts of the law; it is especially marked in the law of property.

2. CAPITAL AND INCOME

Whenever property is given to a person to hold for a limited period some means must be found of protecting the person or persons who are to take it after him. In other words he is entitled only to the income (including in that term the physical use of corporeal things comprised in the property) and must not touch the capital, which must be transmitted as far as humanly possible intact on the termination of his interest. This distinction between income and capital meets the student at many points and, although the rules governing it vary with the various kinds of limited interest, it deserves a brief introductory treatment of a general kind.

Income-tax lawyers, above all other persons, know that the question what is income is not a simple one; but this is largely because Parliament has had to check in detail devious ways of disguising income as a capital gain and so securing exemption from income-tax. Property lawyers do not have to face this mass of repulsive detail, but their task also is sometimes difficult.

Trust funds

The easiest case to understand is that of trustees holding a fund in trust for one person for life, remainder to another person absolutely. Their primary duty is to preserve the capital of the trust fund, and to pay to the tenant for life only the income as it falls due, after deducting the expenses of administering the trust. Formerly the rules governing the various possible situations were fairly clear, though not always easily stated.

If the trust fund consisted from the start of gilt-edged securities, the person entitled to the life interest had to be paid the income from the securities as it fell due. The securities would normally retain their capital value and it was to this alone that the remainderman was entitled.

Nor is the position difficult where trustees have money in their hands to invest. Unless the settlor increases their powers, they must still invest it within the range of securities permitted by statute. For it is the primary duty of trustees to preserve the capital of the trust fund and to apportion income as fairly as possible among the persons successively entitled to receive it.

More difficult questions arise where the trust fund includes other kinds of securities when it comes into the hands of the trustees. Some of them may be speculative and others may be either wasting or reversionary in character. In most cases the trustees will have a discretion whether to retain or to realize them, a discretion with which the Court will not readily interfere, and they must pay the income from them to the persons immediately entitled to interests in the fund. However, if wasting or reversionary securities are settled as residuary personalty on death, the so-called rules of equitable apportionment apply. A wasting security is one which is likely to lose its capital value at some future date, such as an interest in a mine which will probably be exhausted. If such a property were retained, the persons immediately entitled to the income might get a very high rate of interest on the investment, but there might be no capital to transmit to their successors. A reversionary interest is the converse of this. Until it falls in, there is no income and so the person entitled to the capital will be unduly favoured at the expense of the person immediately entitled to the income of the trust fund. Accordingly, the rules say that the trustees must within a year realize wasting and reversionary securities and reinvest the proceeds in property of a permanent and income-bearing character. For it is their duty to hold the scales evenly between those successively entitled to the income. Moreover, until realization, they must not pay the whole income arising from wasting securities to the person entitled to the limited interest, but only a certain percentage on the estimated capital value of the securities, accumulating the residue of the income as capital. Similarly, when reversionary securities fall in, part of the capital must be used to pay arrears of income to the person entitled to the prior limited interest.

Much of this law has recently become unrealistic, for so-called trustee securities are pre-eminently subject to reduction in real value through devaluation of currency and inflation. Accordingly, settlors, if they are well advised, extend the powers of trustees to allow them to invest even beyond the statutory limits in securities of a commercial or industrial kind which, it may be hoped, will adjust themselves to changes in the value of money and maintain their real and not merely their nominal value.[2] But, whatever happens, trustees must try to preserve the capital of the trust fund in order to accord equal treatment to the tenant for life and to successive remaindermen. So, even if the settlor empowers them to invest the fund as if it were their own, they may not take foolhardy risks such as backing a play.

[2] See further pp. 170–5 below.

Waste

The problem of holding the balance even between capital and income is more complicated where the enjoyment of a physical object is divided between several persons successively. It is hardly worth discussing apart from land. In its relation to land the problem first arose in the form of waste. There is an ever-present temptation to the temporary holder of land to waste it by exhausting the soil or letting buildings fall into disrepair. Accordingly, the reversioner or remainderman was given an action for damages against him; but once the Chancellor was willing to grant an injunction restraining the commission of waste, that remedy was preferred to the former. Around these remedies a body of substantive law grew up, simple in its general outlines, but running to complications in detail.

A primary distinction is made between so-called permissive and voluntary waste, the former comprising mere omissions to act, such as failing to repair a farmhouse, the later comprising positive acts diminishing the capital value or changing the nature of the land, such as pulling down a barn. Even the replacement of an old house by a new and more valuable one is voluntary waste, but such *ameliorating* waste would give rise to a claim for only nominal damages and will not be restrained by injunction.

Whether a person is to be held liable for permissive or voluntary waste depends on whether he is a life tenant or a tenant for a term of years such as a lessee. Thus, a life tenant is not liable for permissive waste and is often, perhaps usually, expressly made by the settlor unimpeachable for waste, in which case he may even commit voluntary waste with impunity, though he can be restrained by injunction from committing what is called *equitable* waste, i.e. wanton damage. The liability for waste of tenants holding under a lease or a tenancy agreement, in practice unimportant, varies with the kind of tenancy.

Improvements

The converse of waste is improvement. It might be thought that if the remainderman or reversioner can restrain the holder of a prior limited interest from waste, he should on the other hand have to pay for any improvements made by him. Yet the common law gave the latter no right to compensation and even forced him to leave any fixtures which he had annexed to the soil or buildings. Even when at a later date he acquired the right to remove most fixtures, such as trade fixtures,[3] any unexhausted improvements that increased the fertility of the soil inured to the benefit of the remainderman or reversioner. That was not likely to worry a tenant for life, who would ordinarily be the father or mother of the remainderman and would willingly improve the land for his benefit, but it could enrich a landlord unfairly at the expense of his tenant. Any tenant for an indefinite period did indeed have one privilege, that of taking *emblements*,[4] i.e. of reaping after the termination of his tenancy an industrial crop sown by him. This was to encourage him to cultivate the land properly, free from any fear that he might not reap where he had sown. A tenant for a term of years was not given that privilege, for he was held to have known all along when his term would come to an end.

However, all this learning about waste, improvements, and emblements is now hardly more than the foundation for an entirely different body of law erected by statute or act of parties. Put shortly, the tenant for life has been turned into a manager of the land for the benefit of himself and those coming after him.[5] Accordingly he has been given much wider rights and powers than at common law of making alterations and improvements in the interests of the family and of raising money to finance them, though his beneficial interest remains limited to his life. On the other hand, the relations between landlord and tenant became a matter of contract between them, until various statutes intervened, to protect the tenant against his landlord despite the terms of the contract.[6]

These developments will be considered in greater detail when we treat of leases and life interests respectively.

3. LEASES AND SETTLEMENTS

Although the existence of limited interests in property always gives rise to common problems, of which the most obvious are

[3] See p. 22 above. [4] See p. 25 above.
[5] See further pp. 170–2 below. [6] See further pp. 154–8 below.

those relating to the fair treatment of both capital and income, there are fundamental differences between limited interests arising from business arrangements and those arising under family settlements. Two call for examination here.

Popular notions of ownership

In the first place it is much easier to apply ordinary popular notions of ownership to the former. If A lends or hires out his car to B, he will naturally say that although he has lost the possession of it for the time being, it is his car; and B would neither contest that statement nor claim that the car was his. Nor would the doctrine of estates get seriously in the way if A let his house to B; he would still say it was his house and B would not say that it was his. There might indeed be doubts if B had a long lease with many years to run, for B might then say that the house was his, and A might content himself with the remark that he was entitled to a ground rent.

But when under a family settlement C has a life interest in property followed by a remainder in D, neither would say that the property was his. If indeed the property is land, the tenant for life is usually called a landowner, improperly, for not only has he at best a limited beneficial interest, but he corresponds, not to the lessor, but to the lessee, that is to say, not to the person who claims that the land is his but to the one that admits the other's claim.

Commercial and family interests

The fact is that the essential purpose of a family settlement is to give to several persons the income from property for successive periods. The income may include the physical use of the property, especially if it includes land, but it is not so much the land that is owned by anyone as the temporary income arising from the exploitation of it.

At any rate, that was the point of view that the Legislature took in 1925 when it streamlined the law relating to limited interests. It drew a distinction between cases where one person bargains with another commercially for the temporary physical use of land and cases where several persons enjoy the temporary physical use of land one after another under a family settlement. It said in effect that whereas in the former case the physical use is the paramount consideration, in the latter it is only a way of enjoying the income. Hence comes the second fundamental difference between interests arising from business arrangements and interests arising under family settlements: in the latter case, if for some good reason it is proper to insist that the temporary beneficiary shall enjoy the income in another form, the mere fact that hitherto it has consisted in the physical use of land is to be no obstacle to a sale of the land and the reinvestment of the proceeds in other securities, whereas in the former case such a solution is inadmissible.[7]

Two factors which may have contributed to this decision are perhaps not sufficiently noticed. In the first place, what may be called the commercial interest in land arises from a bargain between two persons, usually a lessor and a lessee or a mortgagor and a mortgagee. Hence any power granted to either party to force the other to submit to a variation in his investment, by selling the land over his head and compensating him with a lump sum or an alternative investment, would have been a power to vary the original bargain without the consent of the other party. The Legislature could indeed have enacted that such a power must be read into every lease or mortgage, but that would have rendered the position of lessees and mortgagors extremely insecure. In fact, as will be seen later, the whole tendency of legislation has been in precisely the opposite direction, to enhance the security of the lessee at a cost to the lessor and of the borrower as against the lender.[8] On the other hand, there is no contractual relationship between the persons successively entitled to income under a family settlement, nor does the obligation which a trustee is under to successive beneficiaries arise out of bargains made between him and them. The beneficiaries have not the same right as a lessee to insist on retaining the land in specie. The most they can do is to ask a court to say that an attempt to alienate the land is bad for the settlement as a whole, that is to say, that the proposed variation of the investment is improvident. Thus the existence or non-existence of a bargain creates a sound distinction upon which to base the distinction made in 1925 between limited interests normally arising

---

[7] See p. 107 above.
[8] See pp. 154, 194 below.

out of a commercial bargain, where the physical use of the land is guaranteed, and limited interests arising under a family settlement, where the beneficiaries may have to submit to a variation of investments, involving a deprivation of the physical use.

Realty and personalty

The other factor is indeed expressed in the title of the Law of Property Act, 1922, which introduced most of the innovations re-enacted in consolidated form in the 1925 Acts. That title, 'An Act to Assimilate the Law of Real and Personal Estate', has been criticized on good grounds, but it does at least help to explain the particular innovation that is now being discussed.

Down to the year 1925 very much the same distinction was in fact observed in relation to personalty as is now observed as a matter of law in relation to land. One person bargained with another for the temporary physical use of a chattel, or a settlor might include chattels in his family settlement. Only choses in possession could be the object of physical use, whereas, apart from heirlooms, such as pictures or jewels, choses in action, especially stocks and shares, were the most likely chattels to be included in a settlement. Where a person bargained for the temporary possession of a chose in possession he usually desired to use it physically or to hold it as security for a loan. As a bailee he was protected against third parties, and in practice his contract gave him sufficient protection against his bailor. If choses in action were contained in a family settlement, they had to be held by trustees in trust for the successive beneficiaries, and in a well-drawn settlement the trustees were given wide powers of sale and reinvestment,[9] for choses in action were then regarded merely as sources of income.

Accordingly, when dealing with chattels, one can make a rough distinction between things which will normally be regarded as objects of physical use and things which are more naturally regarded as producing an income; and one could with no great degree of inaccuracy equate the former class with physical chattels and the latter with some varieties at least of choses in action. However, no analogous distinction could be

[9] See p. 106 above.

146 The Law of Property

applied to land, for two reasons. In the first place, all land is corporeal whereas all interests in land are incorporeal. In the second place, it would have been absurd to regard certain kinds of land as appropriate to leases and others as appropriate to settlements. On the other hand, such a distinction might be properly made among *interests* in land; and such a distinction was in fact made between leasehold estates and limited freehold interests.

It is true that formerly a term of years, the so-called 'portions term',[10] was an essential element in the strict settlement in its fully developed form and that it was not uncommon for a person to take a lease of land for his own life or for the lives of a number of selected persons. In other words, leasehold estates appeared in settlements, and freehold estates less than the fee simple were once objects of commerce. However, the primary and common use of the term of years is to create a lease, which is a matter for commercial bargaining, and freehold interests other than the fee simple came to exist only in settlements. Thus no harm was likely to occur if they were allowed only in settlements and as equitable interest behind the 'curtain' of the legal estate. Moreover, in this way the law relating to real estate was almost exactly assimilated to the practice governing personalty. Oddly enough, as has been explained,[11] the opportunity was not taken of bringing the law governing personalty into strict conformity with that governing land.

[10] This was mortgaged in order to provide for members of the family other than the eldest son.

[11] See p. 113 above.

XI

LEASES AND THE HIRE OF GOODS

1. GENERAL

WHY people hire things is easily understood. They may not want them permanently but only for a time, and it may be inconvenient for them to buy and resell. If they want them for a considerable period of time they may yet either not have the capital to buy them outright or may not want to sink a large amount of capital in them. Sometimes they may be prepared to provide what is called the working capital, whilst hiring the fixed capital from someone else. This is the key to traditional tenant-farming in England.

Why people let things out is also easily understood. They have something that may be made to yield an income and they either cannot or will not exercise the physical use that ultimately produces the income and therefore leave that to someone else who will hire the thing from them.

Where there is hire, each party enters into obligations toward the other. In other words, there is a contract between them, the terms of which are either expressly agreed between them or implied by law or partly the one and partly the other. The contractual aspect of hire is not a matter of interest to the property lawyer as far as concerns physical chattels such as animals or furniture. It is otherwise with leases of land because the benefit and burden of covenants must be made to run with both the lease and the reversion. Leases are ordinarily of longer duration than the hire of chattels and so both leases and reversions are regular articles of commerce. That being so, it is important that any two persons who are lessee and reversioner for the time being should be in the same contractual relation to each other as the original lessee and lessor, in so far as it touches and concerns the land.

In Roman law hire was nothing more than contract. In English law, however, it is much more. Here again we must distinguish between chattels and land. When a chattel is handed over by way of hire a bailment takes place, and thereby the hirer is put in possession of the thing. For land the corresponding transaction is a lease and here too there is a transfer of possession. So far the two are very similar, though whereas the lessor always retains what is misleadingly called 'possession',[1] a bailor who bails goods for a fixed term loses possession, and although a bailor at will, that is to say, one who is entitled to bring the bailment to an end whenever he likes, is said to retain possession, the authority for this proposition is scanty and not universally regarded as sound. The fact is that the real or proprietary, as opposed to the contractual, aspect of bailment has been so little developed that quite a number of possible questions remain unanswered. For this reason it is best to start with leases.

2. THE REAL ASPECT OF LEASES AND BAILMENTS

The property lawyer looks at leases in two different ways. In the first place a lease creates a term of years, which is a leasehold estate. Thus it divides the ownership of the land on a plane of time, between a termor, who holds the land now, and the reversioner, who will come into possession of the land at the expiration of the term.[2]

On the other hand, it divides the present income value of the land between the lessor and the lessee, the former taking a fixed rent and the latter the undefined residue of the profits arising from the exploitation of the land.[3] Thus the interests of the lessor and the lessee are simultaneous in two different senses, first, in the ordinary way in which all estates are simultaneous, in that they have a present capital value although they may give successive rights to possession, but secondly,

---

[1] See p. 150 below.

[2] For leasehold estates see pp. 93–5 above.

[3] It is assumed above that there will be enough income from the land to pay the lessor rent and leave something over for the lessee. This is, of course, not inevitable, and if there is not enough income from the land even to pay the rent, the lessor is still entitled to receive his rent in full. In practice he may find it hard to enforce his claim.

in giving them simultaneous rights to share in the income value.

This second, much more important, aspect of the lease always made it difficult to fit leaseholds into the feudal system. They were indeed, and have always been, a commercial intruder into a way of looking at property which was essentially uncommercial and which was primarily concerned with the public duties owed by holders of land. Thus the medieval lawyers were late in dealing with them and this lateness has caused the word 'possession' to be used in connexion with leases in two very different senses which are apt to cause confusion in the mind of the student.

Originally only freehold tenants[4] were given actions by which they could recover their holdings in case of dispossession. In order to establish their claim they had to prove that they were 'seised' of the land and they were therefore said to have 'seisin of the freehold'. Seisin was possession based on a title which varied with the particular action—of which there were many— but it always served to differentiate the freeholder who had an estate in possession from one who had merely an estate in expectancy, and also the freeholder from the leaseholder, who had originally no action and no estate. When later it became necessary to protect the leaseholder by affording him an action of trespass, the medieval lawyers gave to the relation to the land which he had to establish in himself the name 'possession'.

This distinction between the seisin of the freeholder and the mere possession of the leaseholder was fundamental. Thus if a freeholder seised of the land granted a lease, although the lessee got possession, he did not get seisin, which remained in the lessor. On the other hand, if he gave a particular estate of freehold to another person, say for life, he lost the seisin, which passed to the tenant of the particular estate, and in that case his reversion was incompatible with seisin.

Unfortunately the word 'seisin' has disappeared from the working vocabulary of the real-property lawyer and has been replaced by the word 'possession'. It became the practice to distinguish freehold estates as estates in possession and estates in expectancy according as their holders were or were not

[4] See p. 80 above.

seised of the land. Thus a tenant in fee simple in possession of land who grants a lease of it, though he loses possession of the land to the lessee, is still said to have a fee simple in possession in the sense that his freehold estate is not in expectancy. It is in this sense that section 1 of the Law of Property Act, 1925, includes a lessor among persons who have a fee simple absolute in possession and so a legal estate; it is at pains to distinguish that estate from a fee simple absolute in remainder or reversion which would fall into possession only on the termination of a particular estate of freehold such as a life estate.

This is the historical and technical way of explaining a curious confusion of terminology, but the Act also defines a fee simple absolute in possession in terms of economics, as including the estate held by a person who is entitled to the rents and profits of the land, and this is clearly applicable to a lessor out of possession of the land.

A bailee always has possession of the goods bailed to him, whereas the bailor, except in one doubtful case, namely where the bailment is at will, so that he can bring it to an end at any moment without notice, has not possession. There is no need to attribute an artificial possession to bailors in general since there is nothing in the law governing chattels comparable to the requirements of section 1 of the Law of Property Act that, in order to be a legal estate, a fee simple must be in possession. Hence the possession of goods always has one meaning and is free from the ambiguity attaching to the possession of land.

3. THE REQUIREMENTS FOR A LEASE

There are many different situations in which a landowner may permit another person to occupy his property. If the arrangement amounts to a lease, then the lessee has a property interest —protected against all the world and alienable. In order to count as a lease, however, the arrangement must satisfy certain requirements both of substance and of form.

Substance

As we have explained, the estate concept involves rights *in* space *for* a time. The first requires that the lessee have exclusive possession. Occasional visits by the landlord, say to effect repairs, are, of course, not ruled out; but one who shares occupation with the landowner has no lease, no matter how formal the document enshrining their arrangement. An example is the grant of 'front-of-house rights' by which a theatre owner permits someone else to have the bar, cloakroom, and programme concessions. Such a transaction, even though carried out under seal and to endure for twenty-one years, does not create a property right binding on a new owner of the theatre.[5]

The second factor, that of *time*, inherent in the estate concept means that the grant of exclusive occupation for an uncertain period is no lease. A term of, say, seven years or a yearly or monthly tenancy which can be determined by appropriate notice are both common types of lease. If, however, a landowner grants exclusive occupation 'until my brother needs the land' then the grant does not amount to a lease.

Form

The formalities for the creation of a lease are the subject of much intricate historical and legal learning. Nothing would be gained by explaining it in an elementary introduction to the law. Here it is enough to say that fairly indiscriminate use is made of actual leases and agreements for leases. Leases for not more than three years at a rack rent, that is to say, the best rent obtainable, may be made verbally without any formality; and this rule applies to periodic tenancies, such as tenancies from week to week, from month to month, or from year to year. However, it is advisable to have some sort of document, for otherwise there will be no permanent record of any special terms agreed upon by the parties.

All other leases must be made by deed, i.e. a sealed writing executed by the lessor. There will in fact be a counterpart to the lease executed by the lessee, which will be necessary if, as is invariably the case, the lessee enters into covenants binding him to do or not to do certain things.

An agreement for a lease is nothing more than an agreement between the parties, evidenced in writing, by which the one promises to grant and the other to accept a lease. At common law it confers on the tenant no interest in the land, but merely

[5] Licenses are dealt with in Chapter XVII.

a right of action for damages if the landlord does not grant the lease. However, the tenant is entitled in equity to obtain specific performance of the promise and so, in pursuance of the maxim that equity regards that as done which ought to be done, the tenant has already an equitable interest in the land analogous to a lease. That equitable interest, if registered as an estate contract, is good against all the world. For practical purposes an agreement for a lease is treated as equivalent to a lease and the stamp duties payable in respect of the two are the same.

4. COVENANTS

All leases, besides creating real interests in land, also contain covenants, that is to say, reciprocal promises between the lessor and lessee. But although the real and personal rights so created must, for purposes of analysis, be kept distinct, the latter must in some way or other be made to 'run with' the former so as to bind all persons who acquire the estate of the lessee to all persons who acquire the estate of the lessor and vice versa.

This is not so easy as it sounds. All legal systems are reluctant to allow two persons by contract to burden a stranger. Thus in principle A should not be allowed to promise B that X will do something for him with the effect that X is bound to B. English law, though not most other modern laws, also puts serious difficulties in the way of one person bargaining with another person for a right in favour of a third person. A cannot bargain with B that B will do something for X with the effect of giving X a right against B. Thus if recourse could be had only to the general law of contract, it would be impossible for a lessor or a lessee by covenant to bind to the other party to the lease any persons to whom they might alienate the reversion or the lease respectively. Nor, at the time when the law on this subject was being worked out, could either party bargain for the benefit of the covenants to vest in subsequent holders of their interests. Thus special rules had to be evolved for leases. In the end those rules have become clear and sensible.

Privity of contract and privity of estate

It is said that the rights and duties created by a contract operate only between those who are privy to it, that is to say, the actual parties. Between the parties there is said to be privity of contract. Such privity of contract exists between the original lessor and lessee. An analogous but different institution is privity of estate, which exists between persons who have or have acquired the estates of the original lessor and lessee. Thus there is privity of estate between the landlord for the time being and the tenant for the time being, that is to say, not only between the original lessor and lessee, but also between the lessor and an acquirer of the lease, between an acquirer of the reversion and the lessee, and between any acquirer of the reversion and any acquirer of the lease. As the lessor is the landlord of the lessee, who is his tenant, the substance of the matter is that there is tenure between them and the covenant is, as it were, annexed artificially to the ordinary incidents of tenure.

Now, where there is privity of contract, any covenants which are not illegal, immoral, or against public policy have binding force. On the other hand, persons between whom there is only privity of estate are bound only by covenants which run with the land, and those covenants are, put shortly such as 'touch and concern' the land, or, to put it in another way, have reference to the subject-matter of the lease. In other words, they must not merely affect a person exacting them, but must affect the nature, quality, or value of the subject-matter, or the mode of using or enjoying it.

Where there is neither privity of contract nor privity of estate, covenants do not bind at all. This is especially important where subleases are concerned. If a lessee sublets land, he does not alienate his estate to the sublessee, but carves a particular estate out of his own estate, retaining for himself the reversion to the sublease. Thus there is no privity of estate between the head lessor and the sublessee, but, on the other hand, it does continue between the head lessor and the head lessee. That means in effect that the head lessee retains the benefit of any covenants entered into by the head lessor and he will have to pass it on to the sublessee, though the head lessee alone will be able to sue for an infringement. Conversely, if a covenant entered into by the head lessee is infringed by an act or omission of the sub-lessee, only the head lessee can be sued. He is in fact responsible for his sublessee to the head lessor. The only exception is that *restrictive* covenants in a head lease bind a subtenant; the 'dominant tenement' is the head landlord's reversion but the 'servient tenement' is the land itself.[6] It is worth mentioning that privity of contract survives all alienations of reversion and lease respectively. Thus the original lessor and lessee guarantee each other permanently against the possibility of infringements of covenants by any subsequent acquirers of the lease and the reversion respectively. But a person who acquires either lease or reversion and subsequently alienates it never had any privity of contract, and with the alienation ceases to have any privity of estate, with any lessor or lessee respectively.

5. THE STATUTORY PROTECTION OF TENANTS

Until a hundred years ago the relations between lessor and lessee were almost entirely based on contract, though the lessor had also certain rights, such as that of distraining on the lessee's goods for non-payment of rent, which depended partly on common law and partly on medieval statutes. The lessee made the best bargain he could with the lessor and had to stand by it. His bargaining power varied considerably from time to time and according to the subject-matter of the lease. In days when the business of speculative building was profitable, a house tenant might have his choice of houses and need not be victimized. In times of agricultural depression, when farmers were steadily emigrating to North America or the Antipodes, a landlord might find it difficult to obtain tenants on any but the most favourable terms. On the other hand, landlords of agricultural land, business premises, or houses might, by the force of circumstances, acquire something like a monopoly and could, within reason, impose what terms they liked. Before commenting on such terms it is well to know what forms in general they took.

Standard covenants

The primary and essential term was, and is, that the lessee shall pay an agreed rent to the lessor; and this was sanctioned

[6] Restrictive covenants in leases are not registrable; they are so numerous that such a scheme would be impracticable. In practice anyone taking a sublease should first inspect the head lease, and so have notice.

by a term allowing the lessor to re-enter on the land in case of non-payment and to forfeit the lease. Thus the lessor was not left to bring a personal action on the debt and to exercise his right to distrain on the lessee's goods, but could, if necessary, evict him by bringing an action of ejectment.

The second term bound the lessee to keep the premises in good repair. Here a difference was made between different subject-matters. Tenants of agricultural land, of business premises, and of substantial house property were commonly subjected to full repairing covenants, which threw the full burden of repairs on the lessee. Sometimes tenants of house property undertook merely internal repairs, leaving external repairs to the landlord. Landlords of small dwellings, normally occupied by the working class, found it impossible in practice to throw the duty of repairing them on the tenants. If the houses were not to fall into ruin, the landlord had to do the repairs himself, no doubt endeavouring, as far as possible, to recoup himself by a higher rent.

In the great days of high farming, which lasted for about a century, from about 1770 to 1870, landlords regularly exacted strict improving covenants from their farm tenants. That is to say, they insisted on their tenants improving the land and, incidentally, the farm buildings. At a later date this became much more difficult to ensure.

Very commonly leases of buildings contained a covenant not to assign the lease or create subleases without the consent of the lessor, though generally with the proviso that the consent should not be unreasonably withheld.

All these various covenants were sanctioned, like the covenant to pay rent, by a term in the lease empowering the lessor to re-enter on the land on breach of any covenant and to forfeit the lease.

The contractual aspect of the lease, so apparent and so predominant in what has just been described, has now receded so much into the background that the reader must be warned of the fact that landlords and tenants now look for their rights much less to the terms of their leases than to the statute book. In three important types of property, the legislation waits until the parties have negotiated and concluded a lease and then overrides their agreement by imposing provisions almost all of which are designed to protect the tenant. Thus in these situations the move in legal relations is from contract to status.

Agricultural holdings

Where the old agricultural system was properly worked it was good for the land and not necessarily bad for the tenant. It required the employment by the landlord of an agent who supervised continually the operations of the tenants, and it paid the landlord himself to supervise his agent. It also paid him to have happy and efficient tenants. The great agricultural depression, which started in the late seventies of the last century, did much to make relations between landlords and tenants more difficult, and brought to a head certain possibilities of abuse which had long been present. These were remedied by a long series of Agricultural Holdings Acts, which were eventually consolidated in the Act of 1948.

To put it simply, the basic effect of the legislation is that, whatever the parties may have agreed, a tenancy of an agricultural holding will continue indefinitely while the tenant is alive until determined on one of the grounds permitted by statute, and on his death, a member of his family may succeed to the tenancy. The tenant is entitled to one year's notice to quit from the end of his current period of tenancy. He may, of course, accept the notice and leave but is then entitled to compensation for disturbance of between one and two years' rent. Further, in order to encourage efficient farming he is entitled to compensation for certain improvements made during his term and for any increase in the value of the holding caused by his having adopted a better system of farming than that practised on comparable land.

If, however, he chooses to stay he may usually continue his tenancy by serving counter-notice; disputes are decided initially by the Agricultural Lands Tribunal. Not more than once every three years, either party may require the amount of the rent to be submitted for arbitration and assessed on the basis of open market value. In certain circumstances the tenant cannot claim security of tenure: the most important of these are where the land is used for some approved non-agricultural purpose or the tenant has been in breach of his tenancy or is insolvent. Thus a good tenant farmer usually has the security of tenure which is necessary for efficient agriculture.

Business premises

A similar security is necessary for the conduct of business on leased premises. A person who rents a shop and builds up custom has, through his own efforts, created an intangible but valuable form of property—goodwill. Some of this will be 'cat' goodwill and some 'dog'. The former attaches customers to the premises themselves, because of their situation, lay-out, and the like; the latter attaches custom to the shopkeeper. The total may be a valuable asset for which any buyer of the business would have to pay; it is, however, difficult to divine whether any regular customer is cat, dog, or cross-breed. Here development of the law did not start until the Landlord and Tenant Act, 1927. The present position is rather complicated, and differs a good deal from that of agriculture. In general, if the tenant is given notice to quit he can apply to a court for a new tenancy, which must be granted. When the new tenancy ends the process can be repeated again indefinitely. But here again there are exceptions. Thus an unsatisfactory tenant may be evicted in accordance with the terms of the lease but only at six months' notice; and a landlord can successfully oppose the granting of a new lease if he intends to demolish or reconstruct the premises or, except where he has bought them within the last five years, if he intends to occupy them himself. In certain cases an evicted tenant can obtain compensation for disturbance. On any grant of a new tenancy the rent may be adjusted so as to conform to the open market rent, and other terms of the tenancy may also be revised by the court. A tenant is also entitled in certain cases to compensation for improvements.

Dwellinghouses

In 1914 about four-fifths of the population lived in privately rented accommodation and were subject to the ordinary common law: the rent was that agreed upon and, on the expiry of their lease, they had to leave. The decline in speculative building and the First World War produced a shortage of accommodation which threatened to put tenants at the mercy of landlords. Accordingly in 1915 the first Rent Act was passed which had as its purpose the fixing of rent (and mortgage interest) and also the protection of tenants against eviction at the end of their lease. Designed to be temporary, it proved the forerunner of a large number of statutes which have combined to create one of the most obscure and complex departments of English law. At the same time housing patterns have changed so that today only about a tenth of all dwellings fall within its operation.

The main effect of the statutory regime is to give the private tenant of all save the most luxurious accommodation a status of irremovability. This protection passes on his death to the surviving spouse or, if none, another member of the family who lived in the home; and on that person's death the protection may similarly pass once more.

The landlord may recover possession against a statutory tenant only if the court thinks it reasonable and if one of the specified grounds exists such as the availability of reasonable alternative accommodation or the landlord's own needs for the premises as a home for himself or family. In addition to this security of tenure the legislation sets up machinery to ensure that only a 'fair rent' (assessed by a Rent Officer) is payable.

The main exceptions to the statutory protection relate to such things as holiday lettings and to premises in which the landlord also lives. Further in 1980 the legislature resurrected the old common law under which a tenant had to go at the end of the lease by providing for mandatory recovery of possession of property let on a 'protected shorthold tenancy'— that is a lease of between one and five years preceded by a notice to the tenant that the term granted is such a creature.

XII

SETTLEMENTS

1. GENERAL

So far we have been considering cases where the current income from property is divided between several persons as it accrues, proportionately between tenants or owners in common, or by a reservation of a rent to the owner of a rentcharge or to a lessor, leaving to the owner of the land burdened with the rentcharge or to the lessee the residue of the income. Only in one of these cases is the time element important, namely in leases, where the lessor has a right to retain the whole income on the termination of the lease, and hence has a freehold reversion during the currency of the term.

We have now to consider cases where in principle the current income is not divided, but the whole of the income and the physical use of the objects from which it is derived are enjoyed by more than one person in succession to each other. Where arrangements are made for this purpose there is said to be a settlement; indeed section 1(1) (i) of the Settled Land Act, 1925, defines as a settlement, *inter alia*, any instrument under which any land is 'limited in trust for any persons by way of succession'. Limited interests other than terms of years can only exist as parts of settlements.

Two further observations are called for here. In the first place, the law treats many arrangements as settlements which would not ordinarily be regarded as such, to such an extent indeed as to apply the rules governing settlements to nearly all cases where some obstacle stands in the way of alienation of land. These extensions need be no more than alluded to in an elementary account. Secondly, a settlement is by no means invariably an elaborate document governing large masses of property; a mere indication in a will that one person is to occupy a house after another will be held to create a settlement. Probably very many testators of modest means create settlements unawares.

Large masses of English property law have been built up round family settlements, and it is not too much to say that to the practice of securing the enjoyment of property to several generations the English law of property, especially the law of real property, owes its most peculiar features. The family settlement entered into on a marriage, though private in nature, was the English counterpart of the matrimonial regime imposed by statute in other countries.

But it is the family settlement that causes most difficulty to students beginning the study of real-property law. Why should one person try to make complicated arrangements to make his property go in a particular way? Why should the law allow him to do it? Or, on the contrary, why should the law not allow him to do what he likes with his property, even to the extent of stopping other people doing what they like with it in their turn? Finally, if the law thinks that each person should not necessarily have the full control of his property, unfettered by any arrangements that the previous generation may have tried to make, has the law made an intelligible compromise between the competing interest of successive generations.

It is difficult to avoid treating this subject historically, but the temptation must be resisted as far as possible. In fact some explanation can be sufficiently divorced from history.

Protection of widows

Let us take first the simple case of a man who has a wife some years younger than himself and children. He is about to make his will and he has to contemplate the possibility that his wife may survive him, may remarry, and may have children by her second marriage. He has considerable property but not enough to be able to make an outright gift to his wife to keep her for the rest of her life and sufficiently large outright gifts to his children. He does not want to give his widow the whole of his property, partly for fear lest she should favour the children of a second marriage in preference to his own children. Surely a very natural way of disposing of his property will be to give the whole or part of it to his widow for life with remainder to his children.

From a very early time widows have acquired life interests in property. Sometimes the law itself has secured them such life interests; for instance, the common law of England gave a widow a life interest in one third of her husband's freeholds. This right was known as dower. It persists in many of the States in the United States. Even where the law itself does not give such a right, it is extremely common for testators to give life interests to their widows by will. The arrangement is indeed very natural and requires little justification. What is more natural or more normal than for a man to feel that he has duties to two separate generations, his own in the person of his widow and the next one in the persons of his children? Indeed, if he does not make a will, the standard intestacy regime will often impose such a scheme on his property.

This is a very simple and common form of settlement. Settlements are indeed infinitely various and may be established *inter vivos* or by will. But they tend to conform more or less to a fairly small number of types. It is by examining some of the more complicated of them that we can best become acquainted with the various interests which can be held in succession to one another.

The strict settlement

The most famous is the strict settlement by which the lands of the aristocracy and gentry were kept together in families for generations. Although it is extremely improbable that any new settlements of this kind are now being made, so fatally do they attract taxation, some must still survive. Moreover, so many of the most characteristic institutions of English real-property law are intelligible only as elements of a strict settlement that, in spite of its lack of practical importance at the present day, it deserves some attention even in an elementary book.

It had two main purposes. Firstly to ensure that the land should be kept undivided in the hands of one person in each generation, but that minor interests should be secured to other members of the family, such as wives, widows, and younger children. How those minor interests were secured is a complicated story which lies outside the compass of an elementary introduction. Secondly the scheme sought to resolve the conflict between generations of a wealthy family by giving both father and son bargaining strengths. The primary object of the settlement was affected as follows.

The land was given on marriage to the husband for life with remainder to his sons successively in tail, that is to say, the eldest son to be born was given an entailed interest in remainder, and a similar entailed interest was given to his next younger brother in the event of his dying without issue, and so on. Since an entailed interest is smaller in duration than a fee simple, the settlor, that is to say the person providing the land, has a reversion in the land so that if the husband's line dies out the land reverts to the settlor. This settlement had to be renewed every generation, for reasons which will appear later,[1] with the result that all living persons of full age in the direct line of succession held only life interests, in possession or in remainder, and the entailed interest was vested in an unborn person or in one who was still under age.

The 'trader's settlement'

A much commoner settlement was that made by persons who did not want to 'found a family' but wished to control the property in it for more than a single generation. Since it was not primarily concerned with land but rather with the money that a person had made in business, it was formerly known as a trader's settlement. On marriage the husband and wife (or their parents) transfer property to trustees in trust to sell it and to hold the proceeds of the husband's trust fund to pay the income to him for life and of the wife's trust fund to pay the income to her for life. The survivor is given the income for life from both trust funds. The husband and wife are given a special power of appointment by virtue of which they can, acting together, distribute the trust funds according to their choice among the children of the marriage. If they do not exercise the power in conjunction, it can be exercised by the survivor. If it is not exercised at all, the trust funds are distributed equally among sons of the marriage who reach the full age

[1] p. 167 below.

and daughters of the marriage who reach the age of majority or marry under that age.

Tax avoidance

Many settlements are now made with the express purpose of reducing liability to income-tax and excluding liability to capital transfer tax. Hitherto the most successful types have involved a grant of the property to trustees, who must take no beneficial interest themselves in the settlement, with an absolute discretion to make payments of income or capital at such times as they may choose to such members of a broadly defined class, such as members or servants of a family, as they choose. As such beneficiaries have no right to such payments, no interest can pass to anyone else on their death. Every precaution is taken to prevent the concentration of the beneficial interest that used to be assured to the head of the family by the strict settlement. For, with an income-tax bearing on incomes, not proportionately but so progressively as to be penal in its exactions, such concentration automatically ensures impoverishment of the family property. It is far better to arrange for as much as possible of the expense of upkeep, including payments to servants, to be borne by the trustees. Of course the beneficiaries have to pay for these privileges by committing themselves to the unfettered discretion of the trustees, who may, so far as the law is concerned, stop payments at any moment and for any or no reason.

The beneficial interests which demand more special attention as elements in settlements are life interests, entailed interests, and future interests.

2. LIFE INTERESTS

There is very little to be said about beneficial life interests; indeed most of what is usually said about life interests relates to management and not to the beneficial enjoyment of property. But it is perhaps worth while to contrast the life interest with the Roman usufruct, for thereby its essential nature is brought out.

The Romans thought of the usufruct as inseparably attached to the person enjoying it, so that, although he could, as it were, sublet the enjoyment of the property, he could not alienate his usufruct. Moreover, as if this personal connexion were not enough, a usufructuary was usually made to enter into a personal undertaking by contract towards the owner of the property to hand it over intact and in good condition.

In contrast to this the English life interest is inseparably connected, not with the person for whose life it is created, but with his life. Thus he is in no way prevented from alienating it, but it cannot last longer than his life. In the hands of the alienee it is not an interest for the alienee's life, but is known as an interest *pur autre vie*, that is, for the life of the alienor.

An inalienable life interest may, however, be created and is used to deal with the problem of the prodigal son. It determines automatically if he tries to alienate or becomes insolvent. For the rest of his life, trustees, at their discretion, distribute the income to him and his family. English law calls it a protective trust; in the USA similar devices are known as the spendthrift trust.

3. ENTAILED INTERESTS

Entailed interests are usually explained historically. This is on the whole rather unfortunate, for the emphasis on their history, which is usually given in a highly technical form, tends to thrust into the background the true economic and social reasons which made entailed interests of great practical utility until recent times.

We must start from the point that an entailed interest was used only for the purpose of ensuring that large masses of property should be kept together in perpetuity, so far as the law would allow, in one direct line of descent or, failing such line, in the next nearest line or lines of descent. Thus a person would want most of his property to go for ever to his eldest son, and then to his son's eldest son, and so on in a direct line, but, if the direct line was in danger of dying out, then, for example, to the brother or nephew of the last childless person in the line and to the issue of that brother or nephew, and so on. That is the pattern that the creator of an entailed interest would have in mind; and the next question is, how the entailed interest would help to ensure its continued existence.

Now the nature of the entailed interest is determined by two different factors, first, its essential character and, secondly, what it can be turned into.

A restricted succession

Its essential character can best be grasped if it is compared to the fee simple. It is a question of intestate succession. At common law if a person dies intestate any lands which he holds in fee simple will go to his issue or, if he has no issue, to his ascendants or, failing ascendants, to collaterals, such as brothers or sisters or nephews or nieces. If, on the other hand, he holds an entailed interest at the time of his death, that interest can only go to his issue, and only to the eldest male in each generation or, more exceptionally, to the females equally, It can never go to either ascendants or collaterals but, on failure of issue, will revert to the donor, i.e. the person creating the entailed interest. Thus the original mark of an entailed interest is a restricted succession; and in fact the older name, fee tail, comes from the Latin *feodum talliatum*, that is to say, a cut down or truncated fee or feudal holding.

Barring the entail

Now for what can be done to it. Put quite shortly, the tenant in tail can, if he is of full age and in his right mind, bar the entail, wholly or partially, and so improve his position at the expense of those entitled to take after his death. Three cases must be distinguished.

(1) If the person entitled to the entailed interest has actual possession of the property, if, that is, he would formerly have been called the tenant in tail in possession, he can by executing a disentailing assurance, which may be a deed or a provision in a will, turn the entailed interest into an absolute interest, and so make himself or his devisee, that is, the person to whom he has bequeathed it, tenant in fee simple of such portions of the entailed interest as consist of land. (2) If, however, his entailed interest is in remainder, if, for instance, it will take effect in possession only on the death of some other person, probably his father, who holds the land as tenant for life, there will be a person known as the protector of the settlement, who will usually be the tenant for life. The typical regime is a grant to

A [the father] for life, remainder to B [his eldest son] in tail. Now, if the holder of the entailed interest executes *inter vivos* a disentailing assurance with the concurrence of the protector of the settlement, he can turn the entailed interest into an absolute interest just as though he had been in possession himself. (3) If, on the other hand, he disentails without the concurrence of the protector he can create only what is called a base fee.

A base fee is technically described as a determinable fee simple; that is to say, it is a fee simple which may last for ever but will come to an end on the happening of a certain event, which in this case will be the failure of B's issue. If B dies without issue or if he leaves issue which eventually fails, the land subject to the base fee will pass either by way of remainder to any person entitled to an entailed interest in default of B's entailed interest, that is to say, to one of B's brothers or the issue of that brother, or, if there are no such persons, by way of reversion to the grantor. In other words, a base fee will last only as long as the entailed interest it supplants, but the person entitled to it has during that period the same full control over its subject-matter as if it were a fee simple or an absolute interest in personalty. Thus he can, though with difficulty, raise money on the security of a base fee.

Now, a base fee must always start as a remainder, since if the person executing the disentailing assurance has an entailed interest in possession he will inevitably turn it into a fee simple; and hence its value would in any case depend on the expectation of life of those entitled to any particular estates that precede it. This factor alone might reduce it to something very small. Moreover, although there are ways of enlarging a base fee into a fee simple absolute or an absolute interest in personalty, none of them can be accomplished without the permission of the protector of the settlement until, at the earliest, the time when the base fee ceases to be a remainder and falls into possession—which, in our example, is at A's death. Hence a strong speculative element must enter into the calculations of anyone buying or lending money on a base fee. The owner of the base fee may never live to enlarge it, and in that case it would cease if his issue failed. The purchaser or mortgagee would then get nothing, any more than if he had bought a life interest in remainder, whereas if he had bought a fee simple absolute or absolute interest in personalty in remainder, he would have had something to show for the price he had paid for it, even if it proved ruinous. It follows that base fees are not readily marketable, though moneylenders have been willing to speculate in them.

From what has been said, it must be obvious that if it is desired to ensure that the property be kept in the direct line, no entailed interest must ever be allowed to fall into possession, for then the tenant in tail could disentail and alienate the property. Nor should any entailed interest be even allowed to be for any length of time at the disposal of a remainderman who, being of full age and capacity, could turn it into a base fee; for although he might get very little for it, if he was in great difficulties owing to extravagance or misfortune, he might clutch at any straw. Hence steps must be taken to keep the entailed interest always in the hands of a remainderman who is not yet born or has not attained full age.

Resettlement

Accordingly the practice was to resettle the property every generation. When the tenant in tail in remainder reached full age, the first occasion on which he could perform a valid act, he was induced to disentail the property and immediately make a new settlement to deal with his entailed interest, giving himself only a life interest—which would of course fall into possession after his father's life interest—and successive entailed interests to his own children, born, or to be born. The entailed interest would then be safe for another generation.

Now suppose that the young man was disinclined to play his part. There was an inducement and a sanction. The inducement was a provision in the new settlement he was invited to execute giving him a settled income during his father's life independent of his father's control; the sanction was twofold, first, that his father could keep him on very short commons, and secondly, that he could raise money only on the base fee which was all he could create without his father's concurrence. On the other hand the young man had a bargaining counter for if he simply waited until his father's death he could turn his entail into a full fee simple and sell the land outright.

It remains to be said that the entailed interest, which has been abolished in most other common-law jurisdictions, is hardly used today even in England. The severity with which income-tax bears down on large incomes makes any attempt to keep property together in one pair of hands ruinous, and the general tendency is to divide income among large numbers of members of a family or their servants so that each portion attracts as little taxation as possible. But the learning of entails is something that every student is expected to know, and it affords an interesting insight into the functions that the doctrine of estates was expected to perform.

4. THE FORM OF SETTLEMENTS

Although one must always expect to find physical objects playing a double role, as marketable objects in the hands of holders of the legal estate or legal ownership, and as component parts of a trust fund, the income of which is divided among several persons in succession, the two roles are kept strictly apart. For if they were allowed to get in each other's way, either the existence of the trust might make the task of proving title to the physical object more complicated and the sale of it more difficult, or the protection of those interested in the trust fund might be rendered less secure. For this reason steps are always taken, when it is disclosed in documents relating to the legal estate that its holders are trustees, to prevent any disclosure in them of the terms of the trust. This is called keeping trusts off the title. Any purchaser of the legal estate is, of course, entitled to see documents dealing with the legal estate, for otherwise he would be unable to investigate the title he is about to acquire. But he is not entitled to look behind the 'curtain' to see the trust instrument, as the document is called which sets out the terms of the trust. There is indeed no need for him to see it, for, provided the trustees have a power of sale, as they will always have over land,[2] he will not be bound by any of the trusts contained in the trust instrument. If, of course, he is buying, not the land, but an equitable interest conferred on a beneficiary by the trust instrument, then he will need and will be entitled to inspect the trust instrument.

[2] Apart from the one exceptional case mentioned at p. 103 n. 15 above.

Strict settlements and trusts for sale

So far we have spoken simply of trustees and beneficiaries and have conveyed the impression that all settlements, that is to say, arrangements whereby limited interests in property are created, are of one type. This is not true as a matter of theory, though in practice it is becoming very nearly true. The commonest way of settling property is now to give the legal estate in land and the full ownership of personalty to trustees for sale, who are bound to sell the property vested in them (though they may postpone the sale at their discretion) and to hold the proceeds upon the trusts specified in the trust instrument. But there is another method, which is an adaptation of the aristocratic strict settlement of lands which was gradually developed during the seventeenth, eighteenth, and nineteenth centuries as a means of keeping together great landed estates. In a strict settlement the person in actual possession of the land, who in popular speech was known as the landowner, had only a life estate. As the powers inherent in the life estate were insufficient to allow him to manage the land properly in the interests of himself and his successors, he was in the second half of the nineteenth century given statutory powers to deal with the fee simple, by selling or mortgaging it or by granting leases to endure beyond his own lifetime. In 1925 his powers were further enlarged, but the opportunity was also taken to alter the basis of his powers. Instead of holding a legal estate only for life, he is now given the legal fee simple, which he holds in trust for himself for life and thereafter for the other persons interested in the settlement. The change has made little difference to the actual content of his powers but it made possible a new way of handling the title to the property similar to that employed in the trust for sale. Two documents are now used, the vesting deed and the trust instrument. The former vests the legal fee simple in the tenant for life and contains the names of the trustees.[3] The latter appoints them and gives the property to the beneficiaries by setting out the trusts. Thus in the vesting deed the tenant for life appears as owner of the legal fee simple

---

[3] If the title is registered, the tenant for life appears as proprietor, but a restriction ensures that any capital money, such as on sale, will be paid not to him but to the trustees.

upon trust, whereas in the trust instrument he appears as the owner of an equitable life interest.

The two techniques, of the strict settlement and the trust for sale respectively, are kept carefully apart by the law, and the difference between them must always be borne in mind by would-be purchasers of the legal estate, since in the strict settlement it is the tenant for life who must be made to convey the legal estate, though the purchase money must be paid to the trustees, whereas in the trust for sale it is the trustees who both convey the legal estate and receive the purchase money. However, both are varieties of the same general way of keeping apart the physical object and the rights, sometimes fragmentary, to the income produced by it.

5. THE MANAGEMENT OF SETTLED PROPERTY

It is of the essence of a settlement that it should govern the property subject to it for a period of time. During that period not only may one beneficial interest succeed another, but the property has to be managed. Since the reconciliation between the management and the enjoyment of the beneficial interest is the very purpose of the trust,[4] it might have been expected that all that would need to be done would be to vest the property in trustees with extensive powers of management upon trust to allow the use of it and, where necessary, to pay the income to the successive beneficiaries. In actual fact things did not work out that way.

Until 1925 in a strict settlement the successive beneficiaries in the direct line were given legal estates in the land, trusts being used only subsidiarily for special purposes. For a long time problems of management had to be solved in the difficult and complicated environment so created.

The tenant for life

The law of estate management has been worked out mainly in relation to life interests. This is because under the strict settlement the person who was in possession of a great landed estate and was considered by the outside world as 'landowner' was, in spite of the dukedom or other title he enjoyed, merely

[4] See pp. 101–4 above.

a tenant for life. On the other hand, there was no one else with any power whatever to manage the land. All other persons with beneficial interests in the land had for the moment only rights to future income, whereas any trustees there might be were concerned only to see that subordinate members of the family were secured in their minor interests. Thus the tenant for life was the only manager, and his powers as such were strictly limited. On the other hand, if powers of management were to be enlarged, the additional powers would most naturally be given to him.

Waste caused no difficulty, for the tenant for life could be, and usually was, made unimpeachable for waste and so could be restrained only from committing equitable waste.[5] The real difficulty lay in the duration of the life estate itself. Any lease or mortgage must necessarily come to an end with the death of the tenant for life unless his successor chose to renew it, and accordingly it was difficult, sometimes impossible, for such leases or mortgages to be created. That was not necessarily objectionable as far as agricultural land was concerned, for a common tenancy was from year to year; it made the granting of mining leases and the development of urban property by long building leases almost impossible. The difficulty of raising money on mortgage put great obstacles in the way of improvements.

Things were not always, or perhaps often, as bad as that. Not all of a landowner's property was necessarily settled land. He might, like the Dukes of Bedford, be deeply interested in commerce, as a stockholder in the East India Company, or he might have considerable holdings in the funds, i.e. government stock, which had been a very sound investment ever since the great financial reforms of the Glorious Revolution, or he might, like others after him, marry a rich city heiress with ready money. Even if the personalty so brought in was settled, there would be trustees, who might easily be given extensive powers. However, such expedients might not cover the whole ground.

Express powers

In Scotland, where entails had been deliberately made unbarrable, relief could be obtained only by Act of Parliament. In

[5] See p. 141 above.

England the need for legislative reform was staved off for a long time by the beneficent need to renew the settlement every generation.[6] When the tenant in tail in remainder by barring it converted it into a fee simple, the opportunity could be taken of selling or mortgaging some of the land or of granting long mining or building leases which would bind succeeding holders of the land.

A more effectual remedy was on such occasions to confer on the tenant for life for the time being powers to deal with the land for certain purposes as though he had the fee simple, but to safeguard the interests of remaindermen and others provided for in the settlement by insisting on the co-operation for certain purposes of the trustees of the settlement.

Statutory powers

These powers became the model for reforms by Act of Parliament, at first requiring for the exercise of powers the approval of a court, but eventually making such approval unnecessary and the exercise of the powers possible even despite an attempt to exclude them by the express terms of the settlement. The most striking effect of this legislation, which was to reduce the estates of all except the tenant for life to the status of interests in a trust fund, has already been described. Those concerned with management demand some attention here.

The most important power conferred by the Settled Land Act 1925 on the tenant for life is that of sale; and it cannot be restricted by the settlor or made subject to anyone's consent. As trustee for all the beneficiaries the life tenant must get a good price, but it is in his own interests to do so since it is that money, invested elsewhere, on which he will receive the income. The purchaser will know that he is dealing with someone who, beneficially, has only a limited interest; but he is not in the least concerned with the beneficial interests so long as he pays his money, not to the seller, but to the trustees of the settlement. If the title is unregistered the seller will have to produce the vesting deed for it is that which gave him the fee simple that he is selling—but the very same document gives the trustees' names. If the title is registered the tenant for life will appear on the register as the proprietor of the land—but

---

[6] See pp. 167–8 above.

the same page will contain a warning (called a 'restriction') that the money must be paid not to him but to the trustees.

The most important of the other powers are those of granting leases and of mortgaging or charging the settled property for the purpose of paying for improvements or discharging encumbrances or providing money which is required to be raised under the provisions of the settlement.

These statutory powers of management given to the tenant for life are not confined to the old aristocratic family settlement, which is rarely encountered at the present day; for they are also conferred on tenants for life under much simpler settlements and on other persons who have limited interests in possession. Moreover, whenever the trust for sale is used instead of the strict settlement, the trustees for sale are given the powers of a tenant for life. Indeed, so far have the powers come to be adopted as a standard for management that they are given to the trustees of charities and, with slight variations, to the Crown Estate Commissioners and to the governing bodies of universities and colleges, all of whom are faced with the same problem of preserving capital by using it for improvements or for purposes not immediately remunerative but beneficial to the neighbourhood. They play the part in modern law that was formerly played by the doctrine of waste.

Trusts for sale

Since trustees for sale are directed to sell the land and hold the proceeds upon the trusts of the settlement, it might be thought that they would, if it were possible, be even less restricted than the tenant for life under a strict settlement in the exercise of their powers of selling, leasing, and mortgaging the land, the more so as they are expressly given by statute all the powers both of a tenant for life of settled land and of Settled Land Act trustees. This is, however, not the case, for not only are they given a power to postpone the sale, but the exercise of their powers can be made subject to the consent of specified persons. Where more than two persons are specified, a bona fide purchaser for value of the trust property is protected if the consent of two of them is obtained. Thus, by using a trust for sale, land may be made alienable only with the co-operation of the trustees, the tenant for life, and the persons next entitled to the beneficial interest, whereas, if the land is made subject to a strict settlement, the tenant for life can act alone.

For this and other reasons, largely technical, the trust for sale is now generally preferred to the strict settlement. But the marriage of land and chattel investments is not altogether happy. Formerly the typical trustee was a member or close friend of the family, who was willing to perform a thankless and perhaps dangerous task for nothing. He was far enough away from enjoying the property to take a cool and impartial view of its problems but near enough to understand it and the family and take a personal interest in them. However, for various reasons, such trustees of the old school have largely been supplanted by trust corporations such as the Public Trustee or subsidiaries of the great banks, which charge for their services but provide financial security in the highest degree. Since they are expert in the art of financial management, they fulfil admirably the functions of trustees in so far as the trust comprises stocks and shares or similar chattel investments; for where the only questions relate to money, the quality of detachment outweighs all others.

Such investments are, however, already at least one stage removed from the physical objects which are the ultimate sources of wealth and from the human beings who have them in their care and keeping. Not only is the trust fund an abstraction, but the investments of which it is composed are abstractions also. On the other hand, the management of land and houses brings the managers into immediate contact both with soil and bricks and mortar and with flesh and blood. Moreover, to a great extent the occupier himself must be the manager.

The management of houses and flats has indeed largely fallen into the hands of large companies, which are impersonal enough; but the management of agricultural estates is still mainly personal, by owner-occupiers or by landlords with or without the assistance of professional land agents.

Thus, even where land is settled by way of trust for sale, it is advisable to leave the management of it to the tenant for life. Hence the trustees for sale may delegate revocably to the tenant for life all powers of management (except sale), including that of letting it on leases of periodical tenancies.

Changed conditions

Little attention has been paid here to the details of the tenant for life's statutory powers for two reasons. In the first place, they are inappropriate to an introductory survey, since they cannot be properly understood without some knowledge of estate management. Secondly, they are already largely out of date. They were indeed appropriate only to an economy where the value of money was relatively stable. No wise settlor now wants to prescribe the physical form property subject to a settlement should take, nor does he want to limit a trustee's power of investment to gilt-edged securities. The only way to preserve property nowadays is to invest in equities, that is to say, securities which are likely to adjust themselves to changes in the value of money; and this inevitably means to indulge in discreet and informed speculation. The landowner has learnt this truth the hard way as effectually as the business man. Accordingly, the only way to discover what may now be considered to be the general law of settled property is to examine the best standard forms of settlements, which are more likely to be found in the most up-to-date books on Tax Planning than in the older books on conveyancing.[7]

[7] For a summary description of a typical modern settlement see p. 163 above.

XIII

CONTROL OF THE OWNERSHIP OF CAPITAL AND INCOME: PERPETUITIES AND ACCUMULATIONS

1. PERPETUITIES

THERE is no limit to the kinds of interests that can be created in funds. In other words, the enjoyment of the income from a fund may be made to pass from one person to another on the happening of any kind of event or fulfilment of any kind of condition whatever which is not illegal, immoral, or otherwise contrary to public policy.

Nevertheless, although few limits are placed on the types of interests which may be created, or on the kinds of events or conditions upon which they may be made to depend, they are subject to strict restriction in respect of time. Although these restrictions were first formulated to deal with settlements of land, two points are of absolutely fundamental importance to an understanding of the modern law.

The first is that, for over a century, restrictions have not been needed in respect of the land itself. Since 1882 Parliament has ensured that, no matter how far into the future the interests may arise, they are merely interests in a fund. This may be invested in land, but the land itself can be sold at any moment, and the beneficial interests switched to the proceeds of sale and any investment thereof. The second point is a consequence of the first: the Rule against Perpetuities, which controls the ownership of capital, applies to interests in all other property— stocks and shares, patents, debts, goodwill, and even (although, as we have seen, future interests are rare in them) to tangible movables like pictures and porridge.

In many jurisdictions the control over the future ownership of capital known as the common-law Rule against Perpetuities has been amended by statute. Our 1964 Act (which applies only to England and Wales) does not, however, repeal or restate the common law, but merely builds upon it. Consequently an introductory explanation has to proceed in two stages.

(a) The common-law rule against perpetuities

In an earlier chapter of this book we took the example of a settlor, S, who gave income-producing property to A for life, then to B absolutely.[1] We demonstrated that, immediately after this disposition, S owned nothing; A had a life estate (or interest) which, if he was aged 50, was worth about half a million. B's interest (the 'fee simple in remainder') was also worth about half a million and we explained that, since it was his, he could market it at once.

But suppose S had stipulated that, in order to become entitled to this property, B had to fulfil some condition:

'to A for life, remainder to B absolutely if he qualifies as a doctor; if he does not, then to C absolutely'.

Now this limitation does not make S any richer—he has still given away his million—and does not make A any richer—he is still entitled to the income only for his life and we calculated his present worth at about half a million. The other half million is still there—but who *now* owns it? If B does qualify as a doctor, it will be his; if he does not it will belong to C; but meanwhile we do not know.[2]

The Rule against Perpetuities is designed to permit such ignorance but to confine it within strict limits. Its effect is that the uncertainty as to ownership will be tolerated if, but only if, it must, by the laws of biology, be resolved within the lifetime of someone alive at the moment of the gift and a further twenty-one years. In the example given the application of the Rule is easy. We do not know whether B will ever become a doctor and so take the property and disappoint C, but we do know, and we know *today*, that our uncertainty will be resolved, one way or the other, within a lifetime: for if B is to qualify he must be alive to do so.

---

[1] See pp. 84–7 above.
[2] Both B's and C's expectations may still have a market value but it will not be easily ascertainable from an actuary's mortality tables. B and C together could certainly sell the remainder—but how would they split the proceeds?

The classic statement of the Rule, distilled by the doctrine from countless cases, runs:

> No interest is good unless it must vest, if at all, not later than twenty-one years after some life in being at the creation of the interest.

The limit of twenty-one years was added when that was the normal period of minority and it was not altered when the age of attaining majority was lowered. This terse statement of the rule requires explanation.

Vested and contingent interests

This first point to make is that the Rule applies only to contingent and not to vested interests.[3] The reader may be reminded that for an interest to be vested it need not be *vested in possession*, that is to say, the person entitled to it need not have an immediate right to the income. All that is needed is that the nature and quantum of the interest and the identity of the person entitled to it should be known. It is then *vested in interest* and may be sold at once. Thus in our standard example of 'to A for life, then to B absolutely' we know at once that B is entitled and that the interest is a fee simple absolute in remainder on A's life estate.

If, on the other hand, his identity is not yet known with certainty (in our second example it was *either* B or C), or the quantum of the interest is not yet ascertained, or both, then the interest is contingent. Thus where B has to become a doctor in order to take, his present interest is contingent on that happening and will not vest until it does. When it does, C loses all hope of ever taking the property.

Now the Rule against Perpetuities does not deal with vested interests which can be easily valued and marketed. In other words it does not deal with present interests but only with those which may, or may not, belong to someone in the future. And the event which, under the Rule, must be certain to happen, if it ever does happen, within the perpetuity period is the event which turns the contingent into a vested interest. Thus in our example the event which is to take place, if at all, within B's life is the medical qualification. It does not matter that this never occurs; if B dies unqualified, C will take. But we

[3] See p. 91 above.

know now that our uncertainty must, by the laws of biology, be resolved one way or another by the moment of B's death. If he has qualified he will have taken to the exclusion of C; if not, the property belongs to C.

Lives in being

The 'lives in being' mentioned in the statement of the Rule must be persons who are alive at the time when the instrument takes effect, that is to say in the case of an instrument *inter vivos* at the time when it is executed and, in the case of a gift by will, at the death of the testator. The reason for this is that the trustees must at once be able to look at the gifts, look at the possible beneficiaries, and say: 'we do not know now who will get this property. If, however, we are certain to know sometime within the period, then we can wait and see what happens. If, however, it may happen outside the period we do not wait to see if, in fact, it does occur in time. The gift simply fails at this moment and we must find someone to take at once in default.' If, for instance, the void gift is in an instrument *inter vivos* then that person is the settlor; if it is in a legacy, then the residuary beneficiary; if in a disposition by will of the residue, then the intestacy beneficiaries.

The lives in being may be expressly specified, not in order to make them beneficiaries, but simply in order to create an artificial perpetuity period within which the qualifying event must occur: for instance a gift by will

> 'to the first of my descendants to qualify as a doctor within 21 years of the death of the present descendants of Her Majesty the Queen'.

If, on the other hand, no lives are expressly specified then, at common law, the appropriate lives are those whose existence is biologically relevant to the event. For instance

> 'to Jane when she marries'.

We do not know now if this will happen but we do know now that, if it does, it must happen within Jane's lifetime. Another example is:

> 'to Jane's first son'.

Again, we do not know now whether Jane will ever have a son

but we do know now that, if she does, she must be alive to do so. Similarly:

'to Jane's first son to reach twenty-one'.

We now have two contingencies: Jane must first have a son and then he must live to the age of twenty-one. Since, however, if a son is born at all this must occur within Jane's lifetime then he cannot attain the age specified (if he ever does so) more than twenty-one years after the death of someone alive today, namely his mother.

But consider a gift

'to Jane's first son to marry'.

Here again we have two contingencies. The first, the birth, must happen, if at all, within Jane's lifetime. But the second, although it may well occur, is not bound inexorably to do so within 21 years of her death. So without the Rule our uncertainty might extend longer than the period allowed and, at common law, the gift to the son is void from the start.

If, by the very nature of the gift, there are no lives connected with it, then the perpetuity period is just twenty-one years—for instance a gift

'to the next female MP for Oxford'.

No wait and see

At common law if the event is certain to happen, if at all, within the period then one *must* wait and see if, in fact, it does. If, however, it may happen within or after the period then one *must not* wait and see if, in fact, it happens within. One must be able to predict, when the instrument creating the interest takes effect, whether such vesting, if it does take place, must inevitably do so within the period. Therefore if there is the remotest possibility of its occurring outside the period the gift is void from the start and the interest is not allowed to vest even though, as things turn out, the contingency on which it depends is actually satisfied within the period.

Charities

The Rule is sometimes said not to apply to charities, but this statement is inaccurate. The law permits certain forms of charity, which it regards as beneficial to the community, to be the objects of permanent endowment: that is to say a sum of capital may be tied up for ever with only the income going to the charity.

Any gift to a charity is subject to the Rule against Perpetuities in that it must vest in the charity within the perpetuity period. On the other hand a gift over from one charity to another may be valid even if it is to occur at some remote time in the future. It is said that all charities are regarded as one single object and the change in recipient is merely a matter of internal arrangement. But that is merely a way of restating the exception to the Rule. Probably a true explanation is that the law regards a gift to charity as taking property permanently out of commerce, but has to admit that a particular charitable object may become obsolete.

The Rule against Inalienability

The Rule against Perpetuities is not a rule against inalienability, that is against gifts which transfer property but stipulate that it must not be disposed of.[4] Further, this is emphasized by the fact that the Rule permits the switching of income from one charity to another at any time in the future, although the capital is tied up for ever.

Nevertheless the close control that is exerted over the purposes for which property can be given to charity would be absurd unless the law disapproved in general of arrangements whereby a settlor can take property out of commerce. Further the practical effect of the Rule is to annul gifts which might vest outside the period; so that during the period the gifts saved will vest one way or the other and become readily evaluable and marketable.

The disapproval is announced expressly where property is given in trust, not for human beings and not for charities, but for non-charitable purposes. The danger of freely permitting these is that the trustees will apply the property to those purposes and so keep it out of commerce. The classic Rule against

---

[4] The Rule applies even though the contingent interests are marketable. For instance if a testator leaves property to a hospital, but if the hospital ever closes, then to ICI Ltd., the Rule makes the latter gift void because it may vest too remotely. This is so even though the hospital could convey its interest and ICI Ltd. could sell its executory interest.

Perpetuities can do little to stop this for if the property is vested in the trustees within the period, the Rule is obeyed. Hence a rule has been devised, by analogy with the strict Rule against Perpetuities, which states that it must be possible to spend the capital or wind up the trust within the period or the gift is void. In other words it is not permitted to set up a perpetual endowment for an impersonal, non-charitable, purpose.

Corporations

The same tendency to take property out of commerce would seem to exist whenever property is given to a corporation, for such a body is not subject to the natural incident of death, although it may be dissolved. In truth the accumulation of land in the hands of ecclesiastical corporations has at various times in the past taken too much property out of commerce. As long ago as 1279 legislation was enacted to prohibit the giving of land to corporations without a licence from the Crown. It was called the Statute of Mortmain because the corporation's ownership was like a dead hand on the property. The statutory prohibition was not totally repealed until 1960. Long before then, however, major exceptions had been permitted. Thus municipal corporations did not need a licence for they are able to acquire land only for municipal purposes authorized by Act of Parliament. The acquisition of land by ordinary commercial companies does not take it out of commerce and so, being without danger to the economy, did not require a licence. All corporations have always been free to acquire movable property, whether tangible or not, without authorization.

(b) The Perpetuities and Accumulations Act 1964

As befits an elementary work, the following account will deal only with the major changes wrought by this Act. It must be stressed that, if the gift is valid according to the common-law Rule, there is no need to consider the legislation.

Eighty-year period

To spare settlors the need to incorporate a 'royal lives clause'[5] in order to provide an artificial period to save the contingent

⁵ See p. 179 above.

gift, section 1 of the Act allows for the express use of any number of years up to 80. Thus a gift by will

'to my first grandson to become a doctor within a per- petuity period of seventy-eight years'

will save the gift. The testator has stipulated that qualifying after that period does not count; and so a grandson who quali- fies within it takes the property even though he was never certain to qualify within twenty-one years of the death of the last of the testator's children.

Statutory sterility

At common law trustees were expected to know the facts of death, but not the facts of life and were required to presume that any living person could have a child. Section 2 of the Act sensibly provides for a presumption that the only people capable of having children are males over thirteen and females between 12 and fifty-five. Further in the case of any individual, say a woman who has passed the menopause at the age of fifty, evidence of sterility may be given.

This reform alone saves many gifts from the rigours of the common law. Thus a disposition

'to Jane's first child to marry'

was void since the first child to do so might be born after the date of the gift and marry more than 21 years after the mother's death. If, however, Jane is now sterile, whether by the statute or in fact, then she will have no more children. So the only child who can marry must already be alive and, if the event occurs at all, it must do so within that child's life.

Wait and see

If there is no number of years written into the instrument to serve as a perpetuity period, and if the relevant lives are not statutorily sterile, then section 3 of the Act comes into oper- ation. This allows us to wait and see whether an event which might occur outside, in fact happens within, the period; fur- ther, the section gives a list of relevant lives. Thus in the case of a gift by will

'to Jane's first child to marry'

where Jane is a healthy twenty-year old, we wait and see. If she dies childless, that is that. But if she has a child we wait to see if it marries within her lifetime or twenty-one years thereafter. If it does, the child takes; if not we wait no longer and the gift is void.

(c)   Rationale of the Rule against Perpetuities

Let us now try to see why there is a Rule against Perpetuities. By way of preparation, two points must be recalled.

Firstly, although the Rule does not avowedly strike at in-alienability but only at the remote vesting of property interests, it has very much the former effect. For as soon as a beneficial interest vests in an ascertained individual—which must, even today, occur within the perpetuity period—it becomes easy to evaluate and to market. Moreover once all the beneficial interests are in the hands of living persons of full age and capacity, they can make the trustees wind up the trust and distribute the assets.[6]

Secondly, the original purpose of the Rule has long since disappeared. Having been devised for the purpose of preventing land from being kept too long out of the market, it was subsequently applied to all other property interests without, in all probability, very much thought being given to the changed environment in which it would work. Since the passing of the Settled Land Act 1882, much more efficient means have existed of ensuring that land is freely alienable.[7] Indeed there is no longer a danger of freezing any particular asset, since in almost every case any piece of specific property —land, shares, patents, or goods—in which the fund, or part of it, may be invested can at any moment be sold by a tenant for life or trustees. The price, of course, replaces the asset within the fund.

It would seem, therefore, at first sight that the Rule against Perpetuities can no longer have any relation to the market, in so far as that is concerned with specific physical objects or investments. It relates only to contingent rights to receive income from a fund and to their capitalized value. Accordingly some writers regard the Rule as effecting a compromise between

---

[6] The Variation of Trusts Act 1958 now allows the court to give its consent on behalf of those who are not *sui juris*.
[7] See pp. 107, 171 above.

the living and the dead. If we had no such rule, a person might on his death be able to fix, for all time to come (subject to the vicissitudes of the market for securities) the interests which his descendants are to take. If, on the other hand, he were allowed to give his property only to people alive at his death, that might appear too great a restriction on his power to deal with what is his own. There is no particular virtue in our Rule as it stands. Civil-law countries have different rules which are not obviously worse. But from a comparison of those rules with our own there does seem to be a consensus of opinion that, in some cases at any rate, a person should be able to give his property to persons unborn at the time of his death, but that that power should be strictly limited so as to avoid anything in the nature of a Perpetuity and so as to return to the hands of the living within a reasonable time full control not merely of the specific physical objects contained in his estate but also of the right to receive and dispose of income that is to accrue from time to time. It must be remembered that the right to income for ever is the right to the capital. Such a rationale, then, sees the Rule as a restriction on legal personality. During a person's lifetime he may do with his property as he pleases. Further, for some time after his death, his will (in both senses) can control his property in the world which he has left. But there comes a moment when even the dead must die: and the effect of the Rule is to fix the latest date for this at the time when his grandchildren become adults.

Other writers prefer a different, but not incompatible, explanation. They say that the Rule has still some application even to the specific objects or investments comprised in a settlement. Wherever future interests exist then the present management of the property is confided to trustees; and the purpose of the Rule is to curb trusts. Trust capital and risk capital are very different. In general, even where trustees are given the very widest powers of management, they may not take risks; it is their prime duty to preserve the capital of the trust fund and not to speculate.[8] They may not, for instance, lend money without security, even though investment in a latter-day Leonardo da Vinci might lead to enormous returns through the development of new technology. And since economic

[8] See p. 138 above.

progress in the modern world demands bold speculation, it is a matter of public concern to preserve a proper balance between trust capital and risk capital. The dangers attendant on an excessive accumulation of trust capital produced, for instance, the invention of devices to bar the entail; though, when steps have been taken to restore other trust capital to commerce, as at the Dissolution of the Monasteries, it has not always been with a single-minded intention to redress the balance in the public interest. Fortunately there is a tendency for the balance to redress itself though inflationary finance, and the Welfare State makes charitable trusts both less necessary and less easy to establish. Moreover some of the more enlightened American benefactors have long provided for the progressive spending of capital so as to ensure the winding up even of charitable trusts within a reasonable period. *A fortiori* individuals should not be unduly protected against themselves. They should have ample scope to take risks and, if necessary, go bankrupt. The economic health of a nation is, according to one view, measured by the number of its bankruptcies. Trusts exist to prevent bankruptcies. Hence they should be curbed.

A third explanation, again not incompatible with either of the former is that, even if a settlor be allowed to provide for the future devolution of his property, opportunities for stock-taking should be afforded from time to time. What seemed provident a couple of decades ago may not be wise now. Hence, even if it is desired to keep property in settlement, one settlement should come to an end and another one begin. The need for resettlement every generation[9] was the salvation of the old strict settlement, for it allowed losses to be cut and improvements to be made. The Variation of Trusts Act 1958 allows similar readjustments to be made nowadays. And perhaps the Rule against Perpetuities plays some part to this end.

2. ACCUMULATIONS

A cognate but rather different problem arises where a settlor takes care to vest the *capital* within the perpetuity period but directs that, in the meantime, the *income* should not be paid

[9] See pp. 87–8 above.

out but should be added to capital. Suppose, for instance, that by a will trustees are given property worth £1m. and told to hand it over to the first of the testator's grandchildren to reach the age of twenty-one. Even at common law this gift is perfectly valid. The testator is dead so the beneficiary's parents, that is the testator's children, must be alive; any grandson must be born in their lifetime and so must attain twenty-one, if he ever does, within twenty-one years of their death.

But suppose that the testator also tells the trustees that, until the event occurs, they are not to pay the income to anyone but are to add it to capital—to accumulate it. This has two effects: it ensures a potentially enormous sum for the fortunate grandson who may not yet be born; but does so at the expense of the living who are denied the use, that is the income value, of the fund in the meantime.

The will of Peter Thellusson who died in 1797 took advantage of this gap in the common law to direct that the income of his considerable property be tied up for, as events turned out, fifty-nine years, thereby depriving his widow and children of any benefit from it. Parliament intervened in 1800 to enact a Rule against Accumulations.

In its modern form the basic effect of the statutory rule is to permit accumulation only for certain periods. The first is the life of the settlor—since he could anyway, if he wished, have kept all his money on deposit during his life. The other periods are basically either twenty-one years or the minority of some child alive at the date of the disposition. If attempts are made to accumulate beyond these limits they fail. Thus if a will directs accumulation during the life of the testator's children, it is permitted only for twenty-one years; thereafter the income of the accumulated fund must be paid out to the appropriate beneficiary. Certain accumulations, for instance with the aim of amassing enough money to settle all debts, are excepted from the rule.

Even without the statutory rule, however, if a settlor attempts simultaneously to give property at once to an adult beneficiary and to order accumulation of its income, the donee may disregard the direction to accumulate.

XIV
SECURITY

1. GENERAL

THE point of exacting security from a debtor is to avoid having to prove as an ordinary creditor in his bankruptcy. What does that mean?

If you could be certain, when lending money or selling goods to a person, that he would be solvent when the time for payment came, you would probably not think of taking security from him, except perhaps to be able to put pressure on him if, though able, he was unwilling to pay. To a great extent people do lend money or sell goods without security because they are prepared to trust the borrower or buyer. Nevertheless, the taking of security is a normal part of business.

Personal and real security

Security falls into two broad groups, personal and real security. In the former the creditor insists on having the debt guaranteed by another person; that is to say, he insists on the debtor providing him with another person who agrees to pay if the debtor does not. There may be more than one guarantor, and in the ordinary case the creditor may sue for the whole debt the person who in his opinion is most able to pay. It is also possible for one person merely to indemnify another against the consequences of his giving credit to a third person, with the effect that he too becomes a principal debtor. All these forms of personal security belong to the law of contract and fall entirely outside the field of the law of property. Real security, on the other hand, is certainly a topic of property law.

The purpose of real security is to give a secured creditor something out of which he is entitled to have his debt paid in preference to the unsecured creditors. A segment of the debtor's property, which may be a piece of land, a particular movable chattel, or a number of investments, is set apart as something over which the secured creditor can exercise certain powers enabling him to ensure payment of his debt before any of the unsecured creditors. But lawyers have always been in the habit of saying that the secured creditor has a real interest in the property which is the subject-matter of the security.

Real security can be divided into three classes, namely, possessory security, proprietary security, and charges and non-possessory liens. For ease of exposition two forms of the second—hire-purchase of and retention-of-title clauses in movables—will be treated separately.

2. POSSESSORY SECURITY

Possessory security exists only in respect of tangible personal property, in other words, in respect of movables in the strict sense of the term. It has two main varieties, pledge or pawn, and possessory liens. A possessory lien is the right to retain the possession of the property of another person until a debt owned by that person is paid. In other words, a possessory lien arises only in cases where the thing is already in the possession of the creditor. It may be particular, giving the creditor the right to retain the thing until paid for his work on it, for instance when he has repaired it; or it may be general, giving the creditor the right to retain possession of the thing until the general balance of his account against his debtor is paid, the best-known instance being perhaps that of a solicitor over his client's papers. A lien does not give the person claiming it a right to sell the goods unless that right is expressly given to him by contract or statute.

A pawn or pledge is created, on the other hand, by an actual transfer of the possession by debtor to creditor. It is the only practical way of securing a debt on many kinds of movable objects. For if the whereabouts of a movable object cannot easily be traced from time to time, the only way in which a creditor can take it in security for a debt is to keep it himself under lock and key. It might theoretically be possible for him to acquire a proprietary interest in the thing while leaving the possession with the debtor, but if the latter chose to sell it it would in practice be almost impossible for the creditor to resume control. Pawn or pledge is a form of bailment, but the pawnee has a right to sell the thing if the debt itself is not paid at the proper time. Pawnbrokers, that is to say, persons who carry on the business of taking goods and chattels in pawn, are governed by a special statute, which requires them to be licensed and to observe certain rules in the conduct of their business.

3. PROPRIETARY SECURITY

Although pledge affords excellent security to the creditor, it is awkward for the debtor, for, since he loses possession of the object, he cannot use it. Accordingly, it is not a good way of raising security on anything which, like the plant of a business, should continue to be used if the debtor is to make enough money to pay off the debt. What is wanted in such a case is some arrangement whereby the debtor is left in possession and therefore free to use the object, while the creditor has the right to take possession if the debt is not paid at the proper time, and to sell the object or perhaps even to retain it as owner, free from any rights which the debtor may have in it.

It is easy for us now to think of these various powers as constituting in combination a separate institution which needs no justification for its existence except that it furnishes an excellent form of security. But it was originally difficult to see how one person could confer these powers on another person unless he vested in him either the full ownership of the thing in question or some more limited right in the nature of property. And so this form of security is called proprietary security.

Since the creditor has an actual title to the thing, he can safely allow the debtor to retain possession of it; though, for this kind of security to operate perfectly, both the thing must be readily traceable and the right acquired by the creditor must be good against third parties as well as against the debtor himself.

Bills of sale

Proprietary security can have for its object both movables and immovables. A person may desire to raise money upon the security of his furniture or all the contents of his house. In that case he may execute a bill of sale in favour of the lender. The name is confusing but ineradicable. A bill of sale may have as its purpose the out-and-out alienation of a movable, but may also be merely a transfer by way of security so that the lender's interest ends on repayment.

It is obvious that security of this kind could work serious injustice to the other creditors, who may well have trusted the debtor on the strength of his apparent ownership of the goods in his possession. Accordingly, the Bills of Sale Acts, 1878 and 1882, were passed in order to ensure the publicity of such transactions by requiring them to be recorded in a register. If they are not so registered within twenty-one days, they are void as against a trustee in bankruptcy, and indeed against any person executing judgment against the debtor.

As soon as they are registered they are noted by trade-protection agencies whose function it is to notify such things to their clients; and a registered bill of sale is likely to be the end of the debtor's chances of raising money.

Mortgages

When a landowner desires to raise money, he is not likely to offer *possession* to the lender. A factory is not a gold watch. The lender is merely investing his money on security and would normally rely on the borrower to retain possession and manage efficiently in order to meet the interest payments on the loan. But if he is not to take possession the only other thing he can take (or so it used to be thought) is ownership of the borrower's interest. In the ordinary case this meant that the borrower conveyed his fee simple to the lender in return for the money advanced. The parties do not, of course, intend an out-and-out sale; and so the conveyance would contain an obligation on the lender to reconvey the fee simple on repayment of the loan just as the pawnbroker must hand back the gold watch. From the borrower's point of view he would redeem his property in both cases, but in one he gets back a fee simple, in the other possession. When the mortgage is made, however, the lender needs to know at what date he can, if he wants to, call in his loan. Consequently the practice grew, and still persists, of stipulating for repayment six months after the mortgage. The creditor can, and usually will, leave the money on loan for a much longer period, but, in case his fortunes change, needs a fairly early date on which he may recover. All his major remedies to protect his security still arise on that date.

Just as the lender can call in, the borrower can repay, at any time after this date; and if he dies his successors can repay and redeem. Similarly he can sell his interest in the property to a buyer who may then redeem. Now some name had to be found for this asset which the borrower still owned. If he has land worth £10,000 and, in return for a loan of £2,000, conveys the fee simple to the lender as security, he is still worth £8,000. This asset is his and he can sell at that price; and the buyer, on repaying the £2,000 can recover the fee simple. The borrower's interest came to be known as his 'equity of redemption' and has passed into colloquial American, where a phrase like 'the equity in my Cadillac' is instantly comprehensible.

But a system in which a creditor technically has the fee simple (worth only £2,000) while the asset worth £8,000 is called an 'equity of redemption' is unnecessarily artificial. For practical purposes the debtor was and is regarded as still owning the property and the creditor, or mortgagee as he is called, as having a mere security. The draftsmen of the 1925 legislation knew this perfectly well and tried to put it right. Unfortunately the method they were forced to adopt is largely a waste of mental effort.

They decided to abolish the method of granting a mortgage by conveying the fee simple to the lender. They did not, however, dare to reduce the lender's interest to a mere list of remedies. Mortgagees had always, as security, taken an estate in the land—as real to their lawyers as the watch to the pawnbroker—and the draftsmen feared an outcry and a freezing of the money market if, on 1 January 1926, lenders found themselves deprived of an estate in land. Consequently they had to give the lenders an estate in land; but here they were trapped by their own logic. Section 1 of the Law of Property Act was to say that the only possible legal estates were the fee simple and the lease. So if lenders were still to have an estate there was only one left for them. Mortgages of a fee simple had to take place by the grant of a lease to the lender. The artificiality of this is apparent from the fact that it is no normal lease: it is for a prodigiously long period (such as 3,000 years) at no rent; and when the loan is repaid it dies the death.

A second method—that of granting a security interest which is basically a list of powers and remedies—was provided by the introduction of the 'charge by way of legal mortgage' and this is nowadays the form most commonly used. Its statutory definition, however, provides an even more bizarre creation: the chargee is to have the same protection powers and remedies as if there had been created in his favour a term of 3,000 years without impeachment of waste but subject to a proviso for cesser on redemption.

Enforcement of security

The mortgagee's rights are given him for one purpose only— to secure repayment of his loan and interest. They may seem rather harsh to the modern reader but were designed to do justice in a society of which two things were true: money was readily available for loan on mortgage so that a borrower pressed by one lender could borrow from a second and pay off the first; and the security commonly offered was frequently the business premises of the borrower. Nowadays the private lender prefers the stock market where there is the chance of the capital appreciation which is denied him by a loan on mortgage; and most borrowers mortgage their home.

The mortgagee has three important rights, but a fourth will be added for the sake of historical completeness.

(i) *Sale* Undoubtedly the most powerful remedy is for the lender, having called in his loan without success, to sell the thing mortgaged and pay himself off. In the case of land his sale takes the fee simple from the borrower and vests it in the purchaser free from the mortgage and from the borrower's equity of redemption. These are overreached and shifted to the money in the hands of the selling mortgagee who holds as trustee to pay himself off, then any subsequent mortgages, with the balance (if any) going to the borrower.[1]

[1] The equity of redemption is overreached by LPA 1925 s 2. In other cases of

(ii) *Receiver* The power of sale protects the lender's rights to his capital. He may, however be quite content to leave that on loan but wish to secure prompt payment of the interest. If the property mortgaged is producing an income—if, for example, it is a block of offices—then he may, after due notice to the borrower, appoint a receiver of the rents whose main duties are to collect them, pay the mortgagee his interest, and hand the rest to subsequent mortgagees or the borrower.

(iii) *Possession* If the property involved is business premises, then the mortgagee may well be able to sell the fee simple without obtaining vacant possession. But if it is the borrower's home no one will buy from the lender with the borrower and family still there. Strictly speaking the lender is automatically entitled to possession for he has a lease of the premises, or a legal charge giving him the same rights. In the case of a dwelling-house, however, statute now permits the court to delay a order for possession in his favour if the borrower looks like being able to repay the loan or meet the instalments due.

(iv) *Foreclosure* If the lender wishes to acquire the property as his own and hold it free of the borrower's interest he must apply to the court for a decree of foreclosure. The borrower is then given six months in which to find the money and repay the loan; on his failure to do so the court order takes the fee simple from him and vests it in the lender free for ever of the borrower's rights and of those of subsequent mortagees. In practice this remedy is hardly ever used. If the debtor has any equity at all in the property—that is if its value exceeds the loan—he will either borrow elsewhere or ask the court to order a sale and split the proceeds.

Restraints on the lender

The courts of Equity always kept a tight hold on lenders to ensure that they obtained adequate security but no more and would look closely at substance rather than form. In particular a lender was not allowed to make a mortgage irredeemable: someone who has handed over money in return for a property

overreaching (see pp. 110, 112 above) the section requires payment to independent trustees; but no one lending on mortgage would tolerate that.

interest which is to be his for ever is a buyer, not a lender, and the transaction is a sale and purchase, not a loan of money on security. To this there is one exception where the borrower is not a human being but a limited company. Debentures, which are documents issued by companies to acknowledge their indebtedness and may relate to both secured and unsecured loans, may, by statute, be made irredeemable. The courts restrict the transaction to one of security in two other ways. Firstly an option to buy contained in the mortgage is void because the courts will not permit security to transform itself into sale. Secondly when a loan is secured on any property then a collateral advantage fettering *that* property must end when the loan is repaid and the property redeemed, for otherwise it returns to the borrower in a worse condition than when it was mortgaged. The detriment to him is, of course, balanced by a benefit to the lender; but that benefit is not required to *secure* the loan which, by definition, has been repaid. Thus if A's neighbour lends him money on condition that he be given (*a*) a mortgage of A's house to secure the loan and (*b*) a right of way over the house for ever then, when A repays the loan and redeems the mortgage on his house, the easement dies. If, however, the collateral advantage affects property other than that mortgaged it may be valid after repayment and redemption. If A, on taking his loan, mortgaged one house but gave an easement over another the latter would bind for ever. It was part of the price of, *but not of the security for*, the loan.

In this jurisdiction consumer protection statutes now give the courts wide powers to adjust extortionate credit bargains with individuals.

Priorities

It has already been said that one advantage attaching to proprietory security is that the debtor can retain possession and use the thing mortgaged. Another advantage is that successive securities can be created over the same thing so that, for instance, land may be mortgaged to X to secure a debt of half its value, and then to Y for a quarter. The borrower's equity is thus worth one quarter. This possibility that a thing may be mortgaged successively to several persons may easily give rise to difficult questions of priority.

It is not the practice for lenders to advance money up to the full value of what is mortgaged; indeed trustees are bound to leave a good safety margin. However, the value of the thing may decline seriously and mortgagees may not be able to realize their security in time. Moreover there is always the chance that by some fraud or other a debtor may induce a person to advance money upon a security which the lender thinks is sufficient but which in fact is not. The total value of the thing may then be insufficient to allow the mortgagees to realize their security in full.

If there is only one mortgagee the solution is simple: he realizes as much as he can and, for the rest, falls back on his personal action in competition with other unsecured creditors. But there may be several successive mortgagees and enough to satisfy some but not all of them. The question then arises in what order they are to be paid their debts, if indeed they are not to share and share alike.

Where land is mortgaged then, if it is unregistered, the first mortgagee will take the title deeds. If it is registered the owner's Land Certificate will be deposited at the Registry. Anyone who is approached with a request that he lend money on a mortgage at once asks to see the would-be borrower's title deeds (or Land Certificate) in order to ascertain whether he really has a right to the land that he is offering to mortgage. If he finds the title deeds in the borrower's possession he takes them along with the mortgage deed. If the title is registered then he makes sure that the Register will be altered before he lends a penny.

If, however, the would-be borrower cannot produce the requisite documents then the lender knows either that the borrower does not own the land at all or, more likely, that there is already a prior mortgage in existence. So he will contact the prior mortgagee to learn how much the borrower has already had, whether he is paying interest promptly, whether the first lender is bound to lend more, and so on. He is then one step along the road to knowing how much money he can safely advance on another mortgage. For a first mortgagee who has taken all the proper steps takes priority over all other mortgagees; and it is not unreasonable that he should do so, because the others should have notice of the amount covered by his mortgage and of its terms.

However in the case of unregistered land only one lender—the first—will have the deeds, and he will be safe. But if there are two or more subsequent mortgages some other method must be found of determining priority among them. That method is registration. Thus a person asked to lend money on the security of unregistered land will do two things: ask to see the title deeds and search the Land Charges Register.[2] Given the existence of a register relating to the particular property mortgaged, this technique is cheap and efficient. It is used for registered land, bills of sale, charges by limited companies, and mortgages of ships and aircraft. Indeed—though in a quite different and private way—it is used for dealing in interests in funds as is explained in the next section.

Interests in funds

So far mortgages have been discussed mainly in relation to land itself or, strictly speaking, legal estates therein. But the assets of beneficiaries owning limited interests such as life estates and remainders are, as we have seen, also valuable. Just as they may be given away or sold, so they may be mortgaged.

Thus, to return to our standard example of the £1m. settled on fifty-year old A for life, remainder to B absolutely. The latter's fee simple absolute in remainder is worth half a million (and growing as A ages) and is good security for a loan. B, however, has no documents proving his worth for his remainder was given him by a trust instrument. If the tangible property in which the million is invested is held on trust for sale this document will be in the hands of the trustees for sale; if not there will be a settlement with A having the legal title to any land comprised therein but the trustees of the settlement having the trust instrument.

So the lender will first approach the trustees who, at B's request, must produce the document which made B rich; he will then value the investments in which the fund subsists, ascertain A's age, and calculate the value of B's remainder. On making the loan this remainder will be mortgaged to him by the old method: he will take a conveyance of it with a proviso for reconveyance when he is paid off. To prevent B's

---

[2] These general principles are subject to refinements dictated by banking practice which cannot be considered here.

approaching anyone else and borrowing money from a lender ignorant of the first mortgage there is only one thing that he can do. He cannot register in any public register for the Land Charges Register and the Land Register deal only with mortgages affecting *legal* estates. Thus, in a strict settlement, if the land in which the fund is invested is registered, it is A's name which appears as the proprietor. Our lender, however, is taking a mortgage of B's interest. But he is safe if he gives *notice* of his mortgage to the trustees and perfectly safe if he writes a memorandum of the mortgage on the trust instrument. This protection operates in two ways. In the first place if A sells the legal estate (i.e. the land itself) the purchaser will pay the money, not to A, but to the trustees. In the second place any later lender to B will first examine the trust instrument and will see that B was given the remainder but has mortgaged it.

The same principle in fact applies to gifts or sales of the interests in the fund. Thus the trust instrument forms, as it were, a private register of all dealings affecting interests in the fund.

The function of land mortgages

Since the days when the law of land mortgages was worked out two important changes have taken place. Firstly, ordinary people and not just the wealthy or the business community enter into mortgages to acquire their homes. Secondly, in this field, the private lender has almost disappeared along with the form of the mortgage that expected periodic payment only of *interest* with the capital advanced being repaid in a lump sum.

Nowadays the great mortgagees are the Building Societies who lend money to enable citizens to acquire a home and stipulate for repayment of both capital and income by instalments, so that after twenty or so years the debt and the mortgage are both extinguished. Their business is to earn money in the form of interest on loans made to purchasers of houses and mortgages are merely security for those loans. But they are *trustees* of their funds for their depositors. In one sense, therefore, the great lenders are merely conduit pipes. Ordinary people hand over their savings to them and receive interest on the money; and the funds thus amassed are lent to other ordinary people at interest.

Thus a mortgage looks two ways. The lender benefits the borrower by financing him, usually in the purchase of something like a home; the borrower benefits the lender by offering him a sound and safe investment. Any problems that might arise over a lender who suddenly needs his money back are solved by the interposition of Building Societies so that both lender and borrower are relieved from the anxieties of a one-to-one transaction.

4. EQUITABLE CHARGES AND LIENS

A third type of real security involves no transfer of either possession or property to a creditor, namely equitable charges and liens. These give no right to take possession or to foreclose the debtor's interest, but can be enforced only by sale of the object over which they exist. That sale may have to be by order of a court, though the power of sale may be bargained for by the creditor in the agreement by which it is created.

Such charges or liens can be created by mere agreement between the parties, and in effect create a trust in favour of the creditor. Charges, as such securities are usually called, can be made for any purpose, but will only be enforced if the creditor has given valuable consideration, that is to say, they cannot be enforced against persons who have established them merely by way of gift. A very common way of creating a charge is to deposit the title deeds of property with a bank, which then has full security for the overdraft it has agreed to allow. Incidentally, if the debtor, when depositing the deeds, intends to create a mortgage, an equitable mortgage is at once created. In practice the bank may require a written document, in order to preserve evidence of the agreement between the parties, and if it wishes to acquire a power of sale without the order of a court, will insist on the execution of a deed.

Vendor's and purchaser's liens
The term *lien* is generally used to denote equitable securities which arise not from any agreement between the parties but by operation of law. The best known are the vendor's lien and the purchaser's lien, both of which are confined to sales of land.[3]

[3] The seller's lien over goods operates at common law.

Once an agreement to purchase land has been made, the buyer is entitled, should the vendor fail to convey it to him, to a decree of specific performance, that is to say, a decree ordering the vendor to convey the land to him. But, in contrast to the rule governing the sale of goods, he is not yet the owner of the land at law. However, equity regards that as done which ought to be done and therefore, since the purchaser ought to be made owner of the land, he is already regarded as owner for the purposes of equity, or, in technical language, he has the equitable interest in the land.[4]

If the purchaser is unable or unwilling to pay the price when the vendor is ready and willing to convey, the latter may lawfully withhold conveyance, but even if he does convey, and thus loses both possession and title, he still has an equitable lien on the land for the price. For equity again applies its maxim that what ought to be done is to be regarded as having been done, and since it is only fair that the purchaser should give security for the price, holds that the vendor has an equitable interest in the land to the extent of the purchase-money owing him. He is entitled to be placed in the same situation (so far as a court of equity can place him) as if it had been paid.

Similarly, if a purchaser has paid the whole or part of the price, but for some reason or other the sale goes off, he has a lien over the land to recover what he has paid.

What is the point of these various equitable charges and liens? How and how far do they put persons entitled to them in a better position than unsecured creditors? They really give the creditor a privilege, that is to say, a prior right to be paid his debt out of the proceeds if the thing over which they exist is sold, and if necessary the power to insist on such a sale. Thus if the debtor is insolvent, the creditor can insist on having his debt paid by the trustee in bankruptcy up to the value that the thing on which it is secured has fetched or would fetch on a sale; and he is entitled to be paid this in preference to the ordinary creditors.

This is perhaps not unreasonable; but what if the debtor sells the thing in question to a third party? Does the latter take subject to the charge or lien? Formerly equity applied to the equitable interest created by the charge or lien the regular

[4] See p. 61 above.

principle that an equitable interest binds anyone who takes
the thing subject to it otherwise than as a bona fide purchaser
for value without notice of the interest. Now, since 1925, an
equitable charge or lien over land must be registered if it is to
bind any purchaser, but if so registered it binds him even if
he has no notice.

Floating charges

One special variety of charges should be noted, the *floating
charge*. It is a common practice for companies, if they are short
of money, to borrow in the market in return for debentures
secured by a floating charge. This is a charge on all the assets
of the company, but it does not prevent the company from
disposing of its assets in the ordinary course of business. It
must indeed continually dispose of its products and stock-in-
trade if it is to earn money and to pay the interest on the
debentures. However, the floating charge may at any time become a fixed charge in accordance with the terms contained
in the debentures, the commonest term being that the debenture-holders may produce that result by giving notice if the
interest ceases to be paid or the company becomes insolvent.
The charge is then said to become crystallized and settles on
the specific articles of property belonging at that moment to
the company instead of affecting the changing assets considered as a fund. From that moment the company can no
longer dispose of anything, even in the ordinary course of
business, without the leave of the debenture-holders. In practice they appoint a receiver to manage the business on their
account. The charge gives the debenture-holders preference
over the unsecured creditors.

5. HIRE-PURCHASE

At the present day one of the commonest transactions is hire-
purchase. It is a somewhat complex legal figure much affected
by consumer protection laws; and in an elementary book we
can give only the basic structure. The need for such a type of
transaction arises from two perfectly rational desires. The first
is that of ordinary citizens to acquire goods now and pay later
rather than save up and find that inflation has pushed the price

beyond their means. The second is the need of the supplier until the price is paid to enjoy some security over the goods both in the hands of his customer and of any third party.

If the supplier simply sells on credit then he parts with ownership at once and has merely a personal, unsecured, claim for the price against his customer and no claim at all against anyone else who acquires the goods from the original customer. At the other extreme, if he merely hires out the goods, then he retains full ownership and, when the hiring period elapses, may reclaim them wherever they may be. But he would probably not particularly want the return of used goods and his customer would hope that some day they might be his.

As its name suggests, the contract of hire-purchase is a mixture of two legal figures: hire and sale. The customer hires the goods for a period, at the end of which, if he has paid all the instalments, he has an option to buy them for a nominal sum. The supplier is bound to sell eventually, if called upon to do so, but, since the buyer does not have to exercise the option and cannot do so until he has paid all the instalments, there is no sale until then. Further the option merely empowers, and does not bind, the customer: he has never *agreed* to buy so as to be able to pass title under the Sale of Goods Act.[5]

The traditional analysis of this transaction, then, assumes that only two interests may subsist in chattels—ownership and possession—and that the former remains with the supplier until the customer exercises his option to buy and acquire ownership. Perhaps a more realistic approach, and one known to the law for centuries, is to recognize that there are two *proprietory* interests in the goods: two *estates*, that of the supplier diminishing in value while that of the customer increases. English law applies this with perfect ease to the dwindling life estate or lease and the growing remainder or reversion.

If one hires a television set for three months then one pays only for the value of possession, plus something for depreciation. But if one acquires the same set on hire-purchase over three months each weekly instalment would be far greater. Although, on the traditional view, one still merely has possession for the period with an option to become owner at the

See p. 48 above.

end, some part of each instalment is the price of a fraction of ownership.

The approach put forward has been used by English courts to deal with a very practical problem. Suppose, in our example of the television set on hire-purchase over three months, the customer pays punctually ten weekly instalments but then, in breach of his agreement, sells the set to an innocent purchaser and disappears. In an action by the supplier against this purchaser the traditional view that the original customer had, and could transfer, only possession means that the purchaser must either return the set or pay its value. But this consequence is manifestly unjust, since the plaintiff has already had five-sixths of the value. A recognition that he has merely an estate in the chattel with a present value of one-sixth of the set's worth would protect the innocent buyer and prevent over-compensation of the supplier. The traditional approach would award him money for something he does not own.

6. RETENTION-OF-TITLE CLAUSES

A similar problem arises with a device recently imported from civil law. Under it a seller of raw materials seeks to reserve the ownership of them until he has been paid; and, by further refinements, stipulates that he is to have ownership for the same purpose of any product into which they are incorporated, or of their proceeds of sale. The aim of this scheme is to ensure that if, between delivery and payment, the buyer becomes insolvent then the seller will have a prior claim on certain of the assets. Four points may be made about this device.

Firstly, as we have emphasized earlier, the intention of the parties to a sale of goods as to the moment when property passes may be decisive as between them, but not against third parties.[6]

Secondly, there is something artificial about purporting to retain ownership of property which is organically incorporated into something else. If a seller of hay stipulates that he is to remain owner until paid there must be some point in the digestive tract of the buyer's horse where the seller's ownership comes to an end.

[6] See p. 66 above.

Thirdly, the device proceeds on the assumption that the law admits of only two interests in goods, namely ownership and possession. As we have just argued, there may be circumstances where the estate concept is both more useful and more true to reality.

Finally, the purpose of retaining ownership is only to provide security for payment. There is no objection to this provided that other potential creditors can be warned. The simplest, indeed the only practicable, way to do this is by some system of registration. The USA utilizes such a system and the Uniform Commercial Code cuts through the thicket of concepts by applying it to any transaction (regardless of its form) which is intended to create a security interest in movable property.

XV

SUCCESSION

1. GENERAL

A question which can never be avoided in any system of law is, what is to happen to a person's property when he dies? The question is complicated by a number of factors of which the most important are the facts that, along with corporeal things such as land or goods, the estate of a deceased person may include debts due to him from other persons and, on the other hand, he may have died owing money to yet other persons; moreover, almost all modern states, insist on taking part of the property by way of taxation. It is therefore, very practical, if not absolutely necessary, for the estate to be administered before it is distributed among the various persons, if there are more than one, who are ultimately to benefit from the estate.[1] In other words, debts must be got in and other debts paid, and taxes also must be paid, before the ultimate distribution takes place. It would be possible to choose one or more of the ultimate beneficiaries and impose upon them the duty of administration; and this is done in many countries. It is not the plan which is pursued in England. Here administration is carried out by so-called *personal representatives*, whose duty it is to administer the estate, pay taxes, and then distribute what is left according to the provisions of a will left by the deceased, or, in default of a will, in accordance with rules laid down by the law. To the extent that the estate is not disposed of by will, there is said to be an intestacy.

Accordingly, the law of succession falls naturally into three parts, the administration of estates, wills, and intestate succession. However, the law is most easily understood if one deals first with wills.

[1] In this context the word 'estate' is used to mean all the deceased's property.

2. WILLS

It has long been the custom for most English people of substance to make wills. No doubt the initial impulse came from the medieval church, which desired legacies, but will-making remained a popular and even necessary practice because the old law of intestate succession was felt to be unsatisfactory. Starting with the great reforms enacted in the Administration of Estates Act, 1925, the law has been progressively improved, so that the average person may safely die without making a will and leave the law to take its course; and will-making may possibly be less common than hitherto.

To make a valid will, a person must be in his or her right mind. This is all that is required of a member of the forces or the merchant navy on active service. Any other person must also be of full age and must state his wishes in writing, his signature being attested by two witnesses, present at the same time, who then sign in his presence. The fact that a benefit is given to a witness in the will does not make him an incompetent witness, but neither he nor his spouse can take any benefit which the will purports to give. Thus, in an indirect way, the impartiality of the witnesses is as far as possible ensured.

A will can be subsequently altered. This is usually done by adding a codicil, which must itself be executed in the same way as a will. A will may be revoked either by the making of a subsequent will which expressly revokes it or is totally incompatible with it, or by deliberately destroying the document. The interpretation of wills has given rise to untold litigation, and the rules and principles that have been developed in the resultant case law fill many volumes of abstruse and intricate doctrine. All of this would be entirely out of place in an elementary book of this kind.

A testator need not deal with the whole of his property by will. He may, for instance, distribute only some of the lands in his possession or may give away specific sums of money leaving a balance unaccounted for, although he will normally leave the 'residue' to someone. As to all the things not dealt with in the will, however, there is an intestacy. In other words, unlike a Roman citizen in the ancient world, an Englishman may die partly testate and partly intestate.

Freedom of Testation

The next question is, what may a testator do in his will. We may leave on one side such topics as the appointment of a guardian to look after infant children; our concern is only with property. Now in many countries a testator is not free to give away his property entirely as he chooses. The moral claims of his family are translated into a legal entitlement to some of it, and he can leave by will only what is left over.

The basic principle of the common law, however, is that of complete freedom of testation: a man may endow a college or a cats' home and leave his wife and children to starve.[2] The harshness of this principle was recognized in New Zealand early this century and the statutory amendments to it there adopted have spread throughout the Commonwealth. The new technique does not, however, give the family any automatic right to a share; instead it adopts the more costly course of allowing the courts to intervene. The system was adopted by English legislation in 1938 and has since frequently been amended and litigated.

The current legislation preserves the main features of the pattern. It leaves the testator free to make his will without marking off any property which he may not touch; correspondingly no one in his family is guaranteed a share in the inheritance. Instead they, or other dependants, may ask the court to modify either the will or the rules of intestacy or the combination of both and make the applicant an award out of the deceased's estate.

3. INTESTACY

Although will-making has long been prevalent among persons of substance, the law of intestate succession is very important, not only because persons who have little property do not usually go to the trouble of making a will, but also because there are always a certain number of persons who die possessed of property but, from want of age or sanity, have been unable to make a will.

[2] In the more distant past there were restrictions. Indeed the ancient common law went so far as to forbid any will at all of freehold land, leaving it to devolve on the heir.

There are two different ways of looking at the question what is to happen to a person's property when he dies. According to one school of thought, certain near relatives are entitled, by the mere fact of their near relationship, to shares in the estate, though some compromise may have to be made with the deceased by allowing him to dispose of some portion of it. If, however, he has not chosen to dispose of such portion, they are entitled to succeed. This way of thinking starts from the assumption that the family is more important than the individual, that some at least of the deceased's estate has probably come to him from his family, and should go back to his family on his death. The next question is to decide which persons for this purpose are to be looked upon as the family; and very different solutions are to be found in different countries. But everywhere the rules of intestate succession are derived from the prevailing conception of the family and are, as it were, an appendix to family law.

Now the English point of view is very different. Individualism is strong and the family weak. It seems to be assumed that a person—a man, at any rate—has made his money for himself and should be allowed to dispose of his estate as he wishes. If he derives much property from his family it is for the family to protect itself by means of a settlement, in such a way that no one shall succeed to the settled property whether by will or on an intestacy. It follows as a natural and logical consequence that in laying down rules of intestate succession the legislature should try to find out what the average man of property would naturally have done with his property if he had made a will, and then to lay down rules of intestate succession which will give the result which he would probably have ensured if he had made a will. Obviously the best way to ascertain what the average man of property would have done is to find out what in actual fact a large number of men of property have done. This was what was done before the Administration of Estates Act was passed in 1925. In fact the task of making an average substitute for a will was made easier by the existence of standard forms of wills in the books of precedents used by solicitors and conveyancing counsel. These forms had tended to canalize wills so that their main outlines were fairly uniform; and all that was needed was for the legislature to choose the arrangements which conformed to its ideas of fairness and therefore could be assumed to represent what would have been the wishes of a fair-minded testator. Changes in the value of money, among other factors, have made certain minor changes necessary, but the general structure of the law is the same as in the Act of 1925.

The first point to be made is that there is complete equality between the sexes and that no preference is given to anyone on account of age. Primogeniture, which was once a salient feature of English law, has been abolished apart from the succession to entailed interests.

Secondly, the only persons who can conceivably succeed on intestacy are the surviving spouse, the issue, and the four grandparents of the deceased and their issue *ad infinitum*. Thus, failing issue of the deceased, parents can take, and also brothers and sisters and their issue, grandparents, and uncles and aunts and their issue, the less remote excluding the more remote. If the deceased leaves no relatives within the family group, the estate goes to the Crown as ownerless property (*bona vacantia*), but compassionate allowances may be made to dependants, whether kindred or not.

Thirdly, all other relatives take subject to the rights of a surviving spouse. In contrast to earlier times, that person is now greatly favoured. He or she now always takes all the so-called personal chattels, which correspond to what would usually be called personal belongings, for instance, household furniture and effects. In addition the surviving spouse is entitled to a sum of money (the 'statutory legacy') which ensures that he or she will take the whole of small estates and that his or her share of the estate will be greater if there are no issue than if there are. If the estate is reasonably substantial and the spouse and children survive, the former gets the statutory legacy, half the rest absolutely and the income of the other half until death, when it is divided among the children. Thus the traditional pattern of a life estate (or interest) with a vested remainder in fee simple is still followed in the modern law. The spouse may insist on taking the home instead of the statutory legacy, with any necessary financial adjustment being made.

One other point remains to be mentioned. All these classes, issue and more remote relatives, with the exception of parents and grandparents, may possibly include persons who are under age. Now, it would be awkward to allow a share of the estate to vest in such a person because he or she might then die unmarried under age and there would be a second intestacy, which would thus undo the effect of the vesting; accordingly it is the regular practice in settlements to provide that interests shall vest in persons only upon their reaching majority or on their marriage under that age. The Administration of Estates Act, 1925, copied that practice by providing that the shares of estates devolving on all classes of persons other than the surviving spouse, parents, or grandparents should be held upon statutory trusts for those persons who are alive at the death of the intestate and who either attain majority or marry, with the powers of maintenance, advancement, &c., which are usually contained in such trusts.

4. ADMINISTRATION OF ESTATES

So far we have discussed the ultimate distribution of an estate. If we had followed the chronological order, we should have started by discussing the administration of the estate, for, as we said at the outset, distribution takes place only after administration is complete. However, we have followed the more practical course, because administration varies to some extent in accordance with whether there is a testacy or an intestacy.

In the first place, the manner of appointing the personal representatives will be different. A testator will normally appoint an executor to administer his estate as his personal representative. If there is no will there can be no executor and some other means must be found of appointing a personal representative, who will, in that case, be called an administrator; though an administrator may also have to be appointed in some other cases, especially if a will contains no appointment of an executor.

The executor derives his office and powers from the testator and may at once take various steps which will bind the estate; but to regularize his position he must obtain a grant of probate. This he does by depositing at a Probate Registry the original will together with the executor's oath, i.e. an affidavit verifying the will and the testator's death and undertaking to administer the estate, and an Inland Revenue affidavit giving detailed particulars of the property contained in the estate, to enable the authorities to calculate the taxes payable. He then receives a grant of probate with a copy of the will and is fully authorized to act as the personal representative of the deceased. This, the normal procedure, is called probate in common form; but if there is a dispute about the validity or genuineness of the will, for instance on the ground that the testator was actuated by undue influence when he made it, probate must be sought in solemn form, which is equivalent to an action. A grant of probate may be revoked if, for instance, a later valid will is found but, being a court order, protects the executor until revoked.

If there is no executor, some person interested in having the estate administered applies for letters of administration. He may be a person entitled to succeed on intestacy or even a creditor, if the estate is thought to be insolvent. The applicant must take steps similar to those taken by an executor seeking probate except that he must, if there is no will, swear an affidavit to that effect and, since he has not been entrusted by the deceased with the administration of his estate, one or more sureties may have to be provided. Once letters of administration have been granted, the administrator becomes, like the executor, the personal representative of the deceased. But since there is always some little time between the death and the grant, and in the interval it is not known who will be the administrator, the estate is for the time being automatically vested in the President of the Family Division of the High Court.

The personal representative succeeds automatically to all the rights of the deceased, in so far as they do not die with him, as is the case, for instance, with a claim for damages for defamation. Thus he can claim property which belonged to the deceased and bring actions on debts due to him. He can in the same way be sued to recover property belonging to someone else which the deceased possessed at his death and he can be sued on debts due from the deceased to third persons. In all these cases he acts not in his personal capacity but as a representative. Thus anything he acquires he acquires for the estate and anything he relinquishes or pays he relinquishes or pays in his representative capacity, that is to say, he does not make himself personally liable but only the estate. If, therefore, the estate is insolvent, he must pay all he can out of the estate but cannot be made personally liable for the residue. However, he must pay the debts before distributing the estate to the beneficiaries, or must keep enough in hand to pay them. If he does not, he may find that he has to pay them out of his own pocket.

The administration of an estate may be a complicated business. For a testor may leave his property to different persons in different ways, and he may owe debts of different kinds. He may make specific or general bequests and then leave the residue to another person; a specific bequest will be of some specific thing such as his car, whereas a general bequest will be, for instance, of a stated sum of money. Now, the debts are to be paid in the first instance out of residue, but if the residue does not suffice, then the other bequests must be drawn on according to rules which are too detailed to be set down here. Again, it may be that the estate is insolvent. If all the debts are of one class, then the creditors divide proportionately what is left after funeral expenses and the costs of administration have been defrayed. But if there are several classes of debts, some, for example, being secured and others unsecured, they will rank in order of priority, one class of creditors being allowed to satisfy themselves before the others lower down the list. Again a detailed description of the rules would be inappropriate here.

The crucial point to grasp, however, is that a personal representative is given, by LPA 1925 s. 2, the familiar overreaching powers. If during administration, he needs to sell off any property, a purchaser in good faith who pays the price to the personal representative is fully protected. The interests of the beneficiaries of the deceased's estate are shifted to the money.

XVI

REGISTRATION

REGISTRATION is a familiar device for preserving evidence and guaranteeing its truth, most familiar to the ordinary man in the form of registration of births, marriages, and deaths. Even in that form it is not very old in England so far as the State itself is concerned; before 1837 there was little besides various ecclesiastical registers, the most important of which were the parish registers maintained by incumbents of the Church of England. For property of various kinds it is much younger, younger than in most civilized countries.

Registration has been accepted wholeheartedly for ships, for bills of sale, and for various kinds of companies; and there has been no difficulty in insisting on companies keeping registers of shares and shareholders. Moreover, the practice of proving wills has always carried with it registration.

With land the story has been very different. The obvious advantages attaching to registration have had to fight against many adverse forces, of which the most important have been the desire of landowners and their lawyers to keep transactions secret and the difficulty of placing all the immensely complicated mass of interests that may coexist in land on a single register. During the latter half of the nineteenth century there were among reformers of real property law two opposing schools of thought, the one insisting that registration should be pushed forward as rapidly as possible, the other insisting on its difficulty without a preliminary simplification of the law and on the probability that it would be found unnecessary once the law was simplified. The dispute between the two schools helped to prevent anything being done on either side, but eventually the simplifiers won. Registration has been extended greatly in many ways, but perhaps not so much as if the movement in favour of it had alone held the field.

Registration of incumbrances

There are two forms of registration as regards land. The most limited form goes back for many purposes only as far as the 1925 legislation, and concerns charges and other collateral transactions relating to land, such as mortgages, judgments, restrictive covenants, and estate contracts, but not the central line of documents which go to make a title to land. So far as this form of registration goes, a purchaser's solicitor must search in public registers for all incumbrances on the title, but he must look for evidence of the devolution of the fee simple to the title deeds disclosed to him by the vendor's solicitor.

These registers of incumbrances are so-called 'names registers', that is to say, the incumbrances are entered against the names of the persons creating them. They are therefore not always as easy to search with any guarantee of success as if the incumbrances were entered against the plots of land described in a cadastral survey. This is particularly the case with restrictive covenants, of which the original covenantor's name may no longer be known. Yet the register is conclusive: no registrable incumbrance binds a purchaser unless it is registered, but a registered incumbrance binds him whether he has succeeded in tracing it in the register or not. This form of registration is probably only a half-way house to registration of title, and meanwhile statute provides compensation for certain losses caused by its defects.

Registration of title

Registration of title is the natural culmination of land registration. Before land is put on the register it has to be identified by reference to a map, and if necessary its boundaries have to be surveyed. The holder's title has then to be proved to the satisfaction of the Land Registrar.

The land may be registered with an absolute, a qualified, a possessory, or a good leasehold title. Only the last three require explanation here.

A qualified title is one which is granted when an absolute title is applied for but some particular defect appears in the title which prevents the Registrar from registering it as absolute. It

215 Registration 215

is then registered subject to the specified defect. The Registrar may in certain circumstances later convert a qualified into an absolute title.

A possessory title is subject to any defects which may turn out to have existed at the time of registration, but is guaranteed as regards anything that may happen afterwards. In other words, the title prior to first registration must still be investigated as if it had not been registered. The Registrar may in certain circumstances convert a possessory into an absolute title and must do so after a certain number of years have elapsed.

A good leasehold title is the same as an absolute title except that it does not guarantee the lessor's title to lease the land. This again the Registrar may convert in certain circumstances into an absolute title.

Except for a few reasons, the most important of which is that the registered owner knew of a defect in his title, an owner whose title is registered as absolute normally has an absolute title against all the world and cannot be disturbed. If, however, the Register has to be rectified, monetary compensation may be made. This makes it possible for the Registrar not to spend unnecessary time or trouble in investigating titles which appear sufficiently sound on their face.

Not only the title itself appears on the register, but also anything that prevents or restricts the registered owner from dealing with the land. Matters such as estate contracts and restrictive covenants are protected by notice. A 'restriction' warns the purchaser that overreaching is taking place and that he must pay trustees and not the registered proprietor. The interests to which persons are entitled under settlements are not registrable, for they will in any case be overreached by a conveyance of the legal estate, will not affect the purchaser, and will be transferred to the purchase money.

There are, however, certain so-called 'overriding interests', by which, although they do not appear on the register, a registered holder is bound. Such are, for example, easements, squatter's claims, and the proprietary interests of anyone in actual occupation.

Once a title is on the register a certificate of title is issued to the holder, in lieu of his title deeds, and if he wants to sell the land, he need no longer prove his title in the old way but will point to his certificate and the entry in the Land Register. This ensures a great saving in time and expense.

Voluntary and compulsory registration

Land may be voluntarily registered wherever it may be; and much land has been registered in that way. Registration is very commonly applied for where there is some doubt as to the validity of the title which may be cleared more rapidly if the land is allowed to remain on the register for a sufficient length of time.

However, the Crown has power to issue orders in council making registration of title compulsory within the area under the jurisdiction of any county, and some 65 per cent of the country is now within the scheme. It would, however, be impracticable to require all landowners to apply for registration and submit their title deeds at once. It is compulsory, therefore, only on the first sale after the scheme comes into force.

XVII

THE BOUNDARIES OF
PROPERTY LAW:
LICENCES AFFECTING LAND

ONCE a relation between persons in regard to a thing has been classified as property, certain consequences follow. This statement, however, must be qualified by two important admissions. In the first place there is a danger of arguing in a circle. One can say: because A owns a thing (such as a book or an interest under a trust) therefore he can recover it in the event of the holder's bankruptcy. Or one can reverse the reasoning and say: because A does not have to queue up with the other creditors and take a share of what is left, therefore he has a property right; he is an owner, not a mere creditor.

In the second place, there are relationships on the borders of property law. At its clearest the statement that A owns a thing implies two distinct sets of conclusions, one to the detriment of other people, the other to the benefit of A. As regards other people, they are all subject to A's ownership and he can recover his thing from any of them who has it. As regards A he has power to alienate the thing—what you own you can give away. Thus in the straightforward case where A owns a house and a car he may recover either from any third party[1] and can deal with house and car as he pleases—by gift, will, sale, lease, mortgage, and so on.

There have, however, long been situations which do not correspond to this simple model and yet are, for many purposes, part of property law. For instance a tenant under a properly executed lease is, during his term, fully protected against everyone. Yet if the lease contains an absolute prohibition

---

[1] There are certain exceptions in the case of the car, such as sale by a stranger in market overt; see pp. 47–9 above.

against assignment he owns something which he cannot alienate. A not dissimilar situation obtains for the life tenant under a protective trust,[2] or the statutory tenant of premises within the Rent Acts.[3] On the other hand, if A is owed money by B only the latter is liable—plus, of course, his executors or trustee in bankruptcy. And yet A has something which he can deal with by gift, will, sale, mortgage, and the like. From his point of view the benefit of B's obligation is an asset and has, since Roman times, been treated as a thing which A owns.[4]

The examples just given are of situations which are well known and whose legal implications have long been worked out. At the present time the main problem in this jurisdiction is in drawing the precise boundaries of property law in relation to land. Land can be used in all sorts of ways but one of the main functions of property law has been to define those types of user which will count as 'property' in the sense of being protected against third parties and (though this is, in practice, less important) of being alienable. That class of protected property interests is further divided into those which bind others regardless of notice (such as leases, mortgages, easements) and those which depend on notice (nowadays, registration) either because of the informality of their creation (as in a contract to buy land) or some accident of their birth (as with restrictive covenants, the child of the Chancellor).

In explaining, in earlier chapters, the different types of property interest we have referred to these defining functions—the need for exclusive possession for a lease,[5] or of two pieces of land for an easement,[6] and so on. Recent years, however, have seen the border between property and personal rights in relation to land becoming blurred. We may distinguish two basic types of situation. The first arises where a person is claiming the right to *occupy* land, the second where he is claiming the right to *use* land for some purpose short of occupation, such as driving his car over it.

It is the first group—claims to occupy land—which have caused most difficulty, and that for several, quite distinct,

[2] See p. 164 above.
[3] See pp. 157-8 above.
[4] See pp. 26-32 above.
[5] See pp. 150-1 above.
[6] See p. 128 above.

reasons. Firstly the person occupying another's land for nothing may, if his possession is treated as adverse, bar the title of the landowner although the occupation began through the latter's generosity. Secondly if the occupier is paying the owner, the arrangement may amount to a lease and thus be within the Rent Acts. Thirdly a person given exclusive occupation *for life* looks awfully like the traditional tenant for life; but such a conclusion would attract to what might be a quite informal arrangement the majestic machinery of the Settled Land Act. The fourth problem arises with imperfect gifts. Frequently within a family one member may wish to give another some property interest in his land but fail to use the formal legal machinery: a father, say, allows a son to build on his land intending that the son will own the land; or he 'gives' a house to a child on marriage without any formal transfer but on the understanding that the young couple will pay off the mortgage. The final set of difficult questions concerns the interests of members of a family in the matrimonial home whose legal title is held by one person, usually the husband.

It would be quite impossible in a book such as this to do justice to all the complexities caused by the factors just mentioned. Instead all that can be offered is a rough framework which may at least help to organize the many solutions offered in the case-law.

We are not here particularly concerned with the effect of licences on the legal relations between the parties—whether, for instance, a miner who goes on strike while down the pit can demand to be brought immediately to the surface; or whether a cinema-manager can revoke a paying customer's right to see the film and evict him. The issue to be faced in a book on property is the extent to which such relations may bind third parties into whose hands the land may come; and, to a much lesser degree, the extent to which the benefit of the licence is alienable. As has been said, these issues are complex, often litigated and much discussed in the doctrine. The standard textbooks, however, make the subject complex at the outset. They define a licence as 'a permission given by the occupier of land to do some act which would otherwise be a trespass' or 'permission to enter upon land. It makes lawful what would otherwise be a trespass'. These definitions cover two totally different things.

The first is the ordinary permission given, say, by a shopkeeper to customers to come in and buy, or a cinema owner to patrons who come to see a film. But the definitions as given also cover a grant 'to A in fee simple' or 'to A for seven years' or 'to my neighbour to cross my land'. These latter involve, of course, permission to do an act which would otherwise be a trespass but they are also instantly recognizable property interests. What follows is an attempt at a simple approach.

(1) There is a fixed number of property interests recognized by the land law and it is easy to list them. There are four such interests conferring rights of occupation—the three freehold estates (life, entail, fee) and the lease. There are three such interests conferring rights over land occupied by another—easements, profits, and restrictive covenants. For the purposes of this chapter, entails, profits, and restrictive covenants can be ignored so that we are left with only four familiar figures of property law: life estate, fee, lease and easement.

(2) In order to define the relations which can come within this list of four the law has laid down clear criteria. Further, to subsist as indefeasible interests, these relations must not only satisfy the substantive criteria of their existence but must also be created in a particular way, usually by deed. If they are created only by contract two further conditions must be satisfied before they will bind a buyer of the land: the contract must satisfy the Statute of Frauds (LPA s 40) and the buyer must have notice of it (by its being entered on a register).

(3) The Law of Property Act 1925, by the proviso to section 4(1), forbids the creation of new types of property interest. This means that interests which do not satisfy the criteria required for the existence of a life estate, fee, lease, or easement do not bind third parties. This is so no matter how brilliant the conveyancer who drafted the documents nor how formal the documents themselves. The arrangements falling short of property interests may, of course, be perfectly valid contracts.

(4) With the distinction firmly in mind between relations which, by their content, could amount to one of the four relevant property interests and those which could never do so, it is possible to advance the following propositions.

(*a*) If the arrangement does not contain the elements required for the appropriate property interest—fee, life estate, lease or easement—then it will not be up-graded into some new species of property. A so-called 'lease' of front-of-house rights does not bind the new theatre owner, whether he knew of it or not. The right to fix advertising posters on a wall does not bind a new owner of the wall: it is not a lease of the wall or its surface; and it is not an easement as there is no dominant tenement.

A wife, deserted by her husband and remaining in the matrimonial home has certain rights against him. If the house is in both their names she is quite safe since she is a legal owner. If it is in his name but she has contributed towards its purchase she still has a perfectly recognizable property interest: she is, in equity, tenant in fee simple absolute in possession as co-owner with her husband (or tenant for years if the house is leasehold). But if it is entirely his house then her rights against him do not give her a fee, life estate, or lease: and so the House of Lords held—reversing lower courts—that her claims could not bind third parties who acquire some property interest in the house by purchase or mortgage. Statute has intervened here, however, to allow her, by registration, to affect third parties with notice of her rights to occupation which will endure until a court sorts out what is just and reasonable.

(*b*) Let us now turn to the case where the relation between the original parties could amount to one of the four property interests. If it has been created according to the law's formal requirements there is no problem and it will bind third parties. The difficulty arises where such formal steps have not been taken. All that can be said in an introductory work is that the courts may make up for formal deficiencies to secure protection against third parties but may still wish to avoid all the consequences of the fully fledged estate.

Our examples follow the traditional types of property interest.

(i) *Easement* The right of a landowner to drive his car over his neighbour's land could obviously be an easement since it satisfies easily all the requirements. To be certain of binding third parties who acquire the servient land it should be created by deed or by prescription;[7] if created by contract it should be registered. There may, however, be cases where none of these requirements has been fulfilled but where the neighbour allows the landowner to act to his detriment as if he had a right of way, for instance by building himself a garage, or selling off any other piece of land giving access to the road. The courts may then treat the relation between the parties as if there were an easement. Further any buyer of the servient land with notice of this is bound by it—presumably he paid less for the property. Similarly the dominant owner should be able to sell his right of way together with his land.[8]

(ii) *Life estate* It may happen that the widow of an employee is told that she may stay in her home, the employer's house, for the rest of her life. She thus has exclusive possession for her life—an interest which could be the traditional life estate long known to the law. Here, the courts will want to do two things: on the one hand to protect her against anyone buying the house with notice—once again, presumably the buyer paid less. Simultaneously, however, the courts shrink from describing her interest in the traditional way as this would attract the complexities, and the powers, of the Settled Land Act. We thus find her interest protected as a life estate but, to avoid the Act, described as a 'licence'.

(iii) *Fee Simple* If a landowner wishes to transfer the fee simple in his land, or part of it, he ought to execute a deed. Cases arise, however, where no such document exists but the donee has altered his position in reliance on acquiring a fee simple. In such a situation the courts may well perfect an imperfect gift. For instance, a father buys a house with the aid of a mortgage and tells his son and daughter-in-law that it will be theirs when they have paid off the mortgage. They move in and start paying the instalments. Now if the parties had taken legal advice before undertaking this transaction a conveyancer would have advised them that, since the house was to be the couple's for ever, the parties contemplate the transfer of what

[7] The latter method can be seen as an old form of doing justice similar to what is nowadays called 'estoppel'.
[8] It would probably pass automatically under LPA 1925 s. 62.

the law calls a fee simple in possession. However since their entitlement depends on their paying the mortgage instalments it is not a clear fee simple—a 'fee simple absolute'—but a fee simple determinable on their failure to make the appropriate payments; if they pay off the whole mortgage their fee becomes absolute. Strictly speaking the arrangement ought to be carried out under the Settled Land Act; but, since it looks like an informal grant of a perfectly well-known property interest, it may be treated as such and so bind anyone except a bona fide purchaser of the legal estate from the father without notice. And since the couple are living there such a person is unlikely to appear.

To sum up: in making sense of the present law of licences it is essential to distinguish the *content* of the relation from the manner of its *creation*. If, by its content, it could never be one of the four property interests it will not bind third parties no matter how many deeds are used. If, by its content, it could be one of the four then, despite the lack of formality in its creation, it may in some circumstances bind others.

XVIII

CONCLUSION

IN spite of the streamlining the law of property underwent in the 1925 legislation, it remains very complicated and not entirely free from confusion. Too many kinds of people have had a hand in producing it to admit of a simple orderly system consistent in all its parts. The merchants have built up the law governing the sale of goods, the financiers have moulded the law of stocks and shares, the landed aristocracy and gentry stimulated the activity of the conveyancers. Some parts of the law of property, especially those concerned with possession and title, have grown up around the common-law actions, while elsewhere the judges have thought sometimes like merchants and sometimes like the old conveyancers who presented them with the problems they encountered in creating and manipulating the doctrine of estates; and where trusts occur the trail of the Chancery is everywhere evident.

Where many people start from different points, they do not always meet. So there is a lack of co-ordination in property law. Moreover, so vast is the field covered by it that no mind has hitherto been capacious enough to master it all and at the same time familiar enough with the details to make his opinions acceptable outside a relatively small part of what is a most technical branch of the law.

If property law had been codified after the Continental fashion, the codifiers would have introduced more order into it, and in particular would have asked whether certain generalizations accepted for one kind of property were acceptable for others. A case-law system like ours naturally deals with problems as and not before they occur in practice; and some problems occur for some kinds of property and have not yet

occurred for others. Occasionally lawyers are then found to
say in effect that they will not occur and adopt for that part
of the law a structure which in the end may prove too simple.
It has been suggested above[1] that the law of physical chattels
has been over-hasty in rejecting the doctrine of estates and
adopting a theory of ownership that is less practical than it
might be. To ensure complete harmony in the law legislation
would probably be needed; but writers on the principles of
property law might profitably inquire whether the solutions
found for leases could not be applied to bailments and a uniform doctrine be enunciated to cover all limited interests in
physical objects. They might find that the doctrines common
to all kinds of property are more numerous than is at present
apparent; and where there is doubt, the courts might be per-
suaded to apply to one kind of property by analogy doctrines
which have been developed for the purpose of governing other
kinds of property.

The universalizing tendency of the trust has produced much
more uniformity in the treatment of beneficial interests, whatever the physical object or other investment on which their
value depends. Here beneficial interests in land, goods, and
intangible movables such as stocks and shares are treated alike
and nothing remains to be done, in order to make the law truly
uniform, but to extend the overreaching effect of a conveyance
to goods.[2]

Some distinctions will remain. The land agent will always
be concerned with the course of husbandry, with repairs to
buildings and with servitudes. Mortgages of the fee simple will
always provide a preferable security in the eyes of some people
to assignments of shares; the security provided by the assignment of a bill of lading will always be a matter for specialist
bankers and merchants; and not everybody wants to be a pawnbroker lending money on watches or jewels. More care will be
taken in investigating title and fewer risks assumed in buying
land than goods. But these will usually be differences of fact
and business practice; they need not be strongly reflected as
doctrinal discrepancies in the law. In other words, differences
between land and movables and between corporeal and incorporeal movables should occupy only a subordinate position

[1] See pp. 77, 95, 202 above.   [2] See p. 113 above.

and not interfere with the formulation of a large body of general principle.

It is, however, clear that one distinction now outweighs all others, namely that between physical objects regarded as things to be used and enjoyed physically as specifically identified individuals and what may be in the broadest sense called investments, of which the money value alone is relevant. It may be expressed summarily as one between objects and wealth, or between use-value and exchange-value.

It is not in essence a distinction between different kinds of things but between different ways of dealing with things; though some things are more likely to be thought of primarily, or even exclusively, in terms of their money value and others to be kept and used in their present state. If funds, such as trust funds, can be regarded as composite things, they of course constitute an exception; as funds, they are clearly wealth and nothing else.

Again, it is not in essence a distinction between the kinds of persons who deal with things. The trader, it is true, while he is trading thinks of all the objects he deals in, whether corporeal or incorporeal, as things to be turned into money, and of money itself as something to be turned into things which are themselves destined to be turned into money in their turn. But he thinks of his house, his car, and his television set as things to be used and enjoyed in themselves. On the other hand, although the landowner values his mansion house and family portraits for themselves, he has at the back of his mind the thought that they may be turned into money in case of need. That money value will be what concerns the state when taxes are to be paid, but the state also may on occasion prefer to take some objects in kind, whether because turning them into money may be awkward and even ruinous, or because it is in the public interest to keep a collection together. Stocks and shares may seem at first sight to have only a money value, but some holders may value them even more for the control they afford of an undertaking. Indeed, although one is tempted to say that the ultimate objects of the law of property are always physical, in the sense that everything is derived in the last resort from physical objects and that in the end all satisfaction comes from the enjoyment of physical objects, money being merely the instrument by which the raw materials are turned into the immediate objects of enjoyment, that is not strictly true of our complex world. Many persons obtain intense satisfaction from the process of dealing with money, if by that term we designate all the abstract intellectual creations that intervene between the use of physical objects in the way of production and their eventual enjoyment.

The law is bound to be influenced, and the balance of its parts in large measure determined, by the ways in which the various groups constituting a nation think of property and by the balance existing between them from time to time. If the groups which think of things mainly in terms of their money value predominate, the law will tend to disregard the desire of a person to keep and enjoy a thing in specie and will see no great harm in forcing him to give it up in return for a money compensation. Still less regard will it pay to one person's expectation of succeeding to specific objects under the present but temporary control of another. It will in principle give no effect to attempts to tie up land or anything else in specie. If, on the other hand, the groups predominate which attach peculiar value to the possession of physical objects themselves, the law will be much less inclined to force an acceptance of money compensation or to allow limited interests to be overreached.

Put very crudely, it is a question of how the commercial and the landed interests are balanced in a community; for, with few exceptions such as heirlooms, movables are not permanent enough for the distinction between them and their money value to be very important. A French or Irish peasant will cling to his land at all costs; a business man engaged in land speculation will sell out at what seems to him the most propitious moment and will regard as absurdly old-fashioned any restrictions which prevent the present holder of land from selling to him.

The law does not indeed always conform to what is desired by one group or another, or even express the balance of power between groups. The law may exhaust itself against the strong passive resistance of a stubborn peasantry, or a class may feel no need to translate its economic power into legal terms. It is easy to expect too much of the law; it will seldom break down deeply rooted social habits, nor do they need it for their preservation. But where the commercial and landed interests have battled for centuries with fluctuating fortunes but on fairly even terms, as in England, both have perforce had recourse to the law and the law has reflected pretty faithfully the changing social scene.

Much of the contents of the foregoing chapters is a commentary on what has just been said. It need not be repeated here. It is, however, perhaps worth emphasizing that the student must be prepared at every turn to ask himself what it is that the law of property is really talking about. Is it talking about physical objects as such, as things to be acquired, possessed, and enjoyed in specie, or is it merely talking about wealth? Sometimes it is only by putting this question that any sense at all can be made of the law. For instance, the continued operation of the Modern Rule against Perpetuities can be reconciled with the policy enshrined in the Settled Land Acts and section 1 of the Law of Property Act only if it is realized that it now deals with wealth, whereas that policy governs the alienation of the land itself.

Generally speaking, the distinction between wealth and the things that it will buy introduces order and system into the law. On the whole judges and legislators have had fairly clear in their minds which they were dealing with at a particular moment. Moreover, in the last quarter of the nineteenth century and the first years of the twentieth century it was pretty clear that the law generally took a commercial view of property, in that it favoured the circulation of land as well as corporeal and incorporeal movables. It was bound to secure tenants in their holdings and mortgagees in their security, but only to the extent that they had bargained for their rights. Such interests had from the very beginning been looked on as essentially commercial in character and so the protection of them formed no exception to the general policy of the law.

However, the Rent Acts[3] marked a decided swing away from pure commercialism, albeit it was expected to be temporary. Tenants had their possession protected on grounds of public policy irrespective of their bargains with their landlords. The legislature was forced to pay special attention to the holding

[3] See pp. 157–8 .

of specific physical objects and to refuse to allow landlords to fob tenants off with money as the price of eviction. The essential thing was to secure to a person a roof over his head, and rent restriction was enacted less for its own sake than in order to prevent eviction by forcing tenants to pay a higher rent than they could afford. Here was a direct denial of the general commercial thesis that every physical object can be adequately replaced by its value in money. The statutory protection now given to mortgagors of dwellinghouses[4] and the stream of lawsuits on licences[5] are examples of the same tendency.

Even more far-reaching has been the change which has secured not obviously inefficient agricultural tenants in the possession of their holdings;[6] for here the public interest has been held to demand a permanent policy of protecting farmers in the physical enjoyment and use of the actual means of production. If a tenant farmer could alienate his holdings so as to force his alienee on his landlord irrespective of the terms of his lease or tenancy agreement, and if the landlord did nothing but receive rent, it would be easy to say that the tenant had in reality become owner of the land subject to a perpetual rent. But that is not usually the case; the landlord retains a real interest in the land, he takes responsibility legally for certain repairs and morally for seeing that the rules of good husbandry are observed. Moreover, the tenant cannot, so long as the present policy continues, insist on buying out his landlord. Thus both have interests in the land itself which cannot be overreached.

So far we know where we stand, and the only warning to be given the student is not to exaggerate the effect of the general commercial bias displayed by the law. In spite of its general tendency to favour the free alienation of physical objects, it allows itself to be deflected by considerations of public policy in the direction of maintaining tenants and spouses in their holdings. But sometimes there is real doubt which line of thought should prevail. There are gaps in the powers of sale granted to trustees by the 1925 legislation, which can be filled

---

[4] See pp. 194-5 above.
[5] See pp. 217-23 above.
[6] See pp. 156-7 above.

in only by the benevolent action of the courts. The courts may, however, not be willing to act in such cases where the effect would be to disturb the occupier, and they have in any case power to grant an injunction to prevent trustees from selling where that would be unjust.

It is clearly the occupier whose protection makes the greatest breach in the policy of the Settled Land Acts and the Land Registration Act. Where there is no question of protecting him, English law has progressively leant more and more in favour of the money point of view. It might well have adopted as its motto the famous saying of Louis Philippe, *Enrichissez-vous*, 'Get rich'. This is in full accord with the old policy of Free Trade, which was justified precisely on the ground that in the long run it made the country richer, in the money sense, than any other policy could have done, though it may possibly have made the country weaker in time of war and may have had social consequences that were not entirely admirable. Taken by and large, the law has encouraged people to get rich at the cost of sentimental or aesthetic attachments.

The merits of this general policy are, however, very questionable, though its defects are rendered more conspicuous, and perhaps in some degree are even called into being by the operation of other factors which have removed the social and moral brakes which formerly kept it in check.

The old state of balance, between a landed aristocracy interested in the land as such and a legal policy aimed not merely at economic improvement but also at the replacement of impoverished landlords by self-made men more capable of looking after the land, undoubtedly produced a very beautiful country and one that in the long run did not suffer even from the point of view of wealth. The old landlords often planned with an eye to beauty as well as money. When land came to be treated much more openly as a source of wealth, there inevitably arose a tendency to exploit it by cutting down trees without replacement, by the practice of ribbon development, and in general by treating it as something to be exploited rather than cultivated.

In other words, the Settled Land Acts were originally thought of as a medicine rather than a regular food. They were a necessary safety valve in a society where the landed interest in general wished to keep the land and could be trusted to look after it. With the gradual disappearance of large-scale land-holding by the aristocracy and gentry, the balance was lost. It is in process of being readjusted by planning controls exercised by public authorities.[7] How the results will compare with those produced by the old landlordism is not easy to say. That the burdens dropped by the old landlords should be shouldered by someone else was inevitable. It is also necessary for the student of property law to cast his eyes into what may at first sight appear to be the alien ground of public law if he is to acquire a sense of the way in which equilibrium is, somewhat painfully, being restored.

There is no need to repeat here the remarks made elsewhere[8] about the difference of intellectual atmosphere when one passes from the law relating to physical objects to that relating to what has in an abstract sort of way, been described as wealth. But in summing up, one question deserves attention.

For over a century attacks have been made here and in other countries on what is called *conceptualism*. It may be described roughly as a tendency not to give a direct answer on the merits to a practical question but to interpose between the question and the answer one or more abstract concepts, to work out a number of legal rules and principles defining those concepts and then to see whether the concepts may be made to apply to the situation in respect of which the question arises. Those who attack conceptualism say that to interpose concepts in this way is to interpose wholly unnecessary middle terms and that it does not help in finding the right answer; whereas at worst it may distort the question, by forcing it into a procrustean bed, and so make the finding of the correct answer even more difficult and hazardous than it would be otherwise.

On the whole these attacks have found targets other than property law; they have been peculiarly prevalent in the law of torts. But property law is open to attack, though mainly where it touches on contract and tort.

It is at least doubtful whether it helps, in deciding whether a finder becomes the owner of goods, to ask whether another person was in possession.[9] There is always the possibility that

[7] See pp. 121-2 above.
[8] See pp. 78-9 above.   [9] See p. 43 above.

a judge will decide first of all whether the finder should really become owner and will then decide whether or not to attribute possession to some other person in order to give the right result. If that is the case, the attribution of possession plays no real part in the process of deciding the main question.

In the sale of goods the attribution of what is called *property* may even commit courts to decisions which have no necessary connexion with property. For instance, whether the creditors of a seller can satisfy themselves at the expense of the buyer out of goods sold to him, and force him to prove as an ordinary creditor in a bankruptcy, is made to depend on whether the *property* has passed from the seller to the buyer.[10] Since the moment at which the property passes is in principle determined by the seller and buyer between themselves without any reference to the possible creditors of either, it is not self-evident that the rights of the creditors should be made to depend on whether the property has passed or not. It might be thought better to think out the answer to the question directly as one affecting the seller's creditors and the buyer. At any rate, in dealing with Scandinavian lawyers where a foreign element enters into a sale, it does not help in any way to say that the property has or has not passed from the seller to the buyer. They say that in doing so one is merely inserting an unnecessary middle term which, if taken seriously, may prevent one from finding the right solution to a practical question. Indeed, our merchants also were not prepared to accept the inferences which lawyers drew from the passing of property where goods were left in the hands of the seller and then resold and delivered by him to an innocent buyer, and they insisted on the passing of the Factors Acts.[11]

The whole conceptual structure of mortgages has become little more than a nuisance. All that the mortgagee needs, and all that he really gets, is a bundle of powers over the mortgaged property, namely, to apply to a court for a foreclosure decree, to appoint a receiver, and above all to sell, all of them governed immediately by practical rules suggested by experience.[12] The mortgagor in effect remains owner of the property subject to those powers, and has a right to redeem, governed in its turn

---

[10] See pp. 66, 71 above.   [11] See p. 48 above.
[12] See pp. 193–4 above.

by other practical rules. Yet other practical rules decide to what extent his right to redeem can be restricted and how far the mortgagee can bargain for collateral advantages by making the loan. Nothing would be lost if the notion that the mortgagee has an interest in the mortgage property were entirely given up and the existence of the equity of redemption entirely disregarded. The essence of the mortgage is that it allows the mortgagee to satisfy himself out of certain property in preference to unsecured creditors.

It is also very doubtful whether anything is gained in many of the cases where a trust for sale is implied by the law. Indeed, there is something ridiculous in saying that trustees are under a trust to sell property and hold the proceeds of sale upon certain trusts with a power to postpone the sale, when what is really intended is that they should keep the property unsold as long as possible, should hold the property as such in trust for the beneficiaries, but should have a power to sell it if at any time they think fit. At one time it may have been necessary to frame trusts in this way. It is surely time now to bring them more in accord with reality. This is painfully true of the matrimonial home.

However, this artificiality is a blemish mainly in the part of property law which deals with physical objects. When we are adjusting the claims of the seller's creditors and the buyer, we are really dealing with the goods themselves; when asking whether land can be sold in such a way as to overreach the claims of those entitled to limited interests, we are dealing with the land itself. When we pass into the field dominated by the conveyancer, especially that of settlements, it is clear that the law cannot help dealing in artificial concepts. Only artificiality can give the certainty of prediction that is required.[13] The doctrine of estates is certainly artificial but it serves practical purposes and has been extremely useful. Moreover, the trust fund made up of ever-changing investments is an artificial creation if ever there was one.[14] But it is not merely the invention of the lawyers. Modern finance in England and America could not now dispense with it. Incidentally it is in its application to the trust fund that the doctrine of estates now

---

[13] See pp. 15–16 above.   [14] See pp. 38–9 above.

performs its most useful function. Similarly, the various commercial documents, such as negotiable instruments and documents of title, which have reached a high degree of standardization, are as artificial as they could well be.[15] If they were not artificial they could not be used, as they are used, by bankers as units in a form of commercial mathematics.

It would seem, therefore, that, speaking generally and somewhat crudely, artificiality and conceptualism, though on the whole out of place in the part of property law which deals with physical objects, are essential to that part which deals with wealth. In any case, what is more artificial than money itself?

Property law now needs the attention of jurists who, while seeing the need to give it the orderly and systematic treatment which it receives in books on Continental law, would still refuse to force it into the closed system of Continental categories. Whether they choose or not to adopt ownership as their starting-point is not very important, so long as they are prepared to subject it to a more profound analysis and to admit that it has no prescriptive claim to be considered indivisible. If the English law of property has anything to teach the analytical jurist it is certainly that some place must be found for a discussion first of the *quantum* of interest measured in terms of duration as exemplified by the doctrine of estates, and, secondly, of the separation of management from enjoyment. To consider the doctrine of estates and the trust as English eccentricities is surely misguided. But English property law would be much better arranged, and some of its substance would probably be improved, if jurists could be found who would look at it comprehensively after the manner of Continental lawyers. Hitherto our property lawyers themselves have been too close to it to see it as a whole.

No attempt has been made in this book to deal with the effects on property of what has been called 'The Managerial Revolution'. This is not to suggest that they are unimportant. Much property of all kinds is now owned by corporations such as limited companies, the control of which is often in the hands of small groups of individuals who between them own perhaps less than a quarter of the shares. If we see as the essential part of ownership the power to dispose of property, then such

[15] See pp. 28-32 above.

small groups really own enormous masses of property to which they have no direct legal title. However, what is peculiar to this form of 'ownership' belongs to company law; the rest has already been described.

INDEX

242 *Index*